ColdFusion®

fast&easy™
web development

Send Us Your Comments

To comment on this book or any other PRIMA TECH title, visit our reader response page on the Web at **www.prima-tech.com/comments**.

How to Order

For information on quantity discounts, contact the publisher: Prima Publishing, P.O. Box 1260BK, Rocklin, CA 95677-1260; (916) 787-7000. On your letterhead, include information concerning the intended use of the books and the number of books you want to purchase. For individual orders, turn to the back of this book for more information.

ColdFusion®

fast&easy™
web development

T.C. Bradley, III

A DIVISION OF PRIMA PUBLISHING

A Division of Prima Publishing

Prima Publishing and colophon are registered trademarks of Prima Communications, Inc. PRIMA TECH Fast & Easy is a trademark of Prima Communications, Inc., Roseville, California 95661.

Publisher: Stacy L. Hiquet
Marketing Manager: Judi Taylor
Associate Marketing Manager: Heather Buzzingham
Managing Editor: Sandy Doell
Acquisitions Editor: Kim Spilker
Project Editor: Melba Hopper
Technical Reviewer: Scott M. Sobecki
Copy Editor: Kezia Endsley
Interior Layout: Marian Hartsough Associates
Cover Design: Prima Design Team
Indexer: Johanna VanHoose Dinse

ISBN: 0-7615-3016-9
Library of Congress Catalog Card Number: 00-104839
Printed in the United States of America

00 01 02 03 04 DD 10 9 8 7 6 5 4 3 2 1

To Lisa,
for her faith in me.

Acknowledgments

I would like to acknowledge the editorial staff at Prima for all their hard work. I would like to thank especially Melba Hopper and Kezia Endsley for putting up with this newbie author's inexperience, and Kim Spilker for her confidence in me to get this book done on time. I extend my appreciation to Marian Hartsough for the book's skillful interior layout and to Johanna VanHoose Dinse for a fine index.

Thanks also go to my colleagues at Indiana University for putting up with my absences and unusual hours while writing the book. Special thanks to Scott Sobecki for his superb technical editorial work in the midst of a demanding travel schedule.

I would like to thank my nieces, Sarah and Katie Doyle, for reminding me that "the book" was not my entire universe. Instant messages can be a good thing. My family also deserves special thanks for their support: my sisters, Lisa Doyle and Leslie Michael; my niece, Lauren Michael, and my, nephew, Brad Michael; my brothers-in-law, Johnny Doyle and Kenny Michael; my parents, Lois and Cullen Bradley; and my in-laws, Shirley and Neil See.

And extra special thanks go to my wife, Lisa, for putting up with our curtailed social calendar and my virtual absences—and to our kitty Bilbo for visiting me at the computer.

PART IV
BUILDING APPLICATIONS 249

PART V
GETTING THE JOB DONE 333

PART VI
APPENDIXES 379

Contents

PART III
WORKING OUTSIDE THE BOX 189

Introduction

This book will get you started with ColdFusion as quickly as possible. With a basic knowledge of HTML, your databases in hand, and ColdFusion, you can create Web applications that are easy to build, use, and maintain.

The tasks in this book provide the foundation you need to build more advanced tasks when deploying a dynamic Web site with ColdFusion. I start with the basic, no-frills version. You can follow along with the basic code, which includes concise explanations about what the code is doing. Where appropriate, screen shots illustrate the output of the code. Then I add variations and extensions to the code and show more illustrations of what I've done.

Who Should Read This Book?

This book is for anyone interested in building Web applications with ColdFusion. Although the book focuses on beginning to intermediate users, the examples provide a toolkit so that an experienced ColdFusion developer can pull it off the shelf as needed. The CD with this book contains all the code from the book, evaluation and noncommercial software from Allaire, and links to sites where you can find custom ColdFusion tags.

I assume that you are interested in developing Web applications and may have written a basic HTML page or form. I also assume that you are familiar with a database environment, such as Microsoft Access or Visual FoxPro, and preferably you have some experience creating tables and views with your database product.

ColdFusion can use any database that has Open Database Connectivity (ODBC) drivers. Please refer to your database vendor's documentation for details.

Here is a list of the tools and resources that you need to build your Web applications with ColdFusion and to follow along in the book:

- **ColdFusion.** At a minimum, you need access to a Web server with ColdFusion installed and your datasources configured on it. Also, a text editor of your choice is required to create ColdFusion templates.

- **ColdFusion Studio.** If you intend to do serious ColdFusion development, I strongly urge you to invest in a copy of ColdFusion Studio, a development component much like Visual InterDev for Active Server Pages from Microsoft. Studio uses dialog boxes and wizards to help you write code. All examples in the book were written with ColdFusion Studio.

- **A sample database and database application:** I use the Northwind sample database that ships with Microsoft Access as the basis for most of the examples in the book. Northwind is a fictitious specialty foods company, and the sample database contains employees, products, orders, and so on, referenced in the examples. It may help to have a copy of that database handy to add to some of the examples on your own. You will also need the ODBC driver for your database system.

Conventions Used in This Book

In addition to clear, concise steps and illustrations that form the heart of this book, you will find special elements such as the Note and Tip icons, which provide additional information about a feature of the program and suggest techniques and shortcuts, respectively.

PART 1

Introducing the Fundamentals

1

Learning the Basics

I know you want to jump right in and build dynamic Web pages, but you need to understand a few basics first. Consider this your first vocabulary and grammar lesson in CFML (the ColdFusion Markup Language). Rather than inundate you with examples of syntax, I show you one or two practical examples of each concept to give you the basic idea.

In this chapter, you learn how to:

- Understand the use of templates
- Differentiate between variables and expressions
- Understand tags and functions
- Understand flow control in ColdFusion
- Understand the use of loops
- Understand what ColdFusion Studio does

Understanding Templates

Templates are the basic unit of construction when building a ColdFusion Web application. As a ColdFusion developer, you will construct a set of templates that defines the appearance of the application, how the application works, and how the application interacts with databases, other Web servers, and so on. You will create your first complete template in the next chapter, "Retrieving and Displaying Data."

NOTE

I've written all example templates in the book with Allaire's ColdFusion Studio, but you can use any text editor, such as Notepad or Visual SlickEdit.

You can find 30-day evaluation copies of ColdFusion Studio 4.5.1 and ColdFusion Server Enterprise 4.5.1 on the CD-ROM at the back of this book. You can also find ColdFusion Express 4.0, a free noncommercial product by Allaire.

A ColdFusion template is nothing more than a text file, named with a .cfm extension, that contains CFML tags and functions. The template might not have other text in it. Usually, you place HTML in the template for display on a Web browser. You can include JavaScript to send to the browser, or you can have plain text in the template.

ColdFusion processes templates from top to bottom. Therefore, the tags and functions you place in the template are processed from top to bottom, like reading a list of instructions sequentially, from step 1 to step 10.

Naming and Creating Variables and Expressions

ColdFusion uses variables and expressions to get its work done, like any other programming language. There are rules about how you create variables and about how you use them in expressions. You learn about those rules in this section and see what variables and expressions look like in CFML. Once you have an understanding of ColdFusion variables and expressions, you'll use them in conjunction with ColdFusion tags to create your templates.

Creating Variables

Variables are placeholders for actual values to be filled in later by ColdFusion. Variables have names, but in ColdFusion, they do not have declared types. That is, when you create a variable in a ColdFusion template, you do not have to inform ColdFusion whether the variable represents an integer or a string. ColdFusion determines the variable type by the way in which you use the variable. Therefore, ColdFusion is a *typeless* language.

There are several rules to keep in mind when naming variables. Variable names must begin with a letter. After that, any letter, number, or the underscore (_) character can be used. No other characters can be used in a variable name. For example, a valid variable name is The_Fab4, but 1stBase is not. ColdFusion is case-insensitive, meaning that it ignores case when reading a template. So The_Fab4 is the same as the_fab4 to ColdFusion. Note that spaces cannot be used in variable names.

You can create variables in two ways: using <cfset> or using <cfparam>.

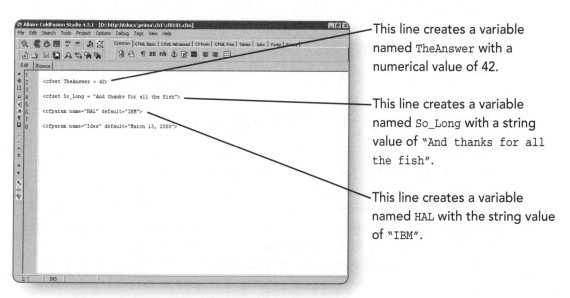

This line creates a variable named TheAnswer with a numerical value of 42.

This line creates a variable named So_Long with a string value of "And thanks for all the fish".

This line creates a variable named HAL with the string value of "IBM".

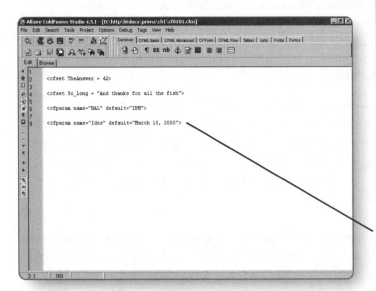

This line creates a variable named Ides with the date/time value of "March 15, 2000".

<cfparam> checks for the existence of the variable named by the name attribute. If the variable exists, <cfparam> stops processing and the template continues. If the variable does not exist and you have used the default attribute, ColdFusion creates the variable and gives it the value in default.

<cfset>, on the other hand, does not check for the existence of the variable. If the variable already exists, ColdFusion will overwrite the existing value with the new value.

Understanding Variable Scopes

In addition to creating your own variables, ColdFusion and your Web server can create variables. These variables belong to different *scopes*. You can think of a scope as a small town. Each town has its own streets and houses, all with their own names and addresses. You therefore can have a street called Main in two separate towns. But if you tell someone you live at 123 Main Street without the town name, he or she might not be able to figure out exactly where you live. Scopes define a community of variables and values that you can access with the proper address.

Using <cfloop> to Control Template Flow

<cfloop> enables you to loop over a section of code many times. The most common use of a loop is to apply a section of code repeatedly to a series of values, like the values in each row of a query result set.

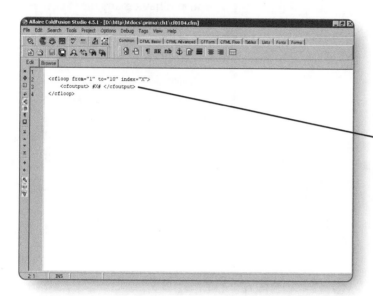

The simplest form of <cfloop> is using the from and to syntax. The flow goes like this: starting from 1, evaluate this section of code, until you get to 10.

Whoa! What are those pound signs (#) doing there? This is how ColdFusion knows that you want to refer to a variable inside the <cfoutput> tags. You learn about this syntax in depth in Chapter 2.

The result of this code looks like this:

```
1 2 3 4 5 6 7 8 9 10
```

The index attribute of the <cfloop> tag specifies the name of the variable to use inside the <cfloop> tags to represent the current loop. In this case, the variable is named X. You can name it anything you want (as long as you adhere to the variable-naming rules).

Using <cfswitch> to Control Template Flow

<cfswitch> is kind of like a big <cfif>/<cfelseif> statement. But the logic of the decision tree is easier to follow than a long list of nested if/then/else statements. In a <cfswitch> statement, you are "switching" to different lines of code based on the value of one expression (called a *case*).

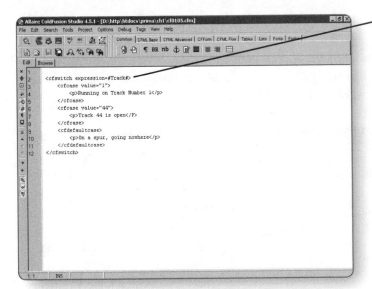

This is an example of a simple `<cfswitch>` statement. Note that each `<cfcase>` clause must have a closing `</cfcase>` tag.

You can have many more cases in the `<cfswitch>` statement to handle more values. Note the `<cfdefaultcase>` tag. This tag enables you to specify a default section of code to evaluate no matter what the actual expression value is.

You'll see practical examples of all these flow control tags throughout the book.

Introducing ColdFusion Studio

The preferred tool for creating dynamic templates is Allaire's ColdFusion Studio. ColdFusion Studio is an integrated development environment application, designed to provide you, the ColdFusion developer, with everything you need to build ColdFusion applications.

You can configure Studio to suit your programming and editing preferences. This chapter doesn't look at all the tools and options that Studio provides, but it does take a look at the most helpful and common tools and operations.

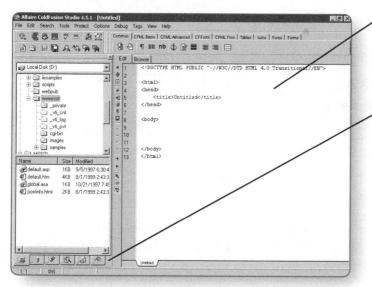

This is the main edit window. The code is colored-coded for CFML, HTML, Java, and JavaScript.

This is the resource tab area. It changes views based on the current tab.

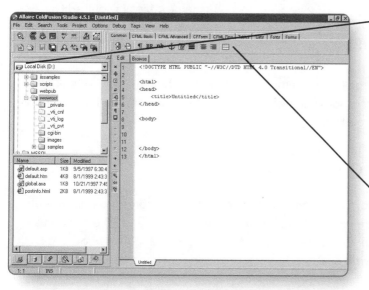

This is the file system view of the resource tab. The top window displays the current drive and directory structure. The bottom window shows the files in the directory that's currently selected in the top window.

The Quick Bar has tabs to hold several toolbars at once. The list of toolbars is configurable.

Studio has new document wizards to help you get started.

Select File, New to get this dialog box.

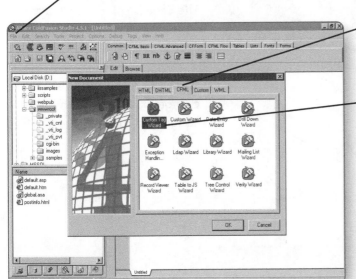

Select the type of document you want to create. CFML documents are selected here.

Select the type of document you want to create by double-clicking its icon or by selecting it and clicking OK.

Each wizard has its own questions, depending on the type of document to be created. Simply answer the questions the wizard asks you. When the wizard is done, Studio will open the new files in your edit window for you to inspect and customize.

Of course, you can also build your templates from scratch. Start with a blank page or a basic HTML page by choosing Basic Document Wizard from the HTML tab in the New Document dialog box.

Getting CFML Contextual Help

The best feature of Studio is its contextual help. Studio has some wonderful tools that help you choose the correct ColdFusion tag or function, and it helps you use the tag or function once you've decided. The Tag Chooser, Tag Inspector, and Expression Builder provide directed help on tags and functions, especially helpful for beginners.

Select Tools, Tag Chooser from the menu.

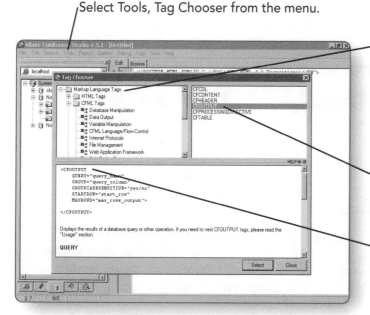

This window separates the CFML tags into categories. It also includes other types of tags, such as HTML, Java Server Page tags, and Wireless Markup Language tags.

This window displays the tags of the category selected in the left window.

The bottom window displays the syntax and definitions of the tag selected in the upper-right window.

With your template in the edit window, select the Tag Inspector tab (the one with the magnifying glass).

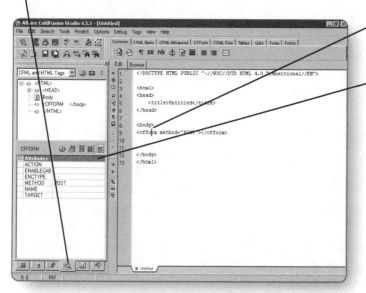

Then place the cursor over a tag to inspect its attributes.

This window shows the attributes for the selected tag in the edit window. You can change the attributes in this window, and Tag Inspector will update your code automatically.

Select Tools, Expression Builder from the menu.

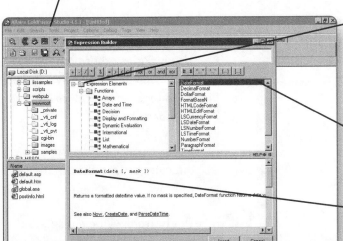

Similar to the Tag Chooser, Expression Builder displays functions, variables, constants, and operators in their appropriate categories.

This window displays the list of functions of the category selected in the left window.

In this window, you can read the syntax and definition of the item selected in the upper-right window.

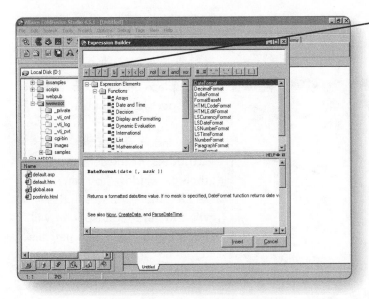

You can build your expression in the window above this button bar using these buttons and the expression elements listed beneath. When you're done, just click the Insert button, and your expression is inserted into your code.

Tag Editor, Tag Insight, and Tag Completion are interactive tools integrated into the editor. They help you while you are typing. Tag Completion completes the tag for you by adding the ending tag. Tag Completion's behavior is also configurable. You can configure Tag Completion's behavior by choosing Options, then Settings from the menu. Click Tag Completion to use the configuration dialog.

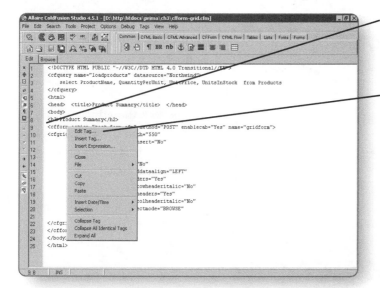

Place your cursor over the tag you want to edit and right-click to get this pop-up menu.

Select Edit Tag from the pop-up menu.

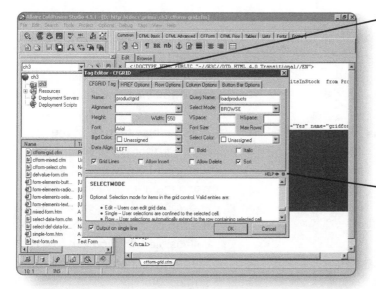

The Tag Editor displays a custom dialog box for the tag you have selected. The tag might have extended options, denoted by tabs across the top of the dialog box. The <cfgrid> tag has lots of options, as you can see.

By selecting one of the two Help buttons, you can get another window with the tag's syntax and definitions. The curly button opens Help in a new window, whereas the arrow button opens an attached window, as shown here.

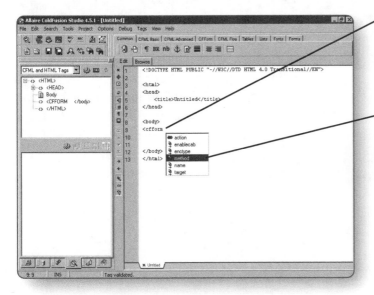

As you type a tag name, Tag Insight presents a selection window with the tag's attributes.

Double-click the attribute to insert it, or use the arrow keys to move up and down and then press Enter to insert an attribute.

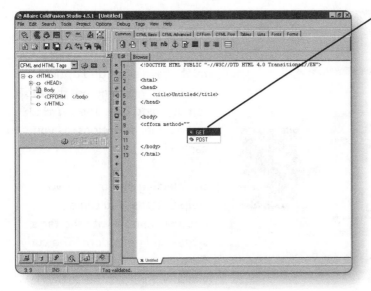

When the attribute has a finite set of values, Tag Insight presents another pop-up menu from which you choose the value you want for the attribute.

Another nice feature of the Studio editor is the collapsible text tool. Sometimes you are working on a very long template and you need to refer to code at the top of the file. With collapsible text, you can fold all the text you don't need into a single icon.

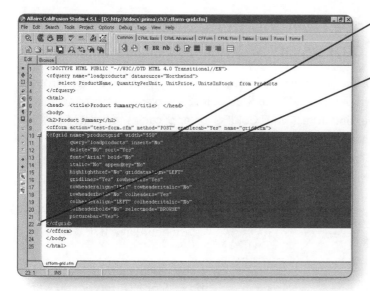

Highlight the text you want to collapse.

Next, click either of the two "minus" buttons at either end of the vertical line that now appears to the right of the line numbers in the editor gutter to collapse the text.

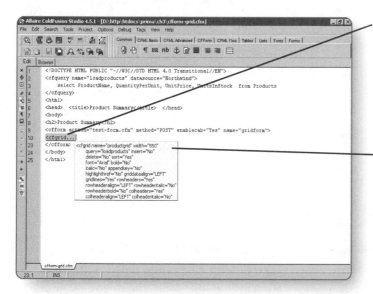

The collapsed text is now replaced by a slightly oval button with the first several characters of the collapsed text on it. To restore the text, simply double-click the oval button.

By hovering your mouse cursor over the button for a few seconds, you get a pop-up window containing the collapsed text. Use this technique for a quick reminder of what is hidden.

Accessing Remote Development Services with ColdFusion Studio

You can develop ColdFusion applications directly on your ColdFusion server through the *Remote Development Services* (RDS) in Studio. RDS enables you to connect to a remote ColdFusion server and access your ColdFusion application templates as though the server were simply another disk drive on your workstation. RDS also offers integrated and interactive debugging of your ColdFusion templates. You'll learn about debugging with RDS in Chapter 25 "Debugging Your Templates."

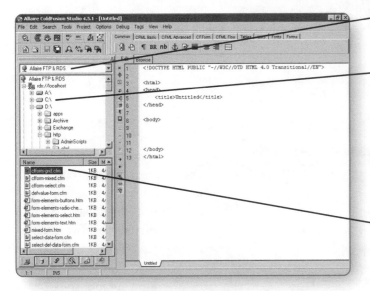

In the Disk Selection drop-down list, select Allaire FTP & RDS.

In the directory window, select the RDS or FTP server you want to open. Navigating the remote file system is just like navigating a local file system. You can right-click the top node in the tree to add a new server to the list.

Here's the file list of the current directory, selected above. To open a file, double-click the filename, or right-click it and select Edit.

Using the Database Viewer

Studio realizes that, as a ColdFusion developer, you will be spending a lot time referring to your database as you write code. After all, putting data on the Web is what ColdFusion is all about. To make life a little easier while you're coding, Studio includes the Databases tab in the resource window. This viewer is actually part of RDS and enables you to browse the datasources on your remote ColdFusion server.

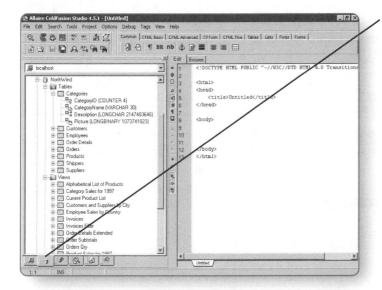

Select the database tab on the resources tab (the yellow cylinder).

Use the drop-down list at the top of the window to select an RDS server. In the lower window, you'll see a list of datasources related to the selected server.

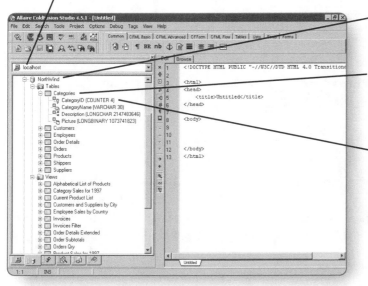

Northwind shows listings for tables, views, and queries.

Opening the Categories table reveals the column names of the table's columns.

In addition to the column names, you can see what kind of data type each column holds. This is great for determining the type of data to expect when processing a query result set.

SQL Builder enables you to build SQL queries for use in your ColdFusion templates. SQL Builder is a query-by-example tool, much like Microsoft Query or the query interface in Microsoft Access.

Select Tools, SQL Builder from the menu to display this dialog

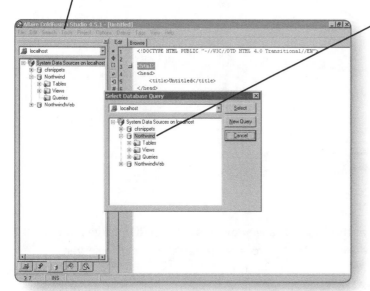

Select a database from the RDS server list, and then click the New Query button. You are presented with an opportunity to select a table for the query.

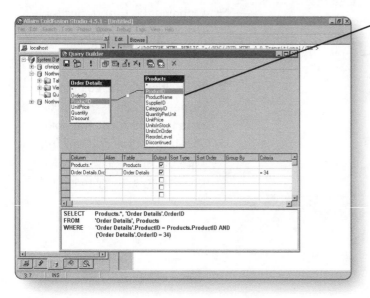

You can add tables in the top window and establish relationships between them. Here you see the Order Details and Products tables from the Northwind database. The ProductIDs of each table are joined (shown by the line drawn between them) to show their relationship.

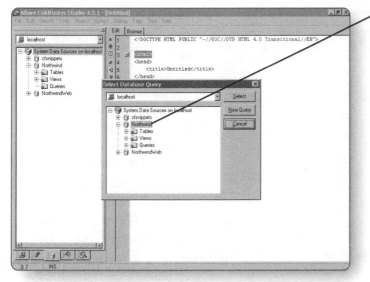

You can add columns to the query in the column grid, set filter values, and set sorting and grouping options. SQL Builder shows you the SQL code in the bottom window as you build the query. Run the query by clicking the exclamation button found on the button bar.

Organizing Your Work with Studio Projects

Studio also helps you organize your work. Studio projects can help you treat a set of templates as a single application and help you with source code control, deployment to remote servers, and organization of the support files.

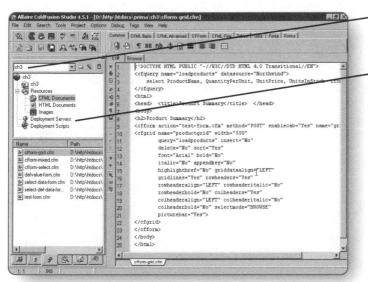

The project view shows you the project files by type.

Studio also helps you write scripts with JavaScript or VBScript in order to deploy your applications to remote deployment servers.

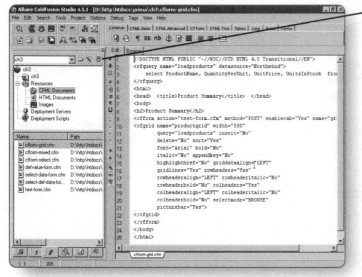

When you're ready to deploy, use the Deployment Wizard to help you send your code off to the world.

This section has only touched the tip of the iceberg in regards to what Studio can do to help you write killer Web applications. I urge you to read the Studio online help and click around a while to learn about this powerful tool. It can save you lots of development time and reduce your learning curve.

2

Retrieving and Displaying Data

Two basic tasks you'll need to be able to do when writing a ColdFusion application are retrieving data from your database and displaying it in a Web browser. Almost all the other templates you write revolve around these two tasks. In this chapter, you learn how to:

- Use `<cfquery>` to retrieve data
- Use different SQL statements
- Use `<cfoutput>` to display variables
- Use `<cfloop>` to display variables
- Use `<cfoutput>` to display query result sets with HTML
- Use `<cfquery>` special variables

Building Simple Queries with ColdFusion

You start with learning how ColdFusion queries the database. You use the
<cfquery> tag to format the SQL query. You also use <cfquery> to tell ColdFusion
what datasource to use. Here is <cfquery> in its simplest form.

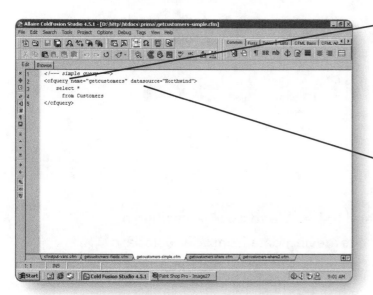

You use the name attribute of
<cfquery> to name the result set
returned by the query. With this
name, you can refer to the result
set later in the template. The
name attribute is required.

The datasource attribute is also
required. It tells ColdFusion to
what datasource to send the
SQL query.

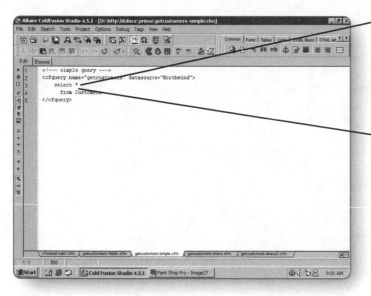

Between the beginning and
ending <cfquery> tags, you
place the actual SQL statement.
This can be any valid SQL
statement or set of statements.

The * (asterisk) here is SQL
shorthand. It means "return all
the columns in all the tables
listed in the from clause." By
using the *, you don't have to
type all the column names (or
even know what they are).

When you write CFML templates, it's important to know what the data looks like in its "raw" form. If you know what to expect from the data, you can write your ColdFusion code to handle the data appropriately. If you have the opportunity, always review the data with which you are working.

Using Filter Queries to Limit Data

You can limit the data that you are handling by filtering the data with a `where` clause in the SQL statement. From ColdFusion's point of view, this query is very much like the previous simple query. In fact, ColdFusion doesn't really care; as long as the SQL statement is valid, ColdFusion will send it along and present the result set back to you.

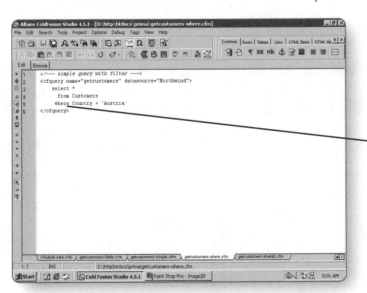

All that has changed is that a `where` clause has been added. The `where` clause limits the number of rows that the database returns by selecting only those records in which `Country` matches `Austria`.

NOTE

The way your database matches strings in `where` clauses depends on how the database is configured. Most default configurations allow for case-insensitive string matching, which means `Austria` will match `austria`, `Austria`, `AUSTRIA`, and `AuStRiA`.

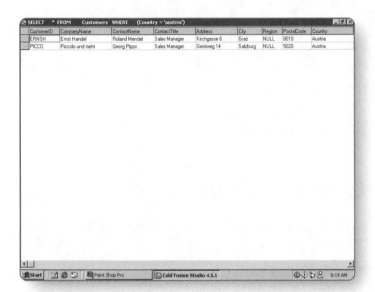

Although you have fewer rows now, you still have a lot of columns. In a full-fledged application, you might have to handle all these columns. But for the examples at this stage, it's better to return fewer columns from the `Customers` table.

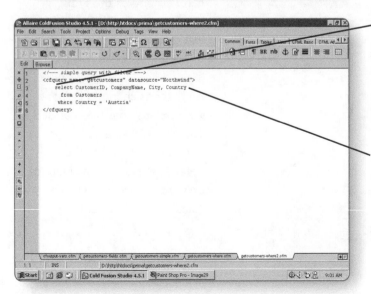

You can specify the columns you want to include in the result set. Note that when you specify the columns yourself, the burden is on you to enter the column names correctly.

Separate column names by commas.

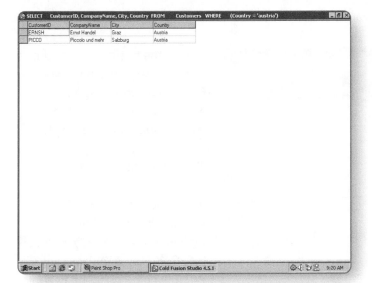

The data that this modified statement returns is much more selective and easier to read at a glance.

Displaying Data

Now you know how to retrieve data from a database using ColdFusion. But this will do your users no good if they can't see the data. You'll have to output the data somehow and do it in a way that is useful. This is where <cfoutput> comes in. <cfoutput> handles all output of ColdFusion variables and query result sets. So the next step in learning to build ColdFusion Web applications is to master <cfoutput>.

<cfoutput> has to interact with other ColdFusion tags and HTML tags to produce interesting and usable Web pages. First, you step through the basics.

Displaying ColdFusion Variable Values

The simplest form of <cfoutput> is used to output simple ColdFusion variables. You might need to output a date value, a loop counter, or perhaps a dynamic page title. Take a look at how that works.

First, you create some variables and set their values.

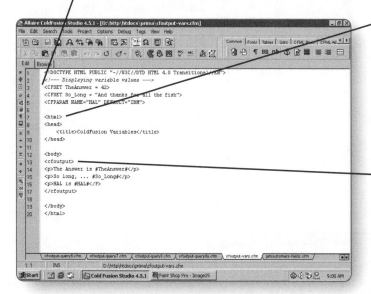

Here is the basic setup for the HTML page. You can put your ColdFusion code just about anywhere with respect to the HTML code, but I usually place variable definitions at the top, above the initial `<html>` tag.

Next, you have the beginning `<cfoutput>` tag. Between this tag and the ending `</cfoutput>` tag, ColdFusion replaces any variable name surrounded by #s with the appropriate value.

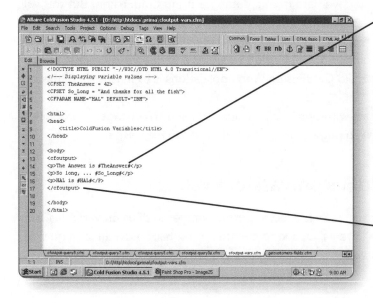

Note that the ColdFusion variables surrounded by #s are interspersed with plain text and HTML formatting tags. ColdFusion passes everything but what's within the pound signs as is. The text and HTML formatting tags are sent to the Web browser exactly as they appear here.

The ending `</cfoutput>` tag tells ColdFusion to stop looking for information to process and just pass the data along. So the ending HTML tags are sent along as they are.

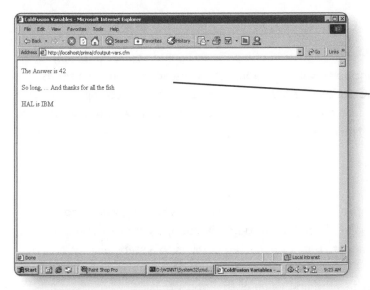

The Web browser receives only the HTML tags and text for display.

The source code of the page gives no hint that it came from anything other than a static HTML page on the Web server.

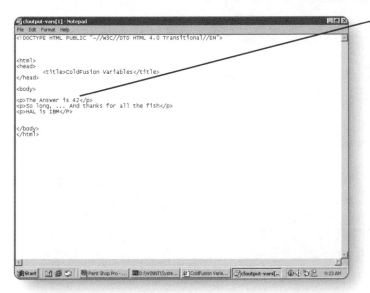

Note that the values of the variables have replaced the variable names in the HTML source code.

Displaying Values in Loops

Often you will need to output a section of a page again and again. For example, you might need to count down values or apply the same adjustment to a series of numbers or strings. ColdFusion provides the <cfloop> tag to accomplish such a feat. You can create these types of loops with <cfloop>: an index loop, a list loop, and a conditional loop. Now check out each type.

Index Loops

An index loop increments a value called the index from a starting value and steps through to the ending value. Each time through the loop, the index value is changed by the step amount. The <cfloop> tag defaults to a step value of 1.

The from attribute specifies the first value of the loop's index.

The to attribute specifies the ending value of the loop's index.

The index attribute specifies the name of the variable that represents the index value inside the <cfloop> tags.

<cfloop> assumes a step value of 1 when recalculating the value of the index each time through the loop.

Note that you must use <cfoutput> inside the <cfloop> tag to display ColdFusion variables.

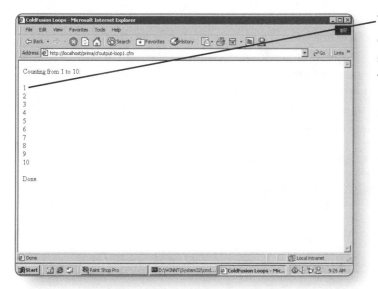

There is one line of output for each iteration through the loop, starting at 1 and adding 1 each time to reach 10.

List Loops

Lists are a great way to organize and manipulate values in ColdFusion. ColdFusion contains a great deal of support for handling lists of various sorts. A list is simply a string containing values separated by a delimiter. The values can be most anything, but typically they are numbers or strings, and the most common delimiter is the comma. The comma is the default delimiter in ColdFusion.

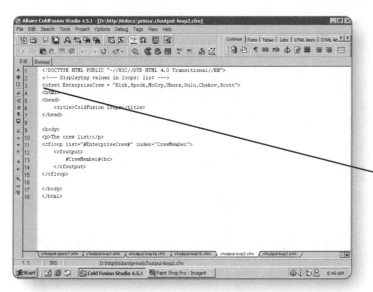

Now, check out how <cfloop> handles a list. This example starts by specifying a list of some TV characters you might recognize.

You can use <cfset> to create a string variable that contains a list of names, separated by commas.

NOTE

You should ignore grammar rules in comma-delimited lists. Spaces between list values are retained in ColdFusion, and you might not want them. In other words, each character between a comma in a list is significant.

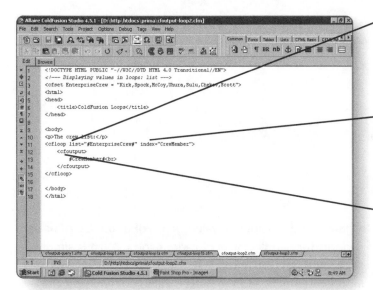

Instead of using the from, to, and step attributes, you use the list attribute to specify the variable that contains the list.

You still need the index attribute to track the index value inside the beginning and ending <cfloop> tags.

Don't forget the <cfoutput> tags if you are going to display variables inside the <cfloop>.

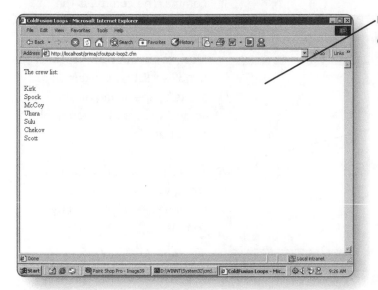

Using this method, you can create the crew manifest.

Conditional Loops

Conditional loops test a statement for a `true/false` or `yes/no` value to see whether the loop should continue. The trick to conditional loops is to design a conditional statement that is affected by something changing inside the loop itself. If the conditional statement does not change, the loop might continue forever, effectively killing your application.

As an example, consider a bidding competition in which there are two bidders and there is a cutoff bid (so you can end the loop). Every bidder must beat the competitor in each round by a set amount. The first one to the cutoff wins the bid.

First, you set a low (starting) bid amount with the variable `LowBid`. You can also use this variable to track the current bid amount in the loop.

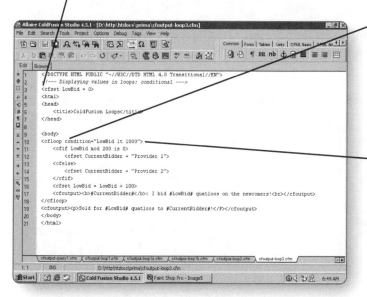

In the `<cfloop>` tag, you only need the `condition` attribute this time. Inside the quotes, you have a valid ColdFusion expression that evaluates to `yes` or `no`.

`lt` is a comparison operator meaning "less than." There are more comparison operators in ColdFusion such as `gt`, `lte` (for `"less than or equal"`), `gte`, `is`, `contains`, and so on. You can also spell them out if you want. Check the ColdFusion documentation for the exact syntax (found under CFML Language/ Operators).

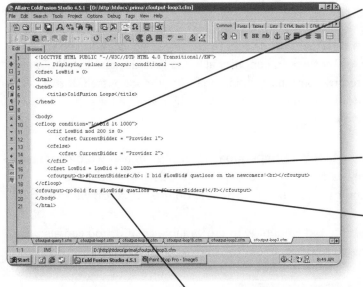

You use the modulus operator (mod) to decide when to change the bidder's name. Every time the current bid is evenly divisible by 200, you set the CurrentBidder to the next bidder.

Each time through the loop, the bid increases by 100.

<cfoutput> displays the current bidder's name and his or her bid for you.

Once outside the loop, you display the winning bid and who bid it with <cfoutput>.

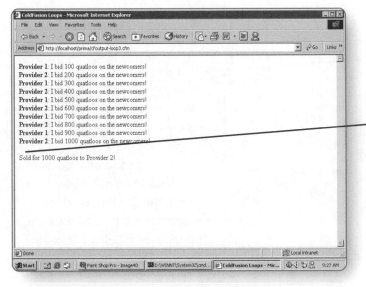

The bidding session in the browser should look like a conversation between the two bidders, with the winner declared at the end.

The loop continues until the conditional statement evaluates to false; that is, once LowBid is more than 1000, the loop ends and the final result is displayed.

Displaying a Query Result Set

Now for the meat and potatoes of `<cfoutput>`: displaying query result sets. Now that you've seen the basics of displaying variables with `<cfoutput>` and using loops to iterate over a set of values, displaying queries will be old news, almost. The mechanics of the `<cfoutput>` tag are identical when displaying query result sets. You simply have more options when outputting result sets.

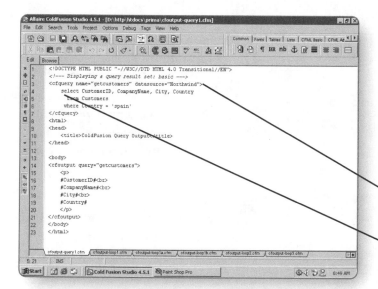

As an example, start with a very simple query using the Northwind database. Assume that you want to see all the customers in Spain, with their customer IDs and their home city. No fancy graphics or formatting, just the facts.

You give the query a name and specify a datasource.

Then specify the columns from the `Customers` table that you want to see in the output.

You set the where clause to filter the query results to include only those rows in which the country is `spain`.

You use the `query` attribute of the `<cfoutput>` tag to tell ColdFusion that you want to output the result set named `getcustomers`. You can have multiple queries in a template, so you have to specify the one you want.

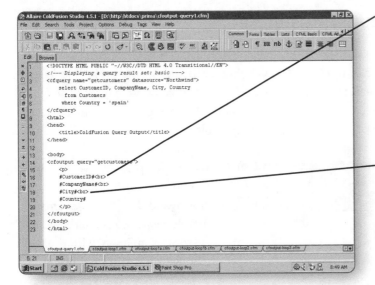

List each column that you want to output between the `<cfoutput>` beginning and ending tags. You surround each column with pound signs (#), just as you do with variable names for output.

No fancy HTML formatting here. Each column value is on a separate HTML line with breaks (`<br>`).

That's it. The output will be one record to a paragraph, with line breaks between the field values.

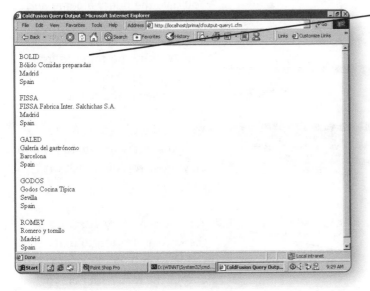

Notice that you have five paragraphs, each containing the values of the columns specified in the SQL statement for each customer in Spain.

Displaying the Query Count

In the previous example, it is pretty easy to see that you retrieved five rows from the Customers table. But what if there are more rows than can be easily counted at a glance? Or what if you need to know which row <cfoutput> is currently displaying?

<cfquery> returns a few special variables along with the result set to handle these circumstances. RecordCount holds the number of records, or rows, returned by the query. CurrentRow can be accessed inside a <cfoutput> (or a <cfloop> over a query). It displays the current row of the result set. ColumnList is a comma-delimited list of all the column names in the result set.

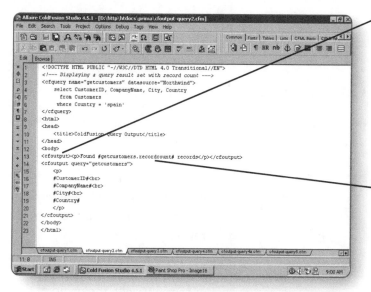

Take a look at the RecordCount variable first. One line has been added to the previous example. Inside the <cfoutput> tags, the special variable RecordCount is referenced to display the number of records found in the query.

You reference special variables by specifying the name of the query, plus a period, and then the special variable name. This amalgam should begin and end with a pound sign.

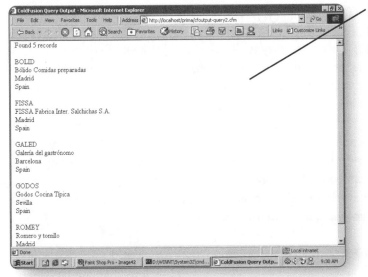

Now you know exactly how many records have been returned by the query.

Displaying the Current Row Number

Sometimes, it is useful to know which record <cfoutput> is currently displaying. You can use the CurrentRow variable of the query to show this value.

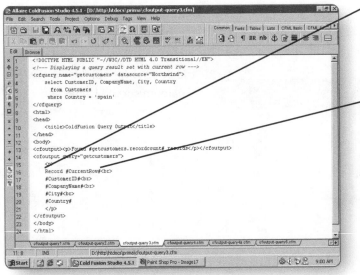

This new line displays the current record number along with the column values of the record.

Note that you do not prefix CurrentRow with the name of the query. Because the code is inside the <cfoutput> tag, the query is assumed to be the one named in the query attribute.

NOTE

The value of CurrentRow has no relationship to the number of the records in your database. The query may be returning, in no particular order, non-sequential rows from a table. CurrentRow numbers the returned rows from 1 to the number of records returned. Therefore, don't rely on CurrentRow to give you the physical or logical record number of a given row in a table or view.

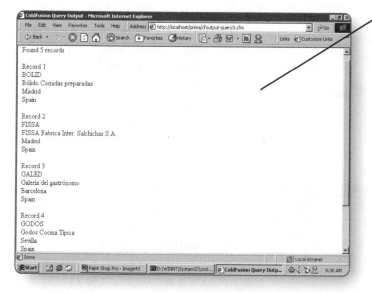

Now you can see the record number of the result set along with each record in the display.

Displaying Results in an HTML Table

Up to this point, you've been displaying these query results with bare HTML formatting. It is more common—and makes for easier reading—to display the output in a table format. You now add an HTML table to the display page, and give each column a header that explains what the values in the column represent. You can also give the table a border to frame the output in the browser window.

Now add one more twist. As a teaser for building dynamic queries, you can change the SQL statement to use a variable for the actual country name. This way, you can change the country name easily to view different customers.

Here you set a variable called CustomerLocation that holds the name of the country you want to display.

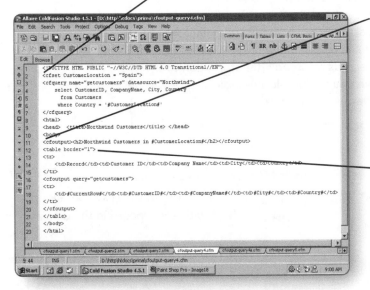

The HTML headline tag now contains the variable holding the customer's country name. The whole line is wrapped in a <cfoutput> in order to display a descriptive headline for the page.

You can start the HTML table outside a <cfoutput> tag. Don't repeat the table tag for each row in the record set. The following table row contains the descriptive headers for each column. Again, this table row should appear only once.

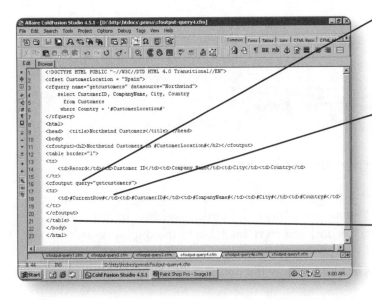

Here, you begin the <cfoutput> display of each row of the result set. One table row is shown for each result set row.

Each column name in the result set becomes a table data cell (using <td>). You place each column name with #s inside <td> tags to form the table columns.

Outside the <cfoutput>, you close the <table></table> tags.

The result of these modifications is an HTML table that provides for easy viewing.

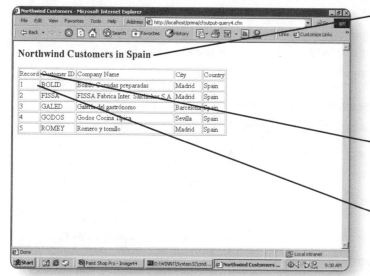

You now have a descriptive name for the information you are viewing in the browser, and it is fully dynamic (it changes when you change the CustomerLocation variable).

The first row of the table is the header that describes the column values.

Notice that each row of the table represents a single row of the query result set. The trick here is to place only the ColdFusion and HTML code you need to repeat inside the <cfoutput> tags.

Displaying a Result Set with Highlighted Rows

When you have large tables with many rows, the information can be difficult to read. This is especially true when you have many columns across the page.

In these circumstances, you need to have more control over the HTML so that you can format the table to make it more visually attractive and useful. One way to do this is to highlight every other row of output with a background color. You can use the CurrentRow special variable to do this.

To accomplish this, try setting the background color of the table row to a light gray if the current record number is even; otherwise, the background color will be white.

This is the line that does the work. Everything else is the same as the previous HTML table example. You have to set the bgcolor attribute of the `<tr>` tag for each row in the result set.

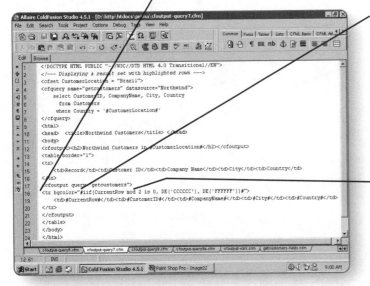

This #iif statement is like a compressed cfif/cfelse statement. Don't worry about the syntax right now. The statement says: "if the current row number is even, use CCCCCC as the background color, otherwise use FFFFFF."

This looks familiar. Review the `<cfloop>` example on conditional loops for information about how the modulus operator works.

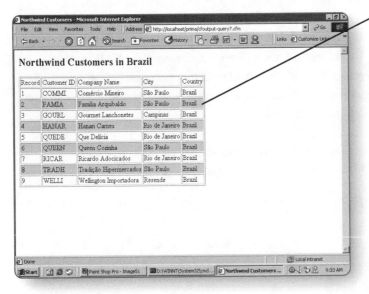

The rows with the even record numbers are now highlighted with a light gray background. This gives the table a nice formatted look, and it helps viewers maintain continuity from left to right in the table.

Of course, you don't have to use gray as your highlight color. In fact, you can use variables to hold the highlight values. That way, you can change the colors easily without having to change the color value on every table in your templates.

Displaying the Query Set Using the Column List

In all the query display examples so far, you have specified the table columns you want to see in the output. Sometimes it is easier to use the * (asterisk) in your SQL select statement to show all the columns. That's nice, but when you want to display the columns on a Web page, you still need to know the names of the columns for the <cfoutput> or the <cfcol> tags, right? Wrong.

You can use the special variable ColumnList from the query to retrieve the names of all the columns in the result set. Remember that ColumnList is just a comma-delimited list of column names in the result set.

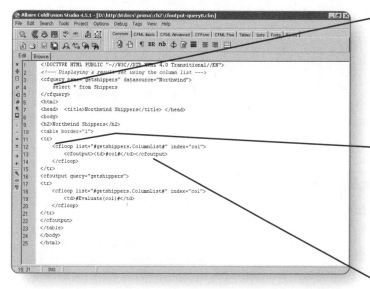

This time, you want to show everything about the shippers in the Northwind database. You use the * to specify that all columns should be returned from the query.

First, to get the table headers right, you loop over the ColumnList to retrieve each column name in turn. The index value is the actual name of the column as a string.

Because you are looping over the list of column names, you only want the individual table cell that's holding the index variable inside the <cfoutput> tags.

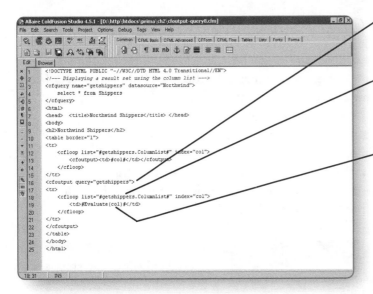

Now you start the `<cfoutput>` loop over the query itself.

You loop over the column list again to access each column name in turn.

The `col` variable contains the name of the column that holds the desired value. So you use the `evaluate` function to tell ColdFusion to evaluate the variable named by the value in `col`. In this way, you can access the value of the column, as in any other `<cfoutput>` situation, without actually knowing what the column name is.

Gee, I don't know. It looks like magic to me. What does this really display?

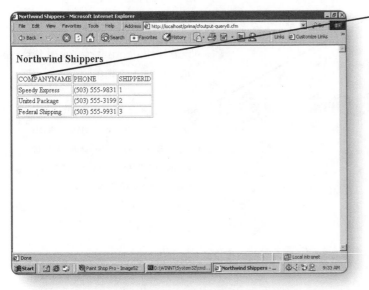

The column list is in an arbitrary order as returned by the query.

To change the order in which the columns are displayed, you have to manipulate the `ColumnList` somehow. You can sort the values of a list in ColdFusion with the `ListSort` function.

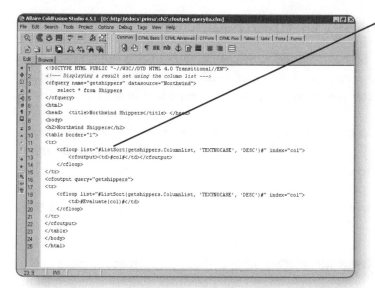

This statement says "sort the list named ColumnList, in reverse alphabetical order, ignoring case."

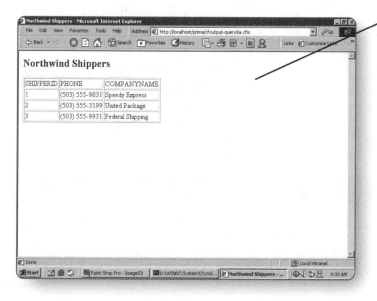

The sorted column list now displays the shipper information according to shipper ID.

Displaying a Subset of the Result Set

The data display has so far been limited to SQL only. You can also use ColdFusion to limit the output of your queries. You can tell `<cfoutput>` to display only a certain number of rows, no matter how many have been returned by the query.

A good example of this is displaying a top-10 list of something. This example has a fairly complex SQL query that asks Northwind for the sum of units of each product sold, sorted from most to least sold.

Examine how you can use this query to display the top 10 Northwind products by total unit sales.

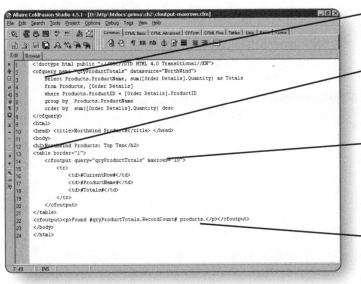

You can learn about these complex queries in Appendix B.

You can skip the headers on this table to keep the code easier to read.

You use the `maxrows` attribute of the `<cfoutput>` tag to limit the display of the query result set to the first 10 rows.

Just to show that the query returns more than 10 products, you can display the `RecordCount` at the end of the table.

You can now view the top 10 sellers.

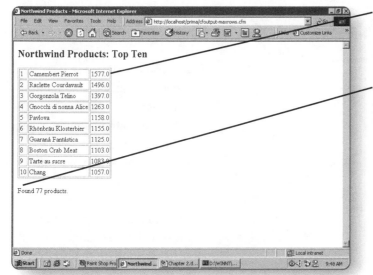

Notice that the numbers of units sold starts with the largest value and decreases.

See, more than 10 products were returned by the query. You are truly only seeing the top 10.

Displaying a Series of Result Subsets Across Multiple Pages

Say that you want to see the sales figures for all the Northwind products, but not all on one page. You need to step through the product sales figures, say, in batches of 10 products per page. No problem.

You need to show only 10 products at a time, starting at a different row each time. You can use the maxrows attribute in conjunction with the startrow attribute of the <cfoutput> tag. You then use a url variable to tell the template which row to start on each time. This way, you can create a navigation link at the bottom of the page to move through the product list.

First, you set a variable named `FirstRow` to a default value of 1.

Next, you check to see whether there was a url variable named `first` passed to the template. If so, the template has been called from a navigation link, and you need to change the value of `FirstRow`.

Now, you need to figure out what row the next page should start with because the program uses this value in the navigation link at the bottom of the page. You can get this value by adding 10 to `FirstRow`.

In the `<cfoutput>` for the query, you set `startrow` to the value of `FirstRow` (don't forget the #s), and set `maxrows` to 10.

Inside a `<cfoutput>`, you create an HTML link that points to this template, with a url variable named `first` having a value of `StartNextPage`. This is your navigation link through the product list.

Check out what happens.

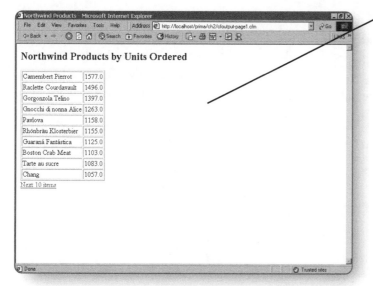

Wow! This looks good. You have the product list showing 10 items at a time, with a link at the bottom of the page so you can view the next 10 items. But you can't go back. Also, if you click the navigation link eight times, you end up with a screen containing only a link on it.

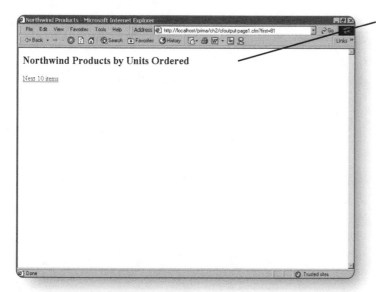

Oops. There is no end to these forward navigation links. They just keep going. You need a mechanism whereby you can stop displaying the forward navigation link when there are no more records to display. You also need to be able to go backward through the list. You add the "Previous 10 items" link first.

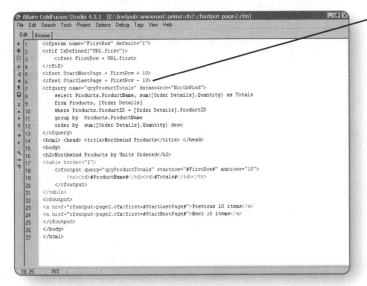

You add a new variable to determine on which row the last set of 10 items should start. You can get this value by subtracting 10 from the FirstRow value.

You add a new HTML link just like the "Next 10 items" but use the StartLastPage value for the url variable instead.

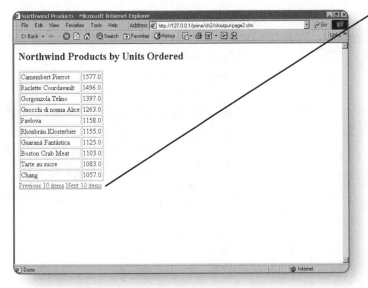

Now you have "Previous" and "Next" links.

You're almost there. But if you're on the first screen and click the "Previous 10 items" link, you get a nasty error from ColdFusion.

This page tells you that you can't use a negative value in the `startrow` attribute of the `<cfoutput>` tag. Well, I guess you knew that didn't make sense. Actually, this is the same boundary problem as the "infinite Next links," but in reverse. By boundary problem, I mean that you have not checked your navigation link URL variable values to see if they are in the bounds of the result set.

Basically, you want to display the forward navigation link only if `StartNextPage` is less than the total number of records, and you want to display the backward navigation link only if `StartLastPage` is greater than 1. Take a look at how to do that.

You wrap the HTML link code for the previous set with a `<cfif>` tag to check whether `StartLastPage` is greater than or equal to one.

You also wrap the HTML link code for the next set with another `<cfif>` tag to determine whether `StartNextPage` is less than or equal to the `RecordCount` of the query.

By wrapping the HTML link code with conditional <cfif> statements, you display the navigation links only if they make sense. Now you try it.

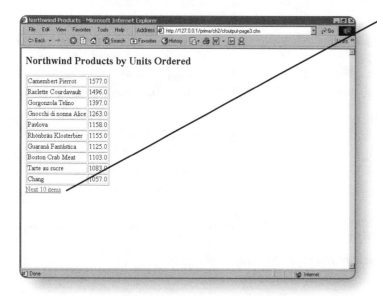

As you might expect, there is no "Previous 10 items" link on the top page of the product list.

Click "Next 10 items" seven times to see the screen that indicates the end of the record set.

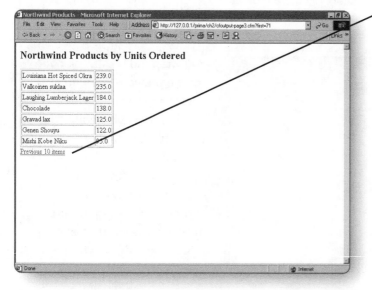

At the end of the product list, you no longer have the "Next 10 items" link, also as expected.

3

Creating ColdFusion and HTML Forms

The Web is fantastic for displaying information in the form of text and images, using the formatting language, HTML. But the real power of the Web is its interactivity. HTML forms (*forms* are the way users commonly interact with a Web page) can go a long way in providing this interactivity. But, with ColdFusion, you can make your forms dynamic and responsive to users' actions.

In this chapter, you learn how to:

- Use different HTML form elements
- Write a simple HTML form
- Write a data-driven form
- Write a form with default values
- Write a form with `<cfform>`
- Write a form with the `<cfgrid>` form element

Working with HTML Forms

An HTML form is an electronic version of a paper form. You have most likely used many paper forms before—consider a change-of-address form at the post office or a credit card application. A paper form has labeled boxes that you fill in with information, or check boxes you mark. An electronic form has the same elements: text fields, radio buttons, and check boxes.

To use forms efficiently, you need to know a few things about how they work. When you fill out a paper form, you hand it to someone for processing. The information is then read and perhaps transferred to another form or computer application (maybe even a database). When you fill out an HTML form and press the Submit button, what happens? How does the form know what to do with the information you entered? The next sections address these questions in detail.

Designing HTML Forms to Gather Information

An HTML form needs two basic attributes: the action and method attributes. The action attribute indicates the Web page to which the form should send the information. This page is usually a Web application of some kind, such as a Perl script, a CGI application, or a ColdFusion template. It is the responsibility of the action attribute to process the information on the form.

If you do not specify an action for an HTML form, it submits the information to itself for processing. This may seem strange, but it is not such a bad idea. By having the form process itself, you have encapsulated the entire submission and information gathering process into one template. This procedure reduces code maintenance and makes your application easier to code. This may not always be feasible, but you should consider it when writing a new form. In the examples in this chapter, you use the same action page: a ColdFusion template that displays the form information back to you. You don't do anything with the form information until Chapter 4, "Processing and Validating Forms."

The other attribute that is important for defining how a form's information is processed is the method attribute. The method attribute defines how the form information is sent to the action page. There are two method types: get and post. The get method sends all the information from the form in the URL of the action page. The form builds a query string of name/value pairs and appends it to the URL. If you do not specify a method, the form uses the get method. The post method sends the information in an HTTP header to the action page. The form builds the same name/value pairs, but the users don't see the header.

The method attribute is important for ColdFusion. It determines how you address form values. If the method is set to get, form fields and values are in the URL scope. If the method is set to post, ColdFusion uses the form scope.

To create an HTML form with a post method and an action of test-form.cfm, type the following:

```
<form method="post" action="test-form.cfm"></form>
```

This is not a very interesting form. There's nothing in it. You need some form elements to give the users something to fill in. That's where the <input> tag comes in.

Using <input> Elements to Build Forms

The basic HTML form element is created with the <input> tag. The <input> tag is used to create the following types of form elements: text boxes, check boxes, radio buttons, password boxes, Submit buttons, Reset buttons, generic buttons, and hidden elements. Take a look at text boxes first.

To create a text box on your form, type the following inside the <form></form> tags:

```
<input type="text" name="textbox1">
```

The <input> tag requires the type attribute. The name attribute is necessary when you want to refer to the value in the text box.

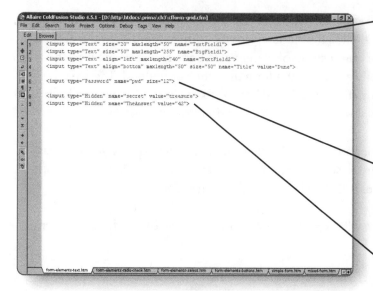

The `<input type="text">` tag accepts attributes that determine how the text box appears on the Web page, such as the size of the box and the maximum number of characters it accepts.

A password `<input>` element is similar to a text box, but when you type in the box, the characters are displayed as asterisks (*).

The hidden `<input>` type enables you to store a value on an HTML form without showing it to users. This is useful when passing a value from form to form, such as the user's e-mail address. This way, you don't have to ask for the e-mail address on each subsequent form. To use the hidden type, specify the type as `Hidden` and use the `value` attribute to give it a value.

To create radio buttons on your form, you use the same syntax as the text box; just specify `Radio` as the `input type` instead of `Text`. To group radio buttons so that users can mark only one button at a time, give all the radio buttons the same name. You can then give each radio button a specific value using the `value` attribute.

Check boxes are like radio buttons, but they are selected independently of one another (so more than one in a group can be selected). You can create a group of check boxes by giving them the same name, just like radio buttons. However, when users select multiple check boxes, the form submits the values of the check boxes as a single, comma-delimited value with the common name given to the group of check boxes. To show a particular radio button or check box already checked, you add the `checked` attribute to the `<input>` tag. You'll see examples of how to process check boxes in Chapter 4.

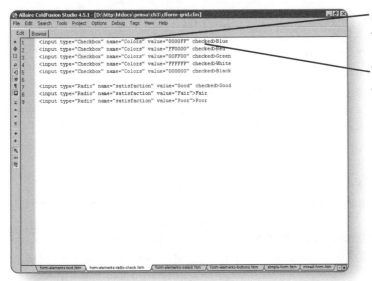

Note that each check box has the same `name`.

The `checked` attribute tells the form to show this check box as checked.

Using <select> Lists to Choose Data

Select lists are powerful form elements that give the users a list of items from which to pick. Select lists can restrict users to picking only one item, or they can allow multiple selections from the list. When a select list allows a single selection, it's often referred to as a *drop-down list*.

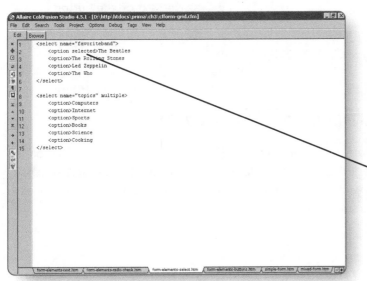

In HTML, you use the <select> tag to create a select list. You specify the list of items, or options, by using the <option> tag between the <select></select> tags. Take a look at some examples.

The selected attribute indicates that an item in the list should be shown as selected.

Creating Buttons for Form Operation

The standard way to submit a form for processing is by using a Submit button. The Submit and Reset buttons are special buttons found on an HTML form. When a Submit button is pressed, a form is sent to the `action` page. The Reset button restores all form elements specified by a `value` attribute to their default values. If a form element does not have a `value` attribute, the Reset button clears the form element.

You can create generic buttons as well. To make the generic button do anything, though, you have to attach an *event* (such as clicking the button) to a script that performs some action. Typically, this script is written in JavaScript or VBScript. You learn how to use generic buttons in Chapter 6, "Modifying and Deleting Data."

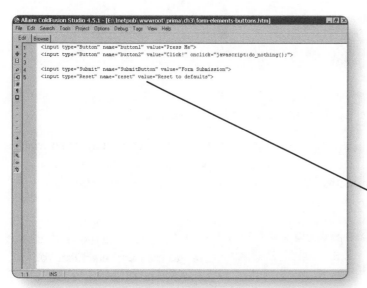

The syntax for all three types of buttons is identical.

Whatever you place in the `value` attribute of a button shows up as the text on the button.

Writing a Simple HTML Form

Now you know how a form works and what kind of information you can place on a form. It's time to put together a very simple form. This form asks the users for their first and last names, as well as their e-mail addresses, so it needs three text boxes. To submit the form, you use a standard Submit button.

The HTML formatting is unimportant, but to keep everything in line with the least amount of fuss, use the <pre></pre> tags, which will preserve all the original text formatting. The test-form.cfm form processor is the action. This example posts the form.

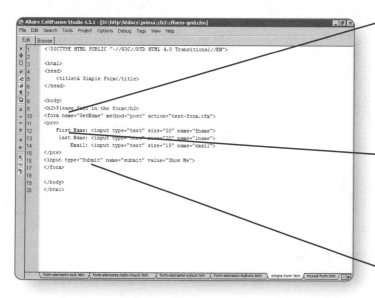

Get into the habit of naming your forms. When you're ready to use scripting to enhance your forms, you'll find it easier if you've already named all the forms on your page.

Because you are using the <pre></pre> tags, the browser displays all white space, including new lines, just as it is laid out in the code.

Make sure that you place the <input> tag for the Submit button inside the <form></form> tags.

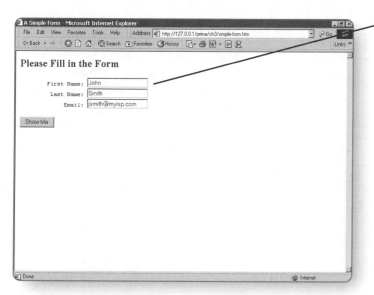

In the browser, the form has a simple interface with three text boxes and a button, just as expected.

To give you an idea what the test-form.cfm form processor does, take a look at the browser after you press the Show Me button.

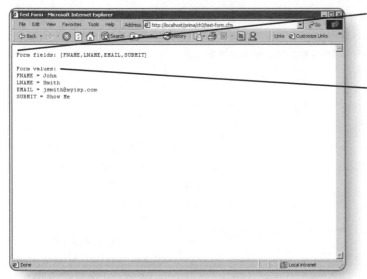

First, it lists the names of all the form fields that test-form.cfm received from simple-form.htm.

Next, it lists the name/value pairs of these form fields. Note that these values match the values typed into the form.

This is a very simple form that performs a specific (and limited) function. Perhaps you want to know how this customer came to your Web site. You can also ask whether the users want to receive e-mail about your products. You can add these features easily with some check boxes and two radio buttons.

Creating Data-Driven HTML Forms

Now you add some data to these forms. Assume that a customer is interested in Northwind products and wants to view more information about a particular category of products. To this end, you can create a form that lists Northwind's products by category. Easy enough—you have already seen the HTML code that places a drop-down list of items on a form.

However, what if Northwind adds another product category to the catalog? You would then have to rewrite the HTML form to include the new category. Likewise, if Northwind discontinues a product category, you would have to remove it from the form.

There is a better way. You can query the database for the appropriate categories and use ColdFusion to build a dynamic HTML form based on the query results. This way, you don't have to rewrite the HTML form when the list changes. The ColdFusion template always displays the correct list.

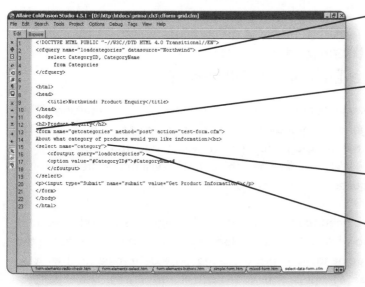

First, use <cfquery> to retrieve all the category names and IDs from the Categories table.

You then create the HTML form with the standard syntax, specifying a name, method, and action.

Start a <select> element and give it a name.

Now, instead of listing all the categories by name, use <cfoutput> to create the <option> list for the <select> tag. Note that each item's value matches the category ID from the database.

The form now updates itself

every time it is requested. The form will never have an incorrect category list (as long as the database is correct, of course).

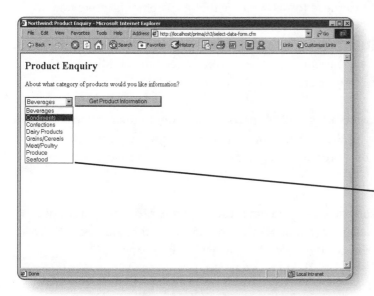

You can use this same technique to create a dynamic list of check boxes, radio buttons, and so on. You can even use a database table to store the list of fields that should appear on the form to create a truly dynamic Web form.

Now you have a dynamic drop-down list based on the database.

Setting Default <select> Values in a Data-Driven HTML Form

Data-driven <select> elements are a great tool for creating self-maintaining HTML forms. But people are generally greedy. We want even more control over our HTML form elements. What if the marketing department wants to feature a particular product category on the Web site each month? Can Web visitors be steered to that category when they request more information? No problem.

The trick here is that you need to show the featured category as the selected item in the drop-down list. So while <cfoutput> is looping through the categories in the query result set, the code needs to check the category to determine whether it is the one to mark as selected. If it is, your code needs to display the selected attribute with the current <option> tag. If it isn't, the template displays no additional attribute.

First, you need to create a ColdFusion variable for the featured category ID as listed in the database. You then use this value to check the current category ID. Before you check for the featured category, you set a variable to hold an empty string value inside the <cfoutput> loop. If the loop is on the featured category, the string is set to selected; otherwise, the string is empty.

The new form has some new variables and attributes, of course.

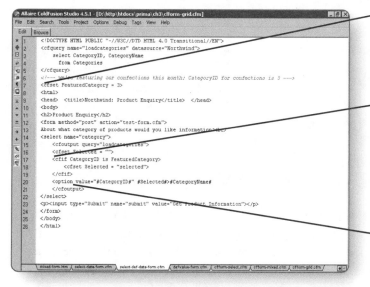

The Confections category is being featured this month, so the FeaturedCategory variable is set to its ID.

This is where the decision about matching the featured category takes place. If the current CategoryID matches the FeaturedCategory, the attribute string is set to selected.

Note that when the featured category doesn't match the current category in the loop, #Selected# evaluates to an empty string, and the option does not appear as selected in the HTML code.

With just five additional lines (and an alteration to one), you've added great flexibility to your form.

Another way to improve this form would be to use a database query to find the ID of the featured category. You could build a tool in the Access database so that the marketing department can specify the featured category when the mood strikes, and you would never have to touch this form again! I'll leave this as an exercise for you at a later time.

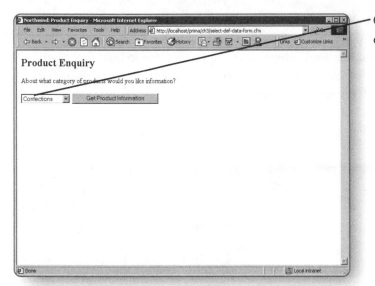

Confections is already selected on the form.

Creating Forms with Default Values

HTML forms are a great way to receive new information from the Web, as you've just seen. However, forms are also a great way to update existing information. By presenting the information you have about existing customers in a Web form, for example, customers can update your data for you. However, by themselves, HTML forms can't help you very much here. You need to fill in the form dynamically so that the users can update it. Static HTML forms were not designed to do this by themselves.

This is where ColdFusion comes in again. By querying your database first, you can retrieve the outdated information and fill in the form dynamically. This kind of form is the bread and butter of many intranet applications because they replace traditional stand-alone applications with updatable forms, such as inventories or product catalogs.

The process is simple. You query the database for the applicable information. In the form elements, you use the `value` attribute to fill in the fields. You learn the hard part of this process—actually updating the database with the altered data—in Chapter 6. For now, you build the form.

You start by establishing some variables to hold the values to edit.

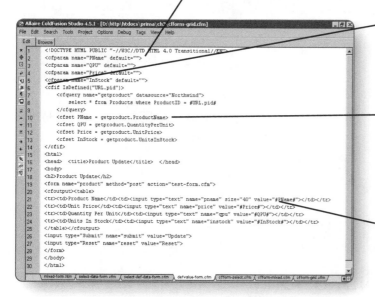

Next, determine whether the form was passed a URL variable named pid, which holds the ProductID of the product to edit.

You set the variables' values to the respective values of the columns in the query. Note the syntax in accessing the values from the query.

Now, use the variable names (with #s of course) in the value attributes of the form elements. Don't forget your <cfoutput> tags.

TIP

The ColdFusion function IsDefined is very useful for determining whether a variable exists prior to accessing it. ColdFusion returns an error when you try to access a variable that does not exist. You can avoid this error if you use IsDefined first.

The key point when building this type of form is that you want to create ColdFusion variables that hold at least a default value for each of the values you intend to edit on the form. By creating these place-holding variables, you can use the form even when the query doesn't return a record to edit.

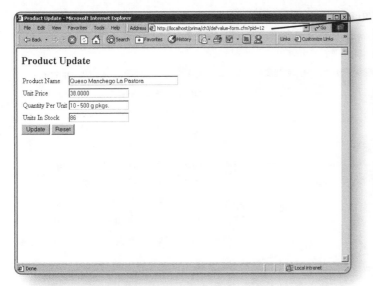

Note that the URL variable has been added to the URL line in the browser. Place a ? after the template name and then add the variable name followed by an = and the value.

Now the form contains all the information about the product, ready to be updated.

Creating ColdFusion Forms with <cfform>

HTML forms give you almost everything you need to interact with users online. Unfortunately, we don't live in a perfect world, and none of us is perfect. People make mistakes, and most assuredly, your users will do the same. If you want an HTML form to hold a date or a phone number, you have to assume that the person typing in the information has done it correctly. But what if they make a mistake? You may end up with dates like 4/68/20000. Wouldn't it be nice if the form could validate the information in the form field? You guessed it: ColdFusion can do that.

<cfform>, <cfinput>, and <cfselect>

ColdFusion provides the <cfform> tag for data validation, which is actually just an HTML form. However, when <cfform> is delivered to the browser, ColdFusion also sends along some JavaScript code that validates the specified form fields. The other benefit of <cfform> is that you can use the ColdFusion versions of other HTML form elements, which provide data validation, special access to queries, and simpler code.

Just like HTML forms, the basic tag for creating most form elements is ColdFusion's answer to the <input> tag: <cfinput>. You use <cfinput> just like <input>, but <cfinput> includes a few more attributes. The most useful attributes are for data validation. You learn about these attributes in detail in Chapter 4.

Check out the <cfform> version of the previous "featured category" form. The code is much simpler using the <cfselect> tag. The value attribute contains the column name from the query that holds the options for the <cfselect> element. The display attribute contains the column name that supplies the values shown in the drop-down list.

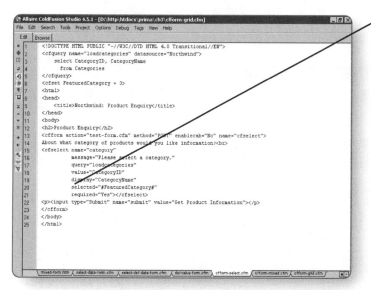

The selected attribute needs a value, not a reference to a value. Therefore, you place the variable name surrounded by #s so that ColdFusion evaluates the variable name for its value.

The browser displays this form just like the previous version.

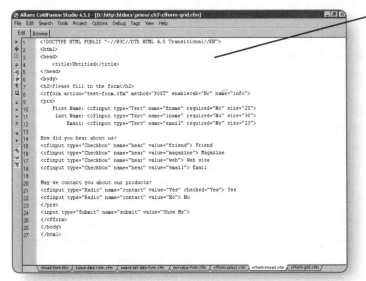

Now take a look at the `<cfform>` version of the mixed element HTML form. The code to create the form elements is very similar. The big difference is that the first name and last name form fields are now required. If either field is left blank, the user is notified.

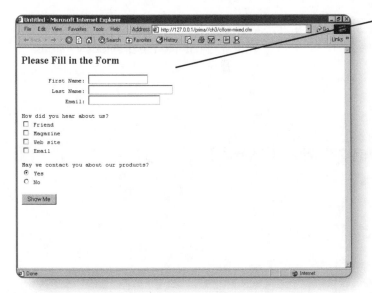

As you can see, the output of this form in the browser looks identical to the straight HTML version.

<cfgrid>

ColdFusion also has some extended form elements. One of the most useful of these for displaying and manipulating data is <cfgrid>. This element is actually a Java applet that ships with ColdFusion. The <cfgrid> element is a grid, much like a table, that holds rows and columns of information. You can use <cfgrid> to display static data in a compact form, or you can use it as an editing tool to provide users with a rich environment in which to change data.

<cfgrid> can be used alone or with <cfgridcolumn> and <cfgridrow>. <cfgrid> provides default formatting for the columns and rows in its display, but if you want more control over the formatting and display of column headers and the like, you need to use <cfgridcolumn> or <cfgridrow>. Note that if you want to use <cfgridcolumn>, such as to format one column in your query display, you have to use a <cfgridcolumn> for each column in the query. You look at examples with <cfgridcolumn> in Chapters 5 and 7. For now, take a look at <cfgrid>.

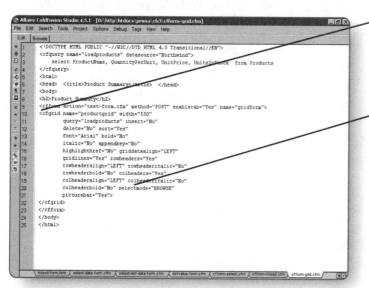

<cfgrid> has lots of attributes. It's best to use the Tag Editor in ColdFusion Studio to configure your <cfgrid> forms.

The selectmode attribute determines whether <cfgrid> allows editing, and if so, what kind of editing is permissible. This grid is set for browsing only.

As you can see, this form is a big step from the simple form created at the beginning of the chapter. With <cfgrid>, you can provide your users with a powerful interface to your database and in a familiar form. The form element created by <cfgrid> is similar to the interface provided by many popular spreadsheet applications. When designing a Web replacement for a venerable, but antiquated, desktop application, providing a familiar setting to the users is often more than half the battle.

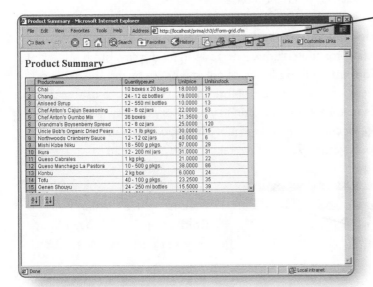

Click the column header of any column to select the whole column. You can then use the sort buttons at the bottom of the grid to sort the selected column.

If you expect to deliver your Web forms to older browsers that don't support Java applets or to browsers likely to have Java support disabled, you won't be able to use these extended form elements.

4

Processing and Validating Forms

Now that you've created all these great Web forms, you'll need to do something with all the data they are generating. Therefore, this chapter focuses on the ColdFusion templates that are the target of the action attribute of your forms. Ultimately, you'll want to send this data to your database. But before you do that, you need to learn how to use ColdFusion to handle form data. You also need to consider the issues related to validating the data you are receiving from the forms. In this chapter, you learn how to:

- Process text box data and radio button data
- Process check box data and text area data
- Validate form data on the server manually and with ColdFusion
- Validate form data on the client with `<cfform>`
- Check for malicious code embedded in form fields
- Create forms that process themselves

Processing Form Elements

When a template is requested from a form using the post method, all the form fields are stored in a header of the request. ColdFusion receives this header from the Web server when the template is requested, and it creates a scope for the fields called form. The form scope has a special variable called fieldnames that contains a comma-delimited list of all the form fields it found in the header. You can use the fieldnames variable to display all the form fields and values submitted with a form without knowing the field names. In fact, the default action template, test-form.cfm, provides a way to test your forms as you build them.

To be absolutely certain that this template was posted, you can check for the existence of the fieldnames variable.

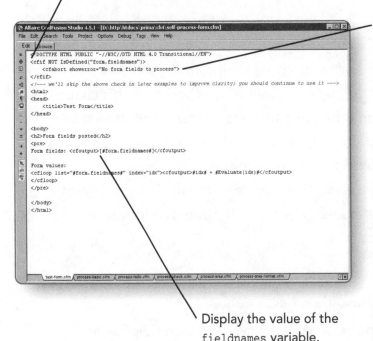

If the fieldnames variable does not exist, you can abort the template and report the error to the browser using the <cfabort> tag.

Display the value of the fieldnames variable.

TIP

<cfabort> stops all processing of the template by ColdFusion. Any code following the <cfabort> tag is not processed, including HTML code. Aborting a template is pretty drastic, but doing so can be useful. You learn about other debugging and error-handling techniques later in the book.

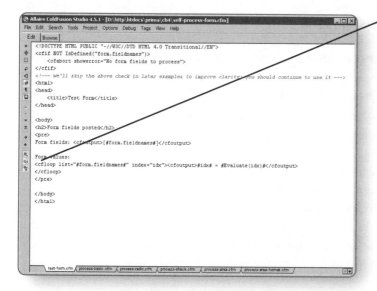

Because `fieldnames` is just a list, you can loop over it and display the field name (the loop index). You can also `evaluate` the field name to display the value of the form field.

The positioning of the code inside the `<cfloop>` looks a little strange because it's inside the `<pre></pre>` tags. To get each name/value pair on a single line in the output, you have to limit the number of carriage returns between the HTML pre-format tags.

Here's what the output of the test-form.cfm template looks like when posted from the simple form built in Chapter 3, "Creating ColdFusion and HTML Forms."

You now have a nice listing of the form fields and their values, one to a line. This is a great debugging technique to use when you are building new forms.

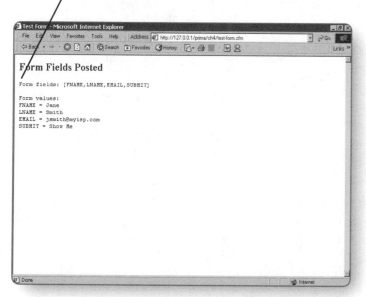

Now you can learn how to process specific types of form elements. In each section that follows, I use the mixed element form from Chapter 3 as the submitting form. This form was the sample survey form with text and check boxes. I've changed the `action` attribute of the form for each processing template featured in the section. Other than `action`, these forms are identical.

Processing Text Boxes

Text boxes are the most common form element that you will process. Generally, there isn't anything special about text boxes with respect to processing (however, see the later section "Checking for Malicious Code in Form Fields" for some other issues related to text boxes). This example uses text boxes to introduce some good coding practices in ColdFusion.

This basic form-processing template contains variables for holding the value of each form field that can be submitted from the form. You then use these variables in the body of the template, instead of using the form scope variables. Doing so enables you to isolate the original values in the form scope variables. Often during form processing, you need to alter the values of the form variables in some way. By using the local variables instead, you preserve those original values, should you need them again.

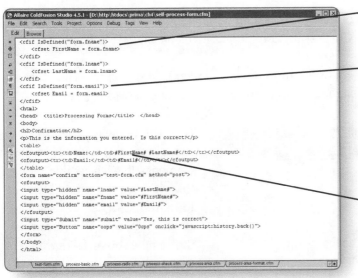

Use this quick check to see whether this form was posted.

It is a good habit to check every form field's existence before trying to access it. After checking for its existence, you assign the form variable value to a new local variable.

When displaying the information back to the users, you use the local variable, not the form scope variable.

There is a bonus in this form-processing template—it has another form! Because this is a confirmation page, the users need to confirm the data by sending it on to the next form processor (in this case, it's sent to the test-form.cfm template).

The new form has three hidden form fields and two buttons. The hidden fields simply hold the values of the previous form's fields. When this new form is submitted, it passes the values on for processing.

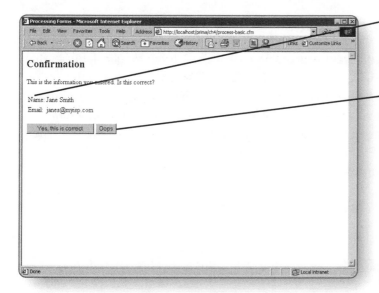

Here is the information that the users typed into the form, displayed for confirmation.

This is a generic button that invokes a small JavaScript command when clicked. The button sends the users back to the original form.

Processing Radio Buttons

Handling radio buttons is very similar to handling text boxes. Because a group of radio buttons that share a form field name returns a single value, accessing that value is identical to accessing the value of a text box. The difference is that you know what the radio buttons' values can be (assuming that you wrote the form with the radio buttons), which gives you some leeway in handling values from them.

I've dispensed with the existence check on the name and e-mail fields for clarity.

To hold the value of the yes/no radio buttons, you set a default variable value. This default assumes that the visitors do not want to be contacted.

You then check for existence of the form.contact variable, and if it's there, set the local variable to whatever the users selected.

Processing Check Boxes

Check boxes present a different processing challenge. A group of check boxes that share a field name returns a comma-delimited list of all the values that were checked on the form. Often, you'll need to process each value individually. You might need to extract one value out of the list for special processing, for example, or you might need to insert the values into separate columns in the database. The good news is that ColdFusion has many functions for dealing with lists of all kinds, some of which you have already seen.

Initially, you treat the check box form field just like a text box. Set the local variable value to the whole list.

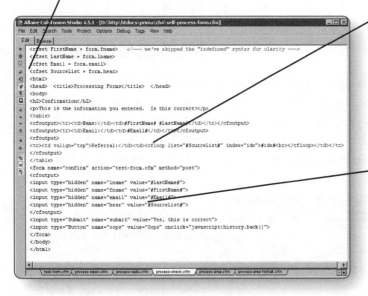

In the confirmation display, you loop over the source list and display each value in the list in turn. By treating the single check box form field value as a list, you have essentially turned it into several values.

The local variable #SourceList# still holds the entire list of values, so you can pass it intact on to the next form.

Now you have a more complete confirmation message.

Note that the list of referrals, as checked off by the user, now appears as separate values on the confirmation page.

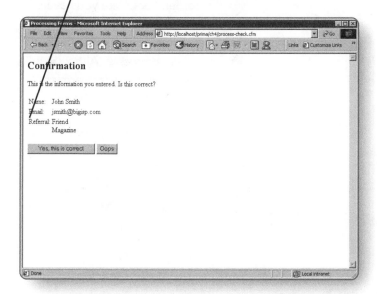

Processing Text Areas

Text areas provide a way for large amounts of text to be submitted using a Web form. You'll find the `<textarea>` tag both a boon and a bane. Although the capability to submit large amounts of text is often required by your Web application, the fact that the users can type just about anything means that you need to be careful about how you handle the submitted text.

For special handling of text areas and security concerns, see the later section "Checking for Malicious Code in Form Fields."

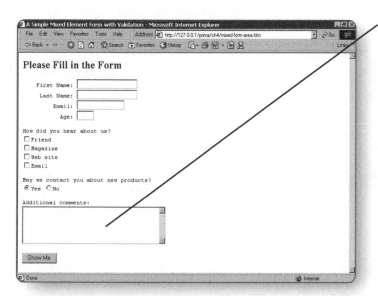

Here is the `<textarea>` form element. The columns and rows visible in the browser can be adjusted with the `cols` and `rows` attributes.

The addition of the comments provides a confirmation to the user of what she submitted with the form.

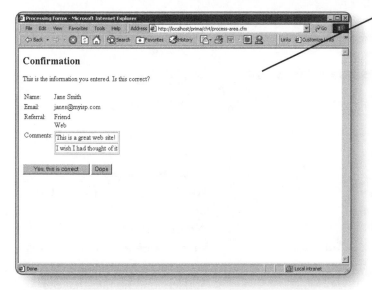

Hey! The comments are displayed in an HTML table with a border. Looks like you have a clever user here who has embedded some HTML code into her comments. Although in this circumstance, it's harmless, you might not always be so lucky.

You can avoid this potential problem by using the `htmleditformat` or `htmlcodeformat` functions to escape all the HTML tags in the Comments field.

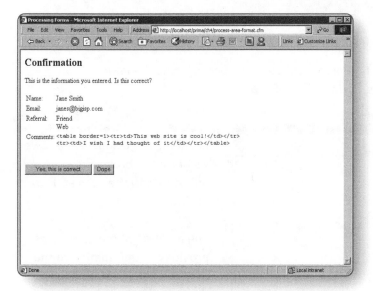

That's better. These format functions convert all <s and >s to the standard escaped HTML format, `&lt;` and `&gt;` respectively. When these codes are delivered to the browser for display, the browser simply converts them back to < and >, with no evaluation of the tag names in between.

NOTE

You can (and should) use a similar strategy with any form field that allows free typing by the users, not just `<textarea>`. This includes ordinary HTML text boxes and `<cfinput>` text boxes.

Validating Form Data

You now know how to deal with unwanted code or scripts embedded in form input fields. But how do you handle data that's inappropriately added to a form? What happens, for example, if you receive "Barney" when you are expecting a date? What if the number entered is out of the database field's range? To avoid these pitfalls, you need to validate the data you receive from the form for its intended use.

You can accomplish this validation in different ways—on the server and on the client. Look at manual server-side validation techniques first.

Manual Server Validation

You can write code into your processing template to perform the validation. That is, for each field you need to validate, you write a segment of code that checks to see whether the data is valid. The processing template needs to check all the fields, indicating any fields containing invalid data. If there is invalid data, the template stops processing the form and informs the users of the problem. If the data validates, the template moves on.

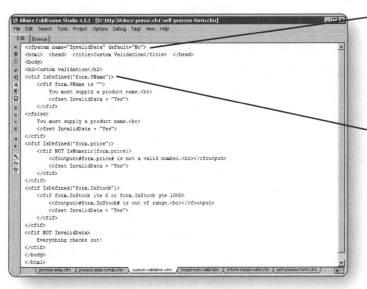

First, you create a variable to track the validation status. This example assumes that all data is valid, so it sets the variable to "No".

Next, you check for the existence of each form variable you are expecting and apply some validation test to the value. For example, the product name cannot be empty. If the validation fails, set the InvalidData variable to "Yes".

TIP

Just because a form field exists does not mean that it contains a value. You can receive empty form field values from a form. You'll need to check the value to see whether it is empty. This example used a simple comparison to an empty string, but you can also use the ColdFusion function len() to check the length of a string.

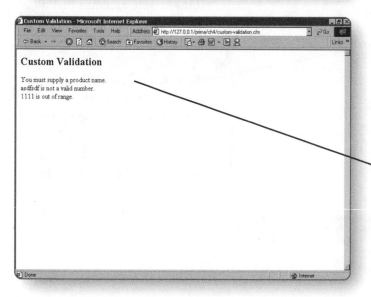

Check to see whether the price field contains a number and whether the instock field contains a number within a certain range.

At the end of the validation checking, you check for invalid code. If there isn't any, you can continue processing the form data. If there is invalid code, you have already output the errors to the browser window. After the code has checked the form fields, it checks the value of InvalidData to see whether invalid information was passed by the form. If all information is valid, no errors have been output to the browser, and the code can continue normal processing.

Entering invalid values in the product update form will produce the error messages from the validation code, one to a line, in the browser window.

ColdFusion Server Validation

Manual validation is great when you need exacting validation routines for the data coming from your form. You can also get a lot of this functionality by using ColdFusion's built-in validation routines. By adding hidden form fields with specific names, you can have ColdFusion do the validation for you. ColdFusion even sends a nice message back to the browser with the error messages you specify.

To validate a given form field, you insert a hidden form field containing the name of the field you want to validate. The hidden form field must also have one of these special validation keywords appended to it:

- _required
- _date
- _time
- _eurodate
- _integer
- _float
- _range

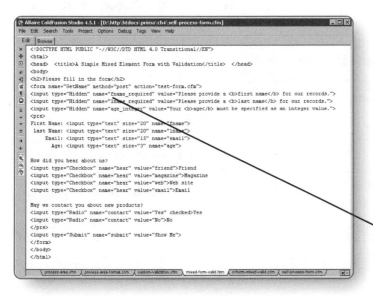

When ColdFusion finds these form fields, it applies the appropriate validation to the fields. The _required suffix is independent of the others. Therefore, if you want to validate that a field is an integer and also require that it be filled in, you need to add two hidden form fields.

A hidden field has been added to the form to require the first name form field. The value of this hidden field contains the message that is displayed if the field is not provided.

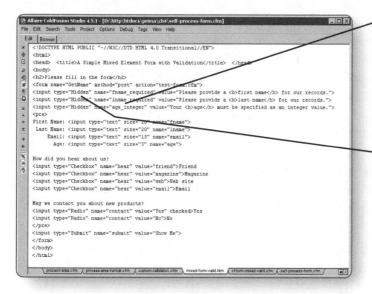

The age field must be an integer. Note that this is the only validation rule applied to age. If you wanted to require this field, you would add another hidden field with the _required suffix.

Inside the <form></form> tags, you insert hidden fields for validation.

Everything else in the form is identical to the original form from Chapter 3. Note also that with this type of validation, the form template itself is standard HTML only; there are no ColdFusion tags, functions, or variables.

Now, submit the form with no first name, no last name, and alphabetic characters in the age field.

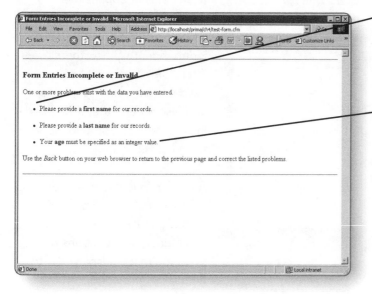

ColdFusion returns a page with a bulleted list of all the validation errors it found on the form.

Note that the error messages here match the values of the hidden validation form fields on the form.

Validating Form Data on the Client

The most efficient way to validate form data is to perform the validation on the client. That way, bad or malformed data never reaches the server. You can validate form data on the client only with client-side scripting.

In other words, your form page must contain a script, usually written in JavaScript, that performs the validation. You can create these scripts in two ways. You can write the scripts yourself, or you can have ColdFusion write the scripts for you. For all but the most demanding of Web forms, I choose ColdFusion. Now, revisit the `<cfform>` tag and its associated elements to see how this works.

Recall that you use the `required` attribute to prevent the form from being submitted without a value in the field. If the field is empty upon submission, the form pops up a small dialog box explaining that the field must have a value.

If you are asking for a numerical value in a text field, you can use the `range` attribute to specify the valid range for the value. To validate a text field for a specific data type, use the `validate` attribute. Data types that `<cfform>` will validate are `date`, `eurodate`, `time`, `float`, `integer`, `telephone`, `ZIP code`, `credit-card number`, and `Social Security Number`.

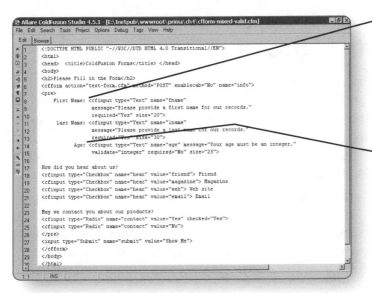

The `required` and `message` attributes are added to the `<cfinput>` tags to require this field and to specify the error message that should be displayed.

To the `age` field, I've added the `validate` attribute and specified that an integer should be used.

When you use <cfform> elements with validation, instead of the form data being validated on the server, ColdFusion writes JavaScript into the form template itself. When the users click the submit button on the form, the JavaScript checks the data in the form fields and pops up an alert box if there is an error.

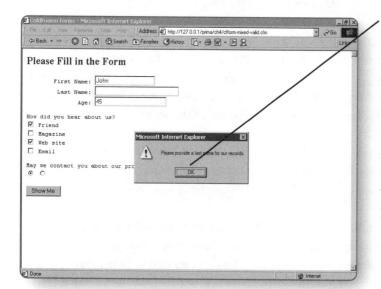

Oops! No last name. Note that the text in the alert box comes from the message attribute of the <cfinput> tag for the fname field.

This is a very clean and robust solution to client-side data validation. And you don't have to write the validation code yourself.

Checking for Malicious Code in Form Fields

The embedded HTML table shown earlier in the <textarea> example is pretty harmless. Unfortunately, not everyone on the Internet is harmless. In addition to embedding ordinary HTML code in form input fields, users can insert scripting code to execute on other users' browsers.

The ColdFusion functions htmleditformat and htmlcodeformat can help with this problem, as you've seen. However, sometimes they are not enough.

To this end, Allaire has recognized this vulnerability and has provided information and developer assistance on its Web site to address malicious code in form input fields. On the Allaire security Web site is a sample input filter written in ColdFusion that you can use with your form-processing templates. You can find a hyperlink to this document on the CD-ROM at the back of this book.

Creating Forms that Process Themselves

Up to this point, the `action` attribute of all the forms you have processed has pointed to a different template than the one containing the form. You therefore end up with a pair of files for each form you want to process. In an effort to reduce your workload of maintaining all these files, you can use the same template to process its own form.

To accomplish this, you simply combine the code of the processing template with the code of the form template. All that's left to do is to instruct the newly combined template how to determine whether the current request should load the form or process it.

You can do that simply by checking for the existence of the `fieldnames` variable in the `form` scope. If the template has not been posted, neither the `form` scope nor the `fieldnames` variable will exist. Therefore, you need to display the form.

First, you create a variable to check whether this form has been posted. This example assumes that it has not been posted.

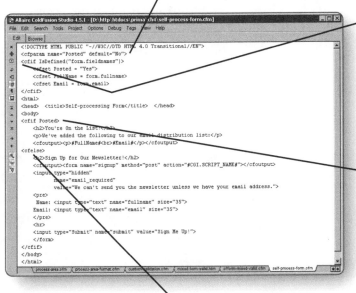

Next, you check to see whether the `form` scope exists (meaning that the form has been submitted to itself). Finally, you set the `Posted` variable to "Yes" and reassign the form field values to local variables.

In the body of the page, you check the `Posted` variable. If it is "Yes", the code processes the form data. In this case, the information is displayed back to the users with a confirmation.

A `Posted` variable value of "No" denotes a request from the browser to display the form.

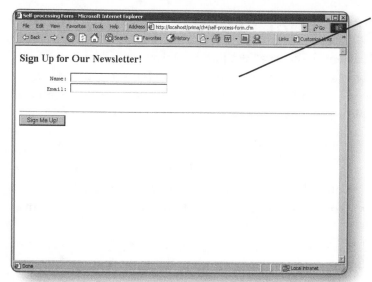

When this template is requested in a browser for the first time, the form is displayed.

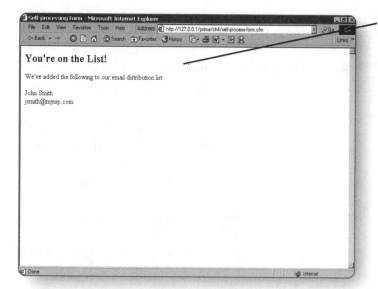

When this template is submitted from its own form, it processes itself and displays the results.

5

Inserting Data

Getting data out of your database and onto the Web is a major accomplishment. However, there has to be data in the database in the first place. You can get data into a database many ways. ColdFusion offers a <cfinsert> tag to help insert data and the <cfgrid> tag to assist you in building a data input form. This chapter looks at a few of the most obvious ways to use ColdFusion to populate your tables, including forms and SQL statements. In this chapter, you learn to:

- Use SQL statements with ColdFusion to insert data
- Use <cfinsert> to insert data
- Use a form to collect and insert data
- Use <cfgrid> to collect and insert data
- Verify an insert operation

Using SQL to Insert Data

ColdFusion provides so many ways to make your life easier that it is easy to forget about the fundamentals. But sometimes the old ways are best. Using straight SQL in your <cfquery> tags offers the most flexibility when working with data and when interacting with the database. The most obvious way to insert data into a database table is by using the SQL insert statement inside a <cfquery>.

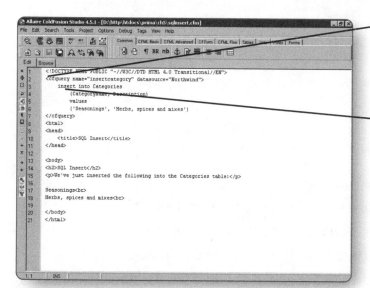

The <cfquery> starts in the standard way. Here, you're simply passing a standard SQL statement to the datasource.

The simple single record entry form of the SQL insert command is used here. After the table name (Categories), you specify the comma-separated column list in parentheses into which you will enter values.

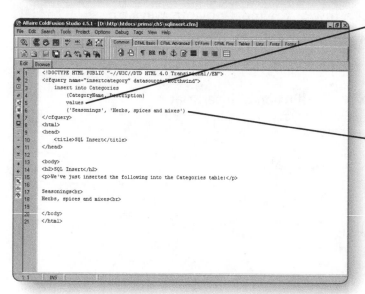

After the column list, you use the keyword values, followed by a comma-separated list of values to be inserted in parentheses.

You specify the values to be inserted into the table as static strings. No ColdFusion variables here yet. Note the single quotes. SQL requires string constants to be enclosed in single quotes.

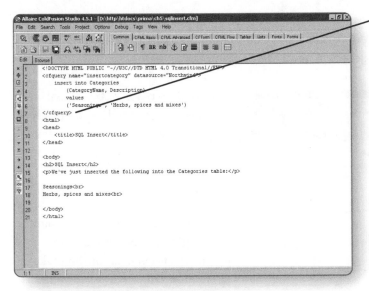

The insert operation is complete once ColdFusion reaches the `</cfquery>` tag. The new data is added to the database at that point. It is important that the format of the insert statement and the data values be correct when this template is loaded. While this may seem obvious in this early example, when you begin building dynamic queries in Chapter 7, "Building Dynamic Queries," this point becomes crucial.

To run the template and insert the data, simply load the page from the Web server into your Web browser.

Note that the information displayed on the HTML page is static and exactly matches the data placed in the insert statement.

You can improve on this template. All the data values are *static*; that is, they are listed directly in the insert statement. A better method is to use ColdFusion variables in place of the static values. That way, you can manipulate the values as necessary before the insert statement gets them. You can also use the variables to refer to the values later in the template. In these simple examples of the insert statement, the use of variables is unnecessary. However, when you move on to using forms to gather data for insert, the techniques shown in this example of using variables will be important for interacting with the form variables.

First, you create variables to hold the values you want to insert. You'll need a variable to hold the category name and one to hold the category description. Because these are strings, you'll need the double-quotes.

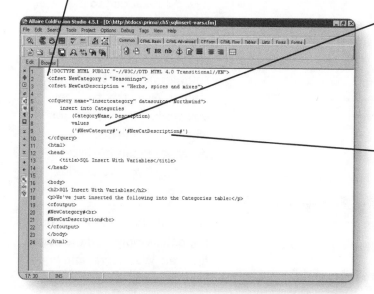

Next, in place of the actual values from the last template, you place the variable names with pound signs (#) to signify that you are referencing variables.

Note that you need to retain the single quotes around these character values for the SQL statement.

You have created variables here for each of the columns in the Categories table. For tables with more columns, you will need to create more variables. What you want to take away from this example is how to use variables with an SQL statement. This same technique is used throughout the book to create SQL statements in your templates.

The data is now inserted into the table in the database. But the process of writing a template with static data values in it in order to add data to a database might be limiting. Wouldn't it be nice if you had a form to fill in instead?

Inserting Data from a Form

You know all about forms from Chapter 4, "Processing and Validating Forms," so this might be old hat. What you need to do is create a form whose form fields correspond to the column values of the table into which you want to insert data. Then, when you process the form, you hand the form values to the SQL insert statement as ColdFusion variables.

Data entry forms can be elaborate, depending on the application. This is where data-validation techniques really come into play—you want to make sure that the data going in to your database is correct. The examples in this section are fairly simple, but keep in mind that you could use the validation techniques covered in Chapter 4.

Consider this simple HTML form, which contains fields for the two columns you need to insert into the Categories table (CategoryName and Description).

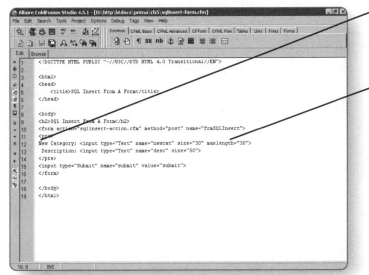

This form has two fields, one for the category name and one for the description.

You can limit the number of characters the users can type into a field. Here, the character length is limited to the size of the database field (30 characters).

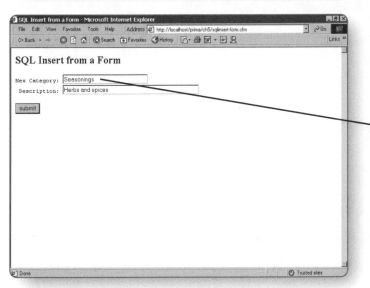

This is not much of a form, but it serves to illustrate that you don't need much fancy stuff to get the job done.

No surprises in the appearance of the form. A category for seasonings has been added in this example.

First, you reassign the form variables to local page variables. The `<cfset>` tag reassigns the values from the form variables to the new variables, NewCat and Desc. This preserves the values of the form variables for later reference, if needed.

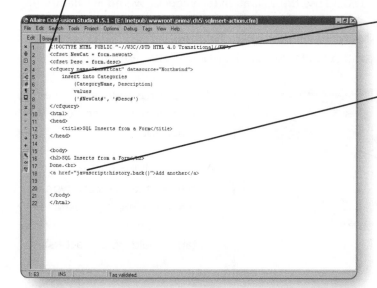

The structure of the insert statement is the same as in the static version.

This is a little JavaScript function for going back a page. It gives the users a way back to the form to add more data.

Again, you invoke the template by requesting it in your browser. After the template has loaded, the insert operation is already complete.

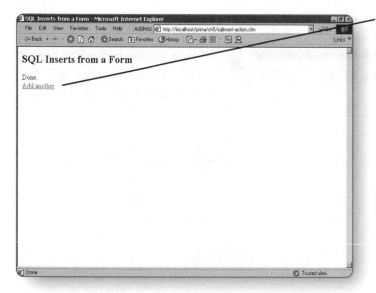

Not much on the results page but the link back to the form. You learn how to improve on this page later in the chapter.

Using <cfinsert> to Insert Data

Although the old ways are sometimes simpler, the new ways are sometimes more handy. ColdFusion's <cfinsert> tag simplifies the use of forms for gathering data. This tag handles all the details of the SQL statements sent to the datasource. You just tell it which form fields to insert into which table in which datasource. This tag is great for simple insert operations like the previous example. As an example, you can convert the previous form and form-processing templates to contrast the two methods.

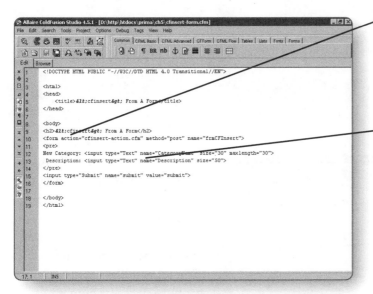

Essentially, the only thing you have to change on the entry form is the action attribute. Now it points to the new form-processing template.

In order for <cfinsert> to work, the names of the form fields must match the column names in the target database. Otherwise, ColdFusion won't know how to insert the field values into the table. These names are not case-sensitive; I've mixed the case here for readability.

NOTE

If a form element in an HTML form does not have a name attribute, it won't show up in ColdFusion's form scope. In other words, only form fields with name attributes can be passed to the <cfinsert> tag. So, in this example, if you had not named the Submit button on the form and the only other fields on the form were also table columns, the formfields attribute of the <cfinsert> tag would have been unnecessary. You use the formfields attribute to limit the named fields to <cfinsert>.

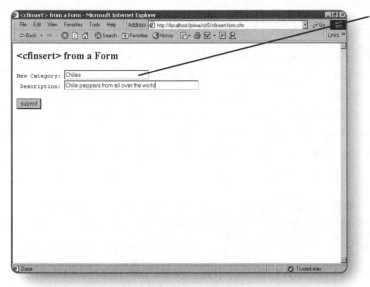

The form looks the same. Here, a specialty category for chiles is being added.

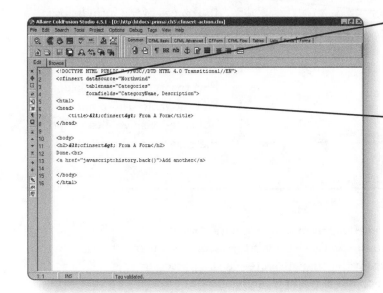

In <cfinsert>, you specify the datasource and table attributes to tell ColdFusion where to put the data.

You can specify the form fields to insert with the formfields attribute. This attribute is optional; if it's not specified, <cfinsert> attempts to insert all form fields into the table.

This example contains significantly less code to write and maintain. In bypassing the SQL code, you have also reduced the possibility of bugs in your code. Another benefit is that if your tables change, changing the form is often all that's necessary to update your application.

Using <cfinsert> is a great way to deliver data entry forms on the Web quickly, particularly when your insert operations are simple. Your needs are not always simple, however. When entering a great deal of data, this simple form is tedious. Never fear, however; there is another way.

Inserting Data from a <cfgrid> Form

You've learned how to use <cfgrid> for displaying data. It's a nice way to display large amounts of data in a small space on a Web page. But <cfgrid> can do a lot more for you.

The real power of the <cfgrid> element is in its editing capabilities. You can use the <cfgrid> element to insert, modify, and even delete data—and all these operations can be done with a single submission. When you use <cfgrid> to insert or update data, you need to process it with the <cfgridupdate> tag. The <cfgrid> tag uses a special format for naming the form fields that it submits; the <cfgridupdate> tag is required to insert these fields correctly.

Start out with a `<cfform>` to hold the grid.

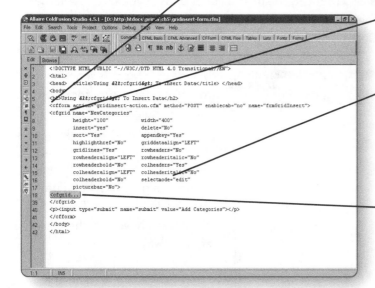

Next, you place a `<cfgrid>` form element inside the `<cfform></cfform>` tags.

As you've seen before, `<cfgrid>` has many attributes, but take a look only at `selectmode` here. You set it to "edit" to allow editing in the grid cells.

The `<cfgridcolumn>` tags for the two columns have been collapsed for clarity. Because this `<cfgrid>` is not based on a query (which would ordinarily provide the column list for display to the `<cfgrid>` tag), you need to specify the columns to be displayed with the `<cfgridcolumn>` tags.

`<cfgridcolumn>` allows you to format the grid in several ways. First, the `name` attribute gives the column a form field name that can be referenced when the form is submitted.

Second, `<cfgridcolumn>` allows you to format the column and column header by setting the font, font style, alignment, and so on.

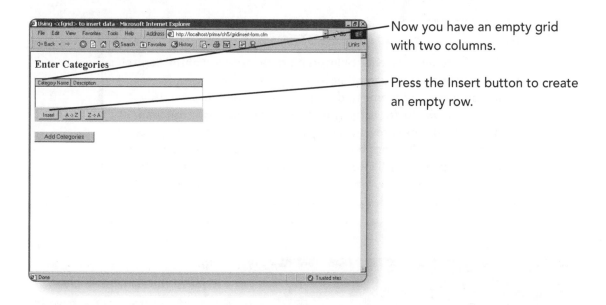

Now you have an empty grid with two columns.

Press the Insert button to create an empty row.

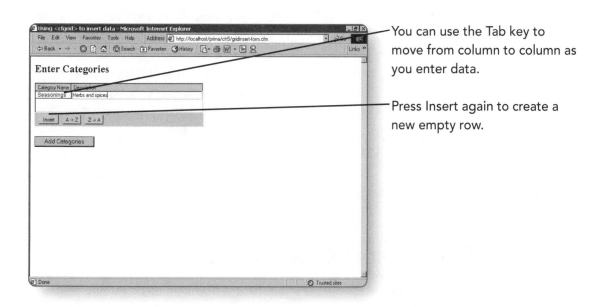

You can use the Tab key to move from column to column as you enter data.

Press Insert again to create a new empty row.

> ### NOTE
>
> An unfortunate behavior of inserting data into a `<cfgrid>` control is that when you add another row by pressing the Insert button, the previous row seems to disappear. Although the previously inserted rows do not actually disappear, this behavior can lead the users to repeat rows when using `<cfgrid>`. The `<cfgrid>` Java applet simply does not redraw the previous rows when the Insert button is pressed. All inserted rows are submitted when the form is submitted. You may want to warn the form user of this behavior when you design a form using `<cfgrid>`.

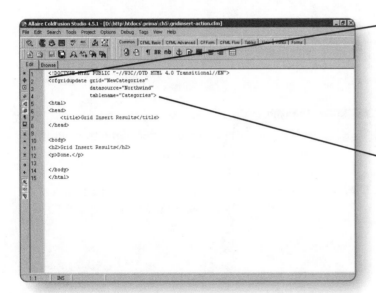

The `<cfgridupdate>` tag takes many of the same attributes as the `<cfinsert>` tag. You have to specify the `datasource`, `tablename`, and the name of the `<cfgrid>` from the form.

As with `<cfinsert>`, once the `<cfgridupdate>` tag is complete, the data has been inserted into the table.

Verifying Insert Operations

Up to this point, you have been inserting data at will with no regard to the actual outcome of the `insert` operation. It might, however, be useful to verify that the information was inserted into the database table properly. If ColdFusion encountered an error, it reports the error back to the browser. But what if the `insert` operation failed silently or the data was altered in some way during the `insert` operation? How would you know whether this happened?

There are more robust and sophisticated ways to verify database operations, but sometimes a quick visual confirmation is all that is required. The simplest way to check the operation is to query the table immediately after the insert for the data just inserted. If it comes back as expected, you're in business. If not, you've got some cleaning up to do.

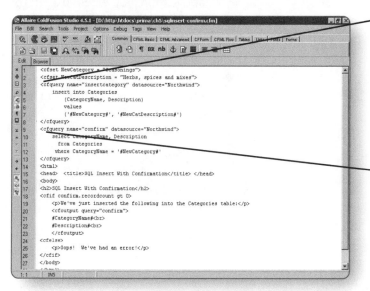

First, you perform the insert operation as normal. This is worth repeating: As soon as this <cfquery> ends, the insert operation has finished. You don't have to worry about updating the data in any way.

Next, you perform a select query on the same table and filter for the data you just entered.

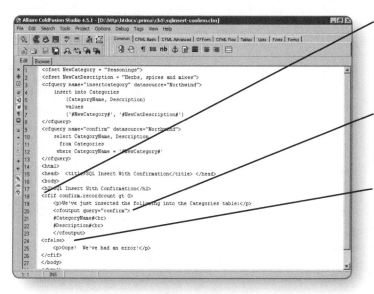

Now, you check the recordcount variable of the confirmation query. If it is more than zero, the data made it to the table.

For a visual check, you can display the data back to the browser with a <cfoutput>.

Uh oh. The confirmation query did not have any records, so the data was not inserted as specified. Here, you report the error.

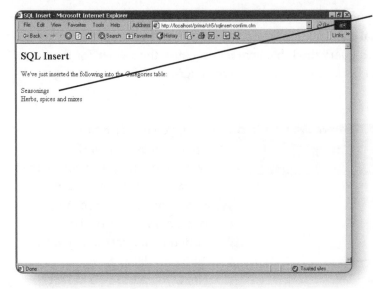

Once you fix the query to insert the correct data and run it again, you'll see success.

Of course, in a more robust application, you would use more sophisticated techniques to make sure that the data was inserted properly. Much of that kind of error checking depends on the database system you are using, but ColdFusion offers transaction tracking and structured exception handling to help out. You'll visit these topics in Chapter 24, "Handling Errors."

6

Deleting and Modifying Data

Databases are rarely static. They change. They grow and sometimes shrink. So far, you have retrieved data from databases using ColdFusion, and you've added data. Now, it's time to change existing data using ColdFusion. The techniques I've introduced up to this point are reinforced in this chapter. Essentially, you will be adding to your ColdFusion vocabulary and, in the process, will extend your expertise to include building Web applications. In this chapter, you learn to:

- Delete data with SQL
- Select data for deletion with HTML forms
- Update data with SQL
- Select data to be updated with HTML forms
- Update data with `<cfupdate>`

Deleting Data with SQL

Deleting data can be somewhat disconcerting. People oftentimes are a little reluctant to press that Delete key. It is surprisingly easy to destroy data—press a key, and poof! There goes your raise. If you are a database administrator, it's your job to protect the data from errant deletion and corruption. And if you're a ColdFusion developer, it's your job to protect users from themselves.

ColdFusion does not have a tag for deleting data, so this chapter uses the SQL `delete` statement to remove data from tables. This does not mean that ColdFusion doesn't have anything to offer in regard to deletions. In fact, this chapter uses techniques from previous chapters to build Web pages that assist users in making that all-important decision: to delete or not to delete.

First, try deleting some data as if you know what you are doing.

This is the basic form of the `delete` statement. Note that `delete` does not require a column list, just a table name in the `from` clause.

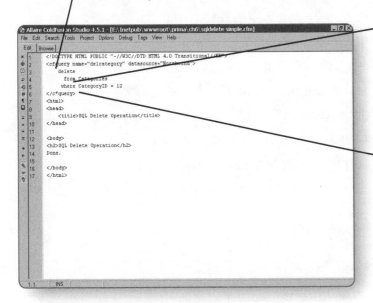

The optional `where` clause is crucial in a `delete` statement. If you were to omit the `where` clause, the `delete` statement would delete all the rows from the table!

Just as with the `insert` statement in the `<cfquery>` tag, the `delete` operation is complete once the `</cfquery>` tag is reached. In other words, this operation does not wait for the completion of the current CFML template. Once the end tag is reached, the operation is complete. Therefore, you should not expect to access any deleted data after the ending `</cfquery>` tag in this example.

There's not much to it, is there? Load this template in your browser, and the appropriate record from the Categories table is gone.

By the time you see this, it's too late to go back.

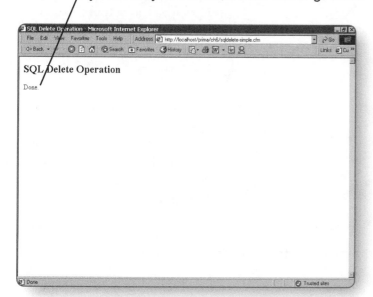

As you can see, this is much too easy. As a developer, you need to anticipate the circumstances under which your application will be used. The most unpredictable circumstances arise from user behavior, and the most important thing to remember about users is that they will make mistakes. You need to anticipate how the users will utilize the application, and what kind of mistakes they are likely to make.

A better way to set this up is to give the users a warning that a deletion is about to take place and give them a chance to change their minds before wiping those electrons off the hard disk. You can start with a form that gives the users a choice about which product categories to delete from the sample database.

First, you need to retrieve all the categories from the database. Note that only the columns needed to display the list are selected.

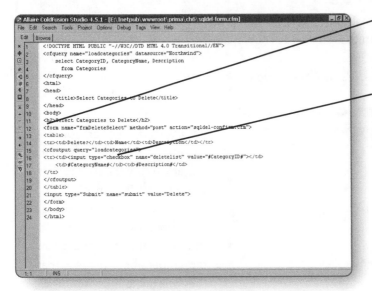

You then create a form and specify the confirmation check template as the `action`.

Now, you can output the query and create a check box for each record. The check box value is the `CategoryID`.

The goal is to give the users an interface that is easy to understand. You want to make it obvious that the users will be deleting information from this form if they continue.

The column headers in the table help the users visually identify what is happening on the form.

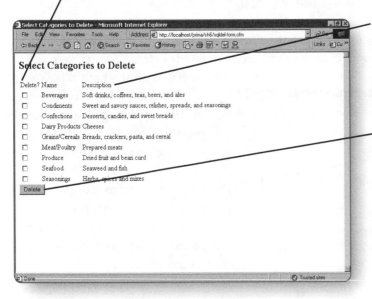

Choose the information you display carefully. It should convey enough information for the users to make a decision about the operation.

There is no mistaking what is going to happen when the users press this button.

The users have now decided where the ax is to fall. The choices are made; the die is cast. Are you absolutely certain about this? No, of course not. There might be a last-minute change of heart, so you need to give the users an opportunity to exercise some restraint.

Show the users what items they have chosen to delete and then give them a
chance to back out or change their selection.

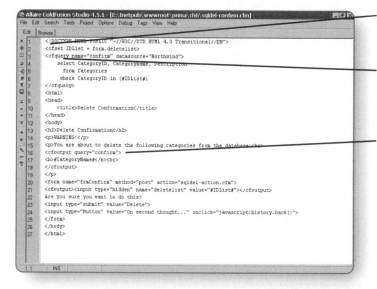

First, reassign the deletelist
form variable.

Next, retrieve the categories
from the database that the
users checked for deletion.

Now, you can loop over the
query to display the selected
categories.

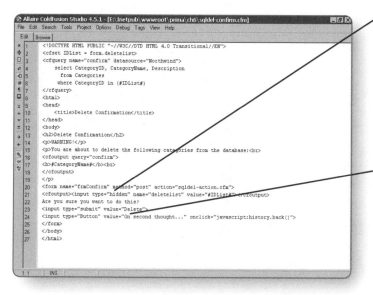

In the response form for the
buttons, add a hidden field to
hold the actual list of category
IDs to delete. When the Delete
button is pressed, the hidden
field is passed to the action
template.

Give the users a way to get back
to the decision form. This
example uses your JavaScript
friend, history.back.

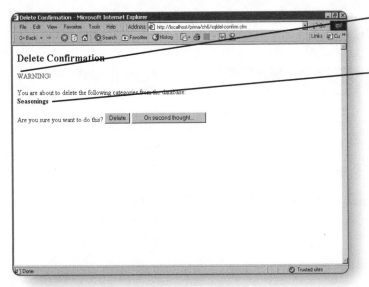

Let the users know what is about to happen.

If possible, you should always describe by name the data the users are about to delete.

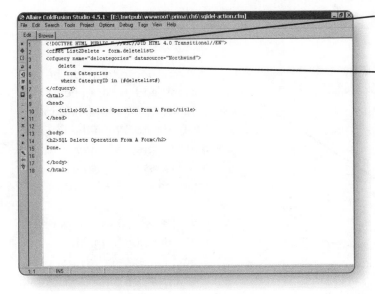

Reassign the form field variable to a local page variable.

Here is the delete query. Note that the where clause is used with the in operator and the list of category IDs. You can review the syntax of the in operator and other SQL operators in Appendix B.

It's all over. The data is gone. They had their chance.

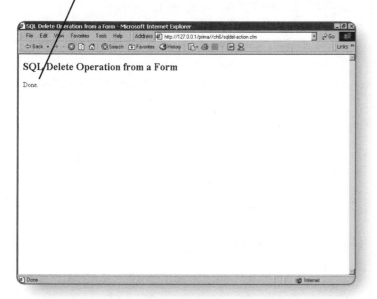

This is just a basic example of protecting data from accidental deletion. This example does not take into account any referential integrity that the database might be using to protect the data, for example. Referential integrity ensures that rows from a table that are referenced by other tables are not deleted. That topic is too database-specific to be included here. ColdFusion, however, can help you design robust user interfaces to protect your data regardless of your database platform.

Modifying Data

People love to change things, and the data in your database will be no exception. Your job as developer is to supply an interface that helps the users make changes without compromising the integrity of the existing data. In this section, you learn how to build such an interface using ColdFusion in conjunction with basic SQL and ColdFusion's built-in tags.

Using SQL to Change Data

Consider the basic SQL update statement first. You can update one or more columns at a time with the update statement. You also need a where clause to limit the selection of records to update, just as you needed the where clause to limit the records deleted by the delete statement. If you omit the where clause in an update statement, the specified columns are updated in all records. This is probably not what you want.

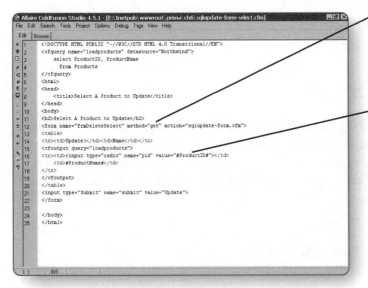

Start by giving the users a list of records to change.

Query the database for all the product records and have it return the ProductID and the ProductName.

Create a form to display the choices and to point to the single-record edit form in the action attribute.

On this form, you set the method to get so that the ProductID is sent to the action form as a URL variable.

For each product record inside a <cfoutput> loop, you create a radio button with the ProductID as the value. Radio buttons ensure that the users can select only one product to update.

The column headers show the users exactly what operation will be performed on the product they select.

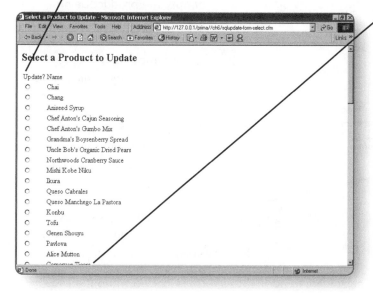

You cannot see the Update button here because the product list is very long.

Now the users have a list of products from which to choose. After the user selects a product, you can move to the single-record edit form. This form displays all the editable fields of a product in the Products table with the current values in the form fields. You saw this form in Chapter 3, "Creating ColdFusion and HTML Forms," when you created a form with default values.

First, you establish variables with default values for all the columns you need to edit. Note that the PID variable has a default value of 0. More on this later.

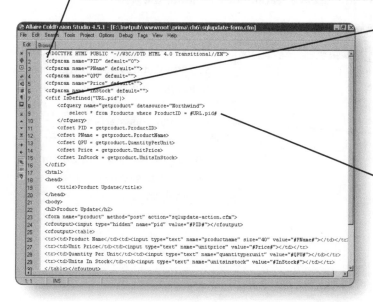

Here, you determine whether the form was called with a URL variable. If it was called from the select form, there will be a URL variable; if not, the form will contain blank values and, thus, be ready for a new product.

If a product ID is specified, you query the Products table for that product and fill in the local page variables with the column values.

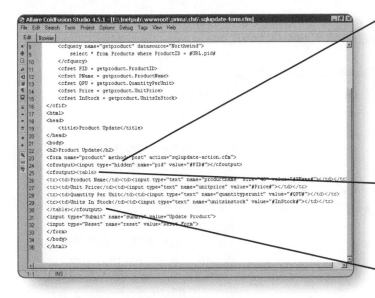

Place a `hidden` form field to hold the product ID value. This will identify the product being updated when this form is submitted. Note that this `hidden` field is wrapped in `<cfoutput></cfoutput>` tags, which enables you to retrieve the value of `PID`.

Next, you simply display form fields, filled in with the values of the product, in a table for the users to edit.

Don't forget the `<cfoutput></cfoutput>` tags around the table.

The default value of `PID` has meaning here. If this form is loaded without a URL variable specifying the product to retrieve, you can use it as a data entry form. If the processing template receives this form with the form field `PID` set to 0, the template assumes that the other values in the form are for a new product. Otherwise, the form is treated like a product update, and the processing template will use the value of `PID` in the `update` statement to update the data.

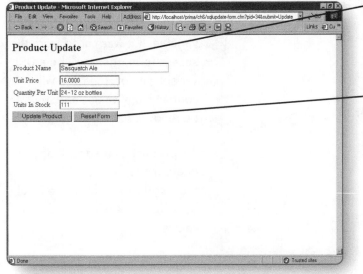

Sasquatch Ale was chosen from the `select` form. Here, you can see the values filled in the form fields for that product.

If a mistake is made when editing the data in the form fields, the Reset Form button can be pressed to restore the original values.

You've done a lot of work already, and you haven't even updated any data. But you have created a reasonable way for the users to select a product to update, and as a bonus, the single-record edit form can double as a new data entry form. You can improve the form by including an option to add a new product, rather than force the users to select one to edit. Code reuse like this can save you a lot of time later.

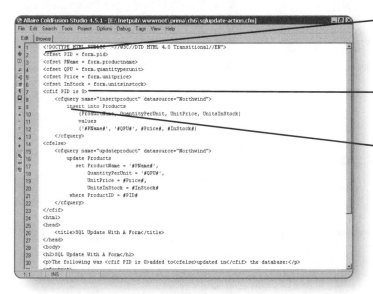

Now, take a look at how you actually update the data in the database.

First, reassign the form variables to local page variables.

Now, determine whether this is a new product entry or an update by testing the value of PID.

If this is a new product, you need to perform an insert statement.

If the PID is not 0, this is an update. You can list as many column/value pairs as you need after the keyword set.

In the where clause, you select the record based on the value of PID.

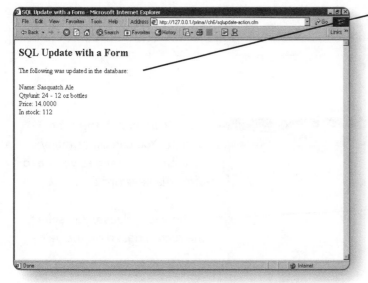

You can use the PID value again to provide context-specific feedback to the users. The following `<cfoutput>` in the next figure displays the values from the local page variables as a confirmation.

The hounds are loose. The data has changed. You now have a dual-purpose database interface. You can add and change data using the same method, and all using a basic SQL statement. ColdFusion, however, provides the `<cfupdate>` tag to ease your burden and streamline your code.

Using <cfupdate> to Change Data

The select form from the previous section is unchanged when using the <cfupdate> tag to update data. The <cfupdate> tag replaces the insert SQL statement in the processing template. The single-record edit form will need to change its action attribute to point to the new processing template.

```
<cfparam name="PID" default="0">
<cfparam name="PName" default="">
<cfparam name="QPU" default="">
<cfparam name="Price" default="">
<cfparam name="InStock" default="">
<cfif IsDefined("URL.pid")>
    <cfquery name="getproduct" datasource="Northwind">
        select * from Products where ProductID = #URL.pid#
    </cfquery>
    <cfset PID = getproduct.ProductID>
    <cfset PName = getproduct.ProductName>
    <cfset QPU = getproduct.QuantityPerUnit>
    <cfset Price = getproduct.UnitPrice>
    <cfset InStock = getproduct.UnitsInStock>
</cfif>
<html>
<head>  <title>Product Update</title>  </head>
<body>
<h2>Product Update</h2>
<form name="product" method="post" action="cfupdate-action.cfm">
<cfoutput><input type="hidden" name="pid" value="#PID#"></cfoutput>
<cfoutput><table>
<tr><td>Product Name</td><td><input type="text" name="pname" size="40" value="#PName#"></td></tr>
<tr><td>Unit Price</td><td><input type="text" name="price" value="#Price#"></td></tr>
<tr><td>Quantity Per Unit</td><td><input type="text" name="qpu" value="#QPU#"></td></tr>
<tr><td>Units In Stock</td><td><input type="text" name="instock" value="#InStock#"></td></tr>
</table></cfoutput>
<input type="Submit" name="submit" value="Update Product">
<input type="Reset" name="reset" value="Reset Form">
</form>
```

Change the action attribute to point to the form processor with the <cfupdate> tag.

The <cfupdate> tag, just like the <cfinsert> tag, requires that the form field names match the column names of the table that you will be updating. You need to pay special attention to this detail.

```
<!DOCTYPE HTML PUBLIC "-//W3C//DTD HTML 4.0 Transitional//EN">
<cfset PID = form.pid>
<cfset PName = form.productname>
<cfset QPU = form.quantityperunit>
<cfset Price = form.unitprice>
<cfset InStock = form.unitsinstock>
<cfif PID is 0>
    <cfinsert datasource="Northwind"
            tablename="Products">
<cfelse>
    <cfupdate datasource="Northwind"
            tablename="Products">
</cfif>
<html>
<head>
    <title>&lt;cfupdate&gt; With A Form</title>
</head>
<body>
<h2>&lt;cfupdate&gt; With A Form</h2>
<p>The following was <cfif PID is 0>added to<cfelse>updated in</cfif> the database:</p>
<cfoutput>
Name: #PName#<br>
Qty/unit: #QPU#<br>
Price: #Price#<br>
In stock: #Instock#<br>
</cfoutput>

</body>
</html>
```

The decision tree is the same in this version. If the PID is 0, this is a new product; otherwise, this is an update.

To be consistent, use the <cfinsert> tag for the new product insert.

The <cfupdate> tag's syntax is nearly identical to <cfinsert>.

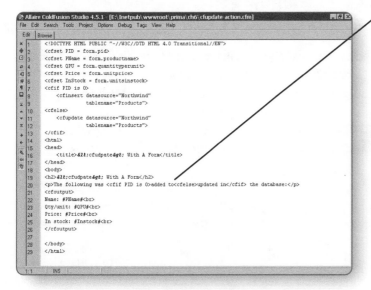

As before, the example displays a message based on the PID value and shows the users what you did.

Using the ColdFusion tag to update your data gives you a nice shortcut. While imposing very few restrictions, the <cfupdate> tag streamlines your code significantly.

7

Dynamic Query Building

You have now been introduced to the basic tools of ColdFusion and Web forms. With a careful approach and some creative thinking, you can use these building blocks—form elements, SQL statements, and variables—to create great Web applications. You do, however, need one more tool in your toolkit to really make these Web applications versatile and exciting.

So far, you have not really tapped the tremendous power of the database itself. That's where dynamic query building with ColdFusion comes into play. In this chapter, you learn to:

- Write a simple dynamic query
- Use a form to create the building blocks of a dynamic query
- Use URL variables to build a dynamic query
- Use the `<cfswitch>` statement to build case statements for dynamic queries

Writing a Simple Dynamic Query

What exactly is a dynamic query? Simply stated, a *dynamic query* is a query in which the parameters change from one call to the next. The parameters can be any part of the query: the column list, the sort order, the grouping, the filter values, and so on. These parameters change based on the directions they get from the variables you define. Almost anything is fair game. You are limited only by your imagination (and the syntax of SQL).

In the fictitious Northwind company, the managers are concerned about shipping costs. They need a set of reports that show the various shipping costs for different customers, shippers, destinations, and so on. As the database administrator and Web developer, it is your job to supply these reports.

You can start with a simple dynamic query using techniques you've already learned. You can use the `Invoices` view in the Northwind database to display shipping information and then vary the shipment date as the single parameter.

First, you can create a variable to hold the changing parameter. In this instance, the changing parameter is the shipping date on the invoice.

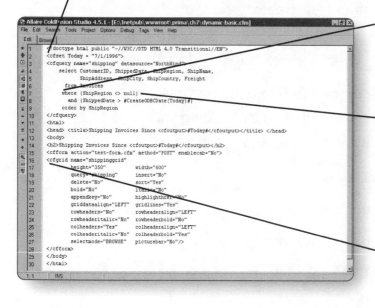

In a dynamic query, the `where` clause is the most likely part of the statement to contain variable parameters.

Two filter parameters are in this query: `ShipRegion` and `ShippedDate`. You want to find any region that is not empty (`null`) and that comes after the `Today` date.

You can display the result of the query in a `<cfgrid>` in browse mode.

> ### TIP
>
> `CreateODBCDate` and `CreateODBCDateTime` are ColdFusion functions that format a date or datetime value with the appropriate syntax so that it can be sent to an ODBC datasource. This syntax is a database-neutral form of a datetime value, which is translated to native format by the driver of the database you are using. Use these functions whenever you are sending datetime data in a `<cfquery>` SQL statement.

You have two criteria for selecting the records from the `Invoices` table in this query. Because you want the two criteria to be *inclusive* (both must be met in order to return a result), use the logical operator `and` to select the records. If you were to want either of the two criteria to be met to return a result, you would use the logical operator `or`.

If you leave the query with just the column list and the `where` clause, you'll get too many rows because in the `Invoices` view, each row is a line item on an invoice. You need to add the `distinct` keyword to the beginning of the column list in this query.

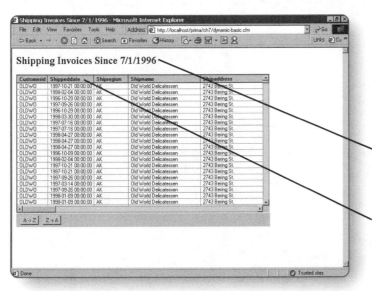

To return only the unique invoice information, you limit the column list to columns common to all items on an invoice and place the `distinct` keyword immediately after the `select` keyword.

Place the variable shipping date value in the header to describe the report.

Note that the column order in the `<cfgrid>` matches the order in which they were placed in the `select` statement.

Of course, this template is only pretending to be dynamic. To be truly dynamic, you need to get the parameters for the query from some other source, such as from a user (or from a manager who likes lots of reports).

Using Forms to Build Dynamic Query Statements

This simple report may not be enough for your report-hungry manager. Now he wants to be able to see the invoices for a single region. You can see it coming— a separate report for each region in the Northwind database. There has got to be a better way.

There is. ColdFusion and Web forms can solve this problem for you. And in the bargain, you can empower your manager to generate the reports himself. Life is good.

The object here is to create a Web form that asks the users for certain parameter values and operations and then sends this information to a form-processing template that produces a report on the fly based upon those parameters. As an example, you can create a form on which the users can specify the shipping region and shipping date, and which includes a choice of sorting options.

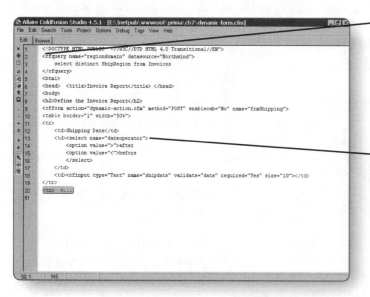

Use a `distinct` query to select all the regions from the invoices. The `distinct` keyword returns a single row for each distinct value from the `ShipRegion` column.

Users can indicate whether the search date is after (">") or before ("<") the date they specify in the next form field.

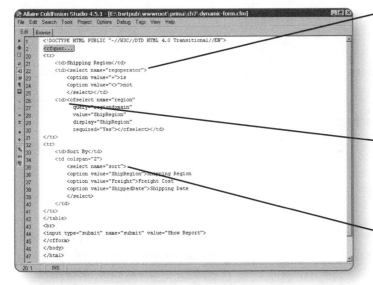

As a bonus, users also can choose to include ("=") or exclude ("<>") a region from the report. Note that the <select> options contain the operators for the SQL statement.

Use a <cfselect> here to display the results of the <cfquery> in a drop-down list on the form.

The three column choices are hard-coded for the sort order <select>. The values are the actual column names.

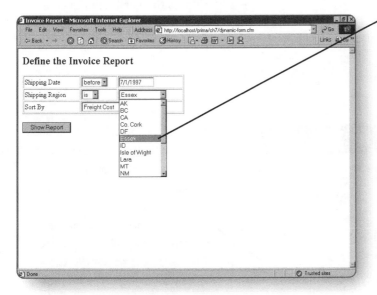

The Shipping Region drop-down list is dynamically created from only the regions that actually exist in the database. Therefore, the form will never present a region that is invalid.

TIP

Whenever possible, provide your users with a prepared list to select from rather than a text field in which to type. Doing so enables you to control and predict what kind of data is entered and returned from a form. It also prevents typographical errors from being introduced into the database.

Not only does a report form like this help you provide timely information in a flexible way, it also gives your users a sense of participation.

First, set a variable to determine the sort order of the query with a default value of the CustomerID.

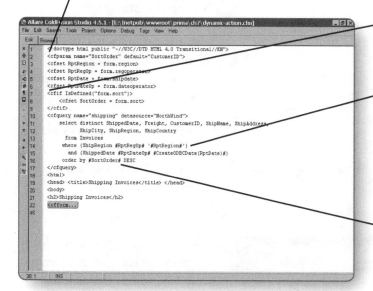

Next, check for the form variable sort and set the local variable accordingly.

Here is the dynamic portion of the query. In place of the operators in the where clause, you use the form variables. In place of the values, you use the corresponding form variables.

Here is the sort order clause using the local page variable, SortOrder.

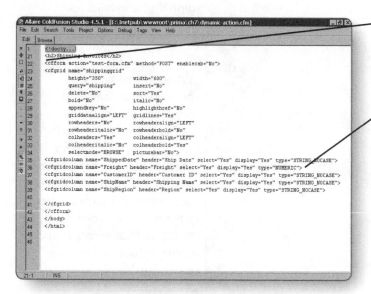

The rest of the setup is familiar. You start with a <cfform> to hold a <cfgrid> for the report display.

Note that the <cfgridcolumn> tag treats the values as numeric. The default is to handle the values as strings. You change this so that the column can appropriately display the freight costs.

As you can see, you can build any part of the SQL statement in this manner. You don't have to limit yourself to the where clause operators or values; these are simply the most common. For example, you could build the report definition form to allow the users to determine which columns are displayed. In fact, the entire SQL statement can be built from scratch.

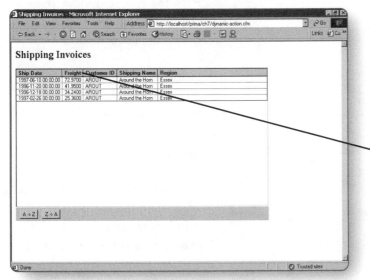

Note the descending order of the freight costs.

Building Dynamic Queries with URL Variables

In the previous example, you passed the report parameters to the processing template as form variables. This method is fine for most circumstances. But what if your manager wanted to share this report with the shipping office? She would have to tell them what parameters she used, and they would have to go to the Web form and regenerate the report. What if your manager could just send the shipping office personnel a URL they could view? Then there is no chance of error or misinterpretation of the parameters.

You can produce such a URL by creating a report template that includes url variables in the dynamic query. In this section, you create a dynamic Web page with links to the reports. Then you modify the processing template to use url variables rather than form variables.

```
<!DOCTYPE HTML PUBLIC "-//W3C//DTD HTML 4.0 Transitional//EN">
<cfquery name="loadinvoices" datasource="Northwind">
    select distinct ShipRegion
        from Invoices
        where ShipRegion <> NULL
</cfquery>
<html>
<head>
    <title>Invoices By Region</title>
</head>

<body>
<h2>Invoices By Region</h2>
Invoices
<ul>
<cfoutput query="loadinvoices">
<li>#ShipRegion#
<a href="dynamic-url-action.cfm?region=#URLEncodedFormat(ShipRegion)#&sort=ShippedDate">
By Shipping Date</a> or
<a href="dynamic-url-action.cfm?region=#URLEncodedFormat(ShipRegion)#&sort=Freight">
By Freight Cost</a></li>
</cfoutput>
</ul>

</body>
</html>
```

First, ask the database for all the distinct shipping regions from the Invoices view. Then use this query result set to create the list of links.

Inside the <cfoutput> loop, you create hyperlinks that point to the processing form, one that sorts by ShippedDate and one by Freight.

You then create url variables by appending the template name with a question mark (?) followed by the variable name. This variable contains the region on which to base the report.

```
<!DOCTYPE HTML PUBLIC "-//W3C//DTD HTML 4.0 Transitional//EN">
<cfquery name="loadinvoices" datasource="Northwind">
    select distinct ShipRegion
        from Invoices
        where ShipRegion <> NULL
</cfquery>
<html>
<head>
    <title>Invoices By Region</title>
</head>

<body>
<h2>Invoices By Region</h2>
Invoices
<ul>
<cfoutput query="loadinvoices">
<li>#ShipRegion#
<a href="dynamic-url-action.cfm?region=#URLEncodedFormat(ShipRegion)#&sort=ShippedDate">
By Shipping Date</a> or
<a href="dynamic-url-action.cfm?region=#URLEncodedFormat(ShipRegion)#&sort=Freight">
By Freight Cost</a></li>
</cfoutput>
</ul>

</body>
</html>
```

Use the ColdFusion function URLEncodedFormat to translate characters in the region name to valid characters for the URL line.

To append another url variable, use the ampersand (&) instead of the question mark. Note that the value of the sort variable is the column name on which you want to sort.

The output of this list is a little cluttered, but it will do for these purposes. You now have a form that you can use as a starting point for many reports.

Each record is a bullet in the list.

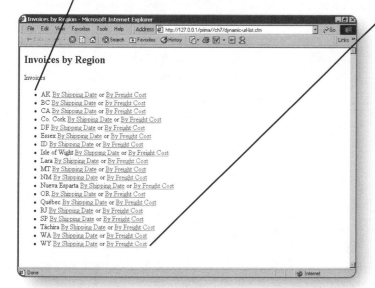

Each region has a hyperlink for information sorted by `ShippedDate` and one for information sorted by `Freight`.

The processing template is familiar in form. You check for `url` variables and then reassign them as appropriate. You then build the dynamic query and display the results. The form details in this template are identical to the previous template, so that part of the code has been collapsed for clarity.

You can set default values—in case this template is called without `url` variables.

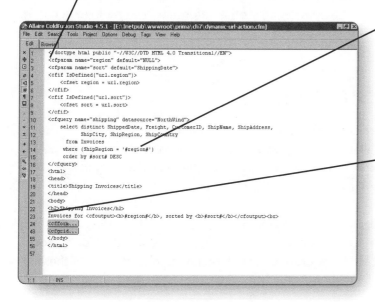

You then build the query in much the same way as the previous example. Note again that you need the single quotes because the SQL query is a string of characters.

This sub-header line describes the report. Simply use the reassigned local page variables inside `<cfoutput></cfoutput>` tags to add this.

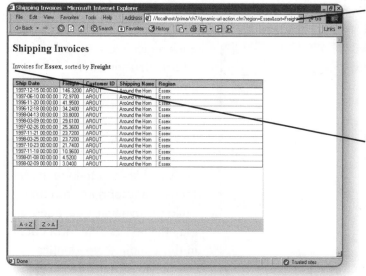

The report specifications are now stored in the URL itself. In essence, the URL has become the report; it can be freely distributed in e-mail and elsewhere.

The sub-header line gives viewers the context of the information they are seeing.

Dynamic queries built with URL variables are very convenient. You can create custom content for a Web page and send the URL rather than the content itself. An order confirmation, for example, can be created with a ColdFusion template that uses the techniques of dynamic query building introduced here. The URL can then be sent to the customer with the order ID or other information embedded in the URL.

Using Case Statements

You can use the <cfswitch> tag to create *case statements*, which are used to combine values into smaller subsets upon which you build your dynamic query. An example of this, along the lines of the previous examples, is combining the shipping regions into larger areas, such as continents.

For this example, you want to combine the ShipRegion values into either North America, South America, Central America, or Europe. You can use the ColdFusion tag <cfswitch> to combine (or aggregate) the shipping regions into one of these four categories.

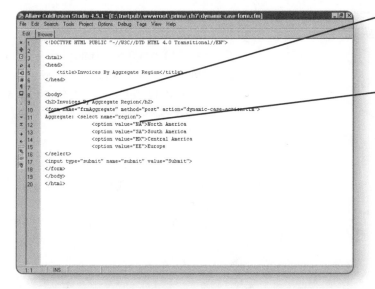

You can use a simple HTML form with a `<select>` element for the aggregates.

The `value` of each `option` element is an abbreviation of the aggregate. This simplifies the code in the case statements.

The form is simple. There are no surprises here. The form-processing template is where all the action happens.

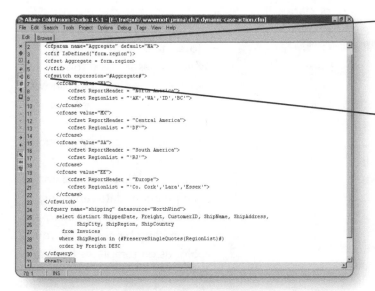

This is the standard default value and reassignment code used so that the variable can hold the aggregate value.

The `<cfswitch>` tag takes a single attribute, `expression`. The `expression` is evaluated, and its value determines to which `<cfcase>` statement the code jumps.

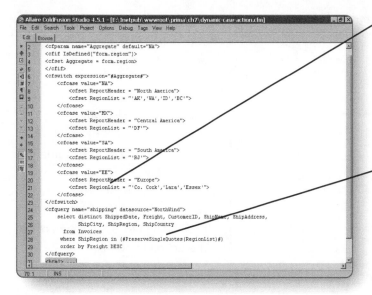

The `RegionList` is a comma-separated list of single-quoted values from the `ShipRegion` column of the `Invoices` view. Note that you need the single quotes because these are string values.

ColdFusion converts the single quotes in this list unless you use the `PreserveSingleQuotes` function to save them.

The page's form display is identical to the other reports, so that portion of the template has been collapsed for clarity.

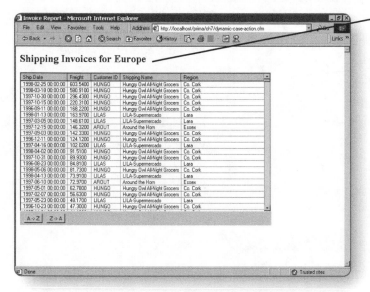

Note the descriptive header, which is based upon the aggregate region being shown.

Now you have all the tools in your toolkit to build dynamic Web applications based on your databases. Web forms, data manipulation, data reporting, and dynamic query building are the building blocks for all your ColdFusion templates from this point on.

PART II

Using the File System

8

Reading Directories

Interacting with databases is ColdFusion's greatest strength as a development platform for the Web. But it doesn't stop at databases. ColdFusion has a full suite of tags and functions to help you work with the file system of your Web server. You can manipulate files and directories, which gives you great flexibility in designing your application. In this chapter, you learn to:

- Use `<cfdirectory>` to get a simple directory listing
- Filter a directory listing for specific file types
- Parse the date stamps on file lists from `<cfdirectory>`
- Walk a directory tree from a Web page

Using <cfdirectory> to Your Advantage

ColdFusion interacts with your Web server's directory structure through the <cfdirectory> tag. Although retrieving a directory listing is the more common operation of <cfdirectory>, the tag offers a complete range of operations for interacting with directories. Anything you can do with a directory from the console, you can do with the <cfdirectory> tag through a Web page.

<cfdirectory> has four operations: list, create, rename, and delete. This chapter explores the list operation in depth. The other three operations make changes to your file system, so you should be very careful how you implement them. Any code that can write to your file system should be regulated carefully, as such code can be a security risk to your Web server. In fact, as the ColdFusion administrator, you can disallow the use of the <cfdirectory> tag in part or altogether—this is discussed in Chapter 19, "Handling Authentication and Security."

With that said, there are legitimate uses for the create, rename, and delete operations. For example, if your application enables the uploading of files to the server, you might want to dynamically manipulate directories to accommodate the uploaded files (file issues are discussed in depth in Chapter 10, "Writing Files"). Another example might be creating a logging system for your application that includes automatic log file rollover with an archiving feature to save old logs in separate directories.

Whatever your requirements are for interacting with directories, <cfdirectory> can help you. However, in the interest of keeping this a discussion of fast and easy Web development, you move on to retrieving directory listings with <cfdirectory>.

Compiling a Simple Directory Listing

You might often need a listing of the files in a directory. Perhaps your application provides a Web interface to an Excel spreadsheet repository on the staff file server. You need to get a listing of those spreadsheet files and display them to the users. Or perhaps you are building an administrative interface into your application for file management; you need to know what files are there.

You can use the list operation of the <cfdirectory> tag. The <cfdirectory> tag is an example of a ColdFusion multiple interface tag. In other words, the tag can do different things, depending on the attributes and values that you pass to it. Its key attribute is action, which tells <cfdirectory> what kind of operation it should carry out. The action attribute is not required (the default action is list), but I recommend always specifying the action attribute for clarity. The directory attribute is the only attribute required for all actions.

Some additional attributes might be required with certain operations. For example, the name attribute is required for the list action. Take a look at the <cfdirectory> tag in action.

The directory attribute must include a physical path on the server. It cannot be a virtual Web path, but it can be a path relative to the location of the this template.

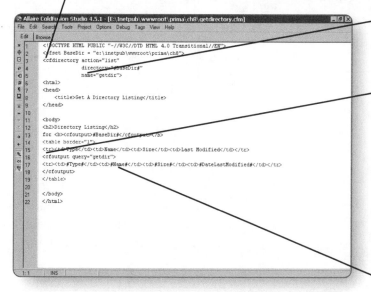

The name attribute is required because this is how you refer to the directory operation results.

The <cfdirectory> tag returns information in the same form that a <cfquery> returns the results of an SQL statement. So you display the directory results just like the results of a query using the name of the <cfdirectory> results as the result set.

The information about each file is displayed just like column names in a query are.

The results of the <cfdirectory> tag can be treated exactly like a query results set. Each listing from the directory operation becomes a row, and each item of information about the file becomes a column name.

The results from a `<cfdirectory>` list operation provide the following information about a file:

- Type
- Name
- DateLastModified
- Size
- Attributes
- Mode (UNIX only)

This example uses the `Type`, `Name`, `DateLastModified`, and `Size` information to display the directory listing.

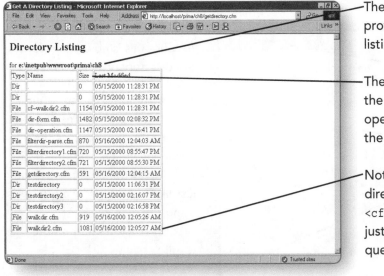

The directory name is shown to provide context to the following listing.

The `size` value is displayed in the units of the server's operating system. In this case, the units are bytes.

Notice that each row is a file or directory listing from the `<cfdirectory>` list operation, just like each row in a database query is a unique record listing.

This display is pretty useful. You have a listing of directories and files in a format similar to a console display. You can see whether the entry is a file or directory, its name and size, and when it was last modified. Consider what else `<cfdirectory>` can do for you.

Filtering the Directory Listing

It is often useful to list only certain types of files in a directory. Therefore, you might want to eliminate items you are not interested in viewing. The `<cfdirectory>` tag can do this for you. Use the `filter` attribute to specify a filename filter that limits the directory listing.

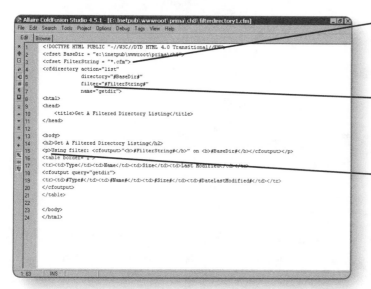

You set a variable to the string of the filter you want to apply to the listing.

The `filter` attribute is added to the `<cfdirectory>` tag in order to filter the directory listing.

You then use the local variables of `FilterString` and `BaseDir` to show the users what filters are set.

The `<table>` and `<cfoutput>` sections are identical to the simple directory listing in the previous example. The only difference is the addition of the `filter` attribute to the `<cfdirectory>` tag. The `filter` attribute limits the listing to files with the .cfm extension.

You can use any filter string in the `filter` attribute that you can use with a command-line utility, including wildcards. Check out this more elaborate filter as an example.

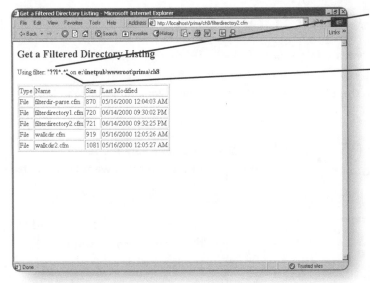

The filter now includes only files with an "1" in the third position.

To change the filter value, simply change the FilterString variable's <cfset> value in the template.

Parsing File Dates

I've mentioned before that the value returned in the DateLastModified column of the <cfdirectory> output is a string, not a datetime value. This is important to know if you ever want to apply date or time functions against this value. You might want to create a custom filter for the output of the directory listing. For example, you might want to limit output to only those files modified within the past 24 hours (1 day).

To accomplish this, you need to check the DateLastModified value to determine whether it falls within the past day. This section uses the ColdFusion functions DateCompare, DateAdd, and Now to manipulate the datetime values. You do have to convert the DateLastModified value to a datetime value by using the ParseDatetime function. The ParseDatetime function attempts to read a string, and if it matches a known date and time pattern, it converts the string to a datetime value. Once converted, this value can be used in the ColdFusion date and time functions mentioned previously.

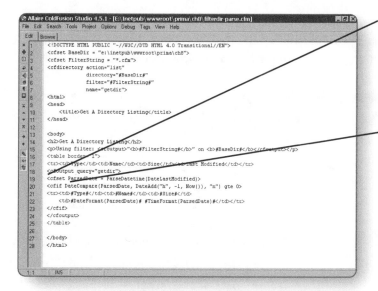

Inside the `<cfoutput>` loop, you convert the `DateLastModified` string value to a `datetime` value and store it in the `ParsedDate` variable.

Next, you need to determine the date and time corresponding to 24 hours ago. You use the `DateAdd` function to add a negative day to the value of `Now`, a function that returns the current date and time.

Now, you compare the `ParsedDate` with the value corresponding to 24 hours ago using `DateCompare`. This function compares two `datetime`s and returns a –1, a zero, or a 1 if the first date is before, equal to, or after the second date, respectively.

The "n" argument of the `DateCompare` function specifies the precision of the comparison. In this case, precision to the minute is used.

Here, a lot is going on in a short amount of code. For one thing, you're taking advantage of the fact that `DateAdd` and `Now` are expressions that evaluate to `datetime` values—you can plug them right into the other functions that require `datetime` arguments. This saves you a lot of intermediate local variables in the template.

The important point here is that the `DateLastModified` needs to be converted so that you can do this kind of comparison on the date and time of the file. Without the `ParseDatetime` function, you cannot perform this type of comparison.

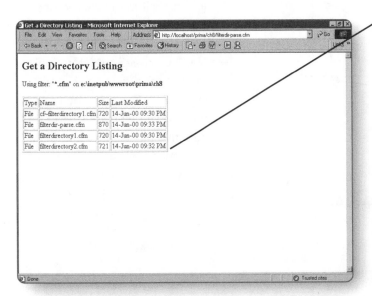

The listing is now a little shorter after applying the custom filter to the directory listing.

You are not limited by the `filter` attribute of the `<cfdirectory>` tag when filtering the output. You can also apply your custom filters during the actual output of the directory listing information. You can filter on the `size` or the `type` of the row or any combination of the values. These custom filters come in handy in the next example.

Walking a Directory Tree

Consider a repository of files belonging to your staff Web site. You can easily end up with hundreds, if not thousands, of files. Obviously, the best way to organize a file repository like this is to use a directory structure that sorts the files by some logical hierarchy. Once you have this directory tree in place, the staff should be able to browse the directory tree and easily find the files they want.

Sounds pretty easy. With `<cfdirectory>` and a judicious use of `url` variables, it is.

The trick here is to turn the listing of a directory into a hyperlink. When the users click the link, it takes them to a listing of that directory. You can then track the path in a `url` variable and pass that path along with each request.

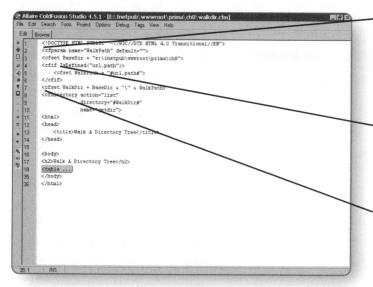

First, you set a default value for the variable WalkPath. This value is used to build the directory name passed to the <cfdirectory> tag.

Next, you determine whether this template is called with a url variable; if it is, you need to walk the directory tree.

Here, you build the directory by adding the directory path that's been passed on the URL line to the base directory path. You pass this value to the <cfdirectory> tag.

Determine whether this is a directory. If it is, you need to create a hyperlink for it.

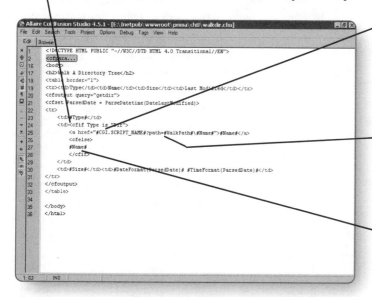

You use the cgi variable script_name to refer to this template in the hyperlink. Then you add a url variable named path to the end of the link.

Build the path variable by appending the current directory name to the directory you are listing (WalkPath).

If this is not a directory, you simply list the name of the file (using #Name#).

Each time the template is called with a new directory, the url variable path gets longer, because it adds up a path from the base directory to display. The path variable becomes a history of the path that the users have walked, starting from the first time the template was requested, which becomes the base directory.

Three subdirectories of the base directory are here. Notice that they are hyperlinked.

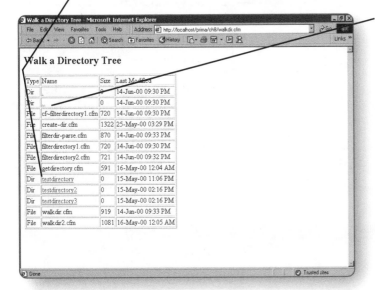

Hmm. Notice the "dot" directories listed here. They are here because you didn't filter them out, but this state of affairs can be a problem. Stay tuned.

This is exactly what is expected. All the directories (including the "dot" directories) are hyperlinks that take you to new directory listings. Try following one link to prove that you really are getting the correct listing.

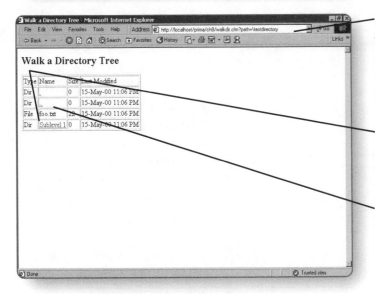

In the address line, notice that the path variable holds the name of the directory you clicked, and now you see a listing of that directory.

You can follow another level. Notice also that the text file foo.txt is not a hyperlink.

Those pesky "dot" directories appear again (as expected).

If you follow the "dot" directory links, you get the correct listings. However, look at the URL that is produced after traveling up and down the directory tree using these directory links:

http://localhost/prima/ch8/walkdir.cfm?path=\testdirectory\..\testdirectory2\..\test directory\Sublevel%201\Sublevel%202\..\..\..

Youch! That's pretty ugly. But that's not the half of it. Remember the .. directory listed at the top page? It allows the users to navigate to the tree above the base directory of the template. This is probably not what you want to happen. In fact, this can be construed as a security hole. It is generally unwise to provide access to the entire physical structure of your Web server's directory tree. Knowledge of your server's directory structure can give a would-be hacker a leg up in compromising your server's security.

Never fear. You can fix this problem by using a custom filter, as you explored in the previous examples. The basic idea is simply to eliminate the "dot" directory listings so that they cannot be used to navigate the directory tree. That way, the users can never go above the base directory you set in the template.

One other change is necessary. Because you are passing the target directory path on the URL line as a variable, you need to determine whether someone is attempting to use .. to travel up the tree. You can handle the problem very simply; if there is a .. in the url variable path, you reset the WalkPath local variable to the BaseDir.

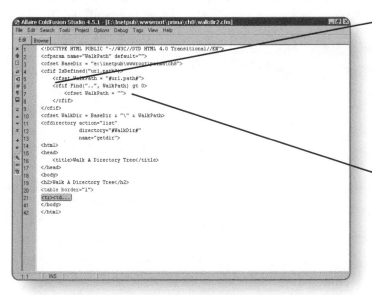

Here is where you determine whether someone is trying to pass an illegal path. Find returns the starting position of the substring in the string to be checked. A zero is returned when there is no match.

Note that setting WalkPath to an empty string results in WalkDir having only the value of the BaseDir.

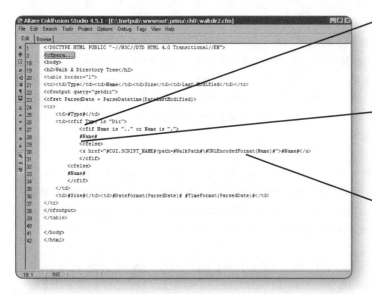

After checking for the file type, perform a simple check on the name to see whether it is one of the "dot" directories.

If it is a "dot" directory, you simply display the name; otherwise, you create the hyperlink for navigation.

Here's a bonus. If the directory name has odd characters in it, you need to encode it for inclusion on the URL line. This line ensures that this is done.

So what have you wrought? The basic display is unchanged, but now the "dot" directories are no longer links. When you attempt to place a .. directory in the path variable now, you simply get dumped back the base directory. You haven't displayed this functionality here, but you can try it with the code from the CD.

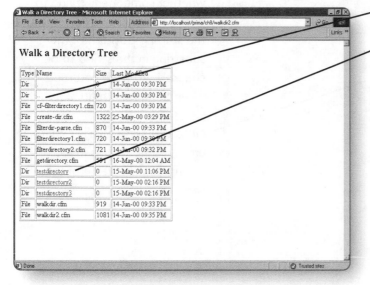

No links!

Yet the valid directories still have their links.

One feature to consider adding to this application is one to enable the users to download the files from the directories. To make this happen, you turn the listing of the filenames into hyperlinks as well.

Creating Directories

Assume for a minute that you have been requested to set up some FTP-accessible directories on the Northwind Web server. Each staff member will have a directory with the same username that each has on the staff file server. The username format on the staff file server is the first name plus the first letter of the last name. So John Smith is johns.

If there are a lot of staff members, setting up these directories can become tedious. But you have an edge. All the staff members are listed in the Employees table of the database. Recall that ColdFusion can create directories for you. Why not let ColdFusion compile the usernames from the database and then create the directories on the Web server for you?

First, you can have ColdFusion retrieve all the first name/last name pairs from the database. Then ColdFusion can create usernames from these names, based on the file server username scheme, and make a list. Next, ColdFusion can simply loop over this list and create the directories with the <cfdirectory> tag.

You need to avoid certain pitfalls when creating these directories. For example, you need to check for the existence of the directory before attempting to create it. Therefore, you should track which usernames already have directories and which ones will get new directories.

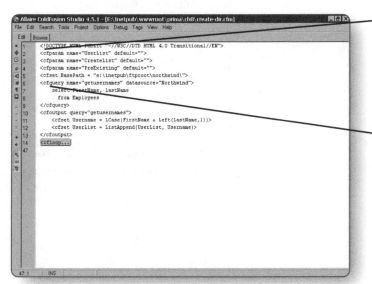

To track your progress, you can have ColdFusion create empty lists to hold the directory names as you check them for existence and create them.

This query finds the first and last name of all records in the Employees table.

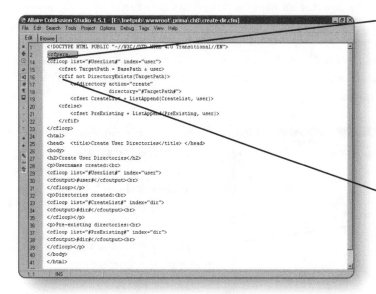

The program loops over the query and creates a list of usernames. ColdFusion gets the first letter of the last name with Left and adds it to the end of FirstName. Lcase reduces the result to all lowercase letters.

Here, the program loops over the UserList of usernames. It sets the TargetPath of the operation to the BasePath, which was set at the top of the template. Then it adds the username from the list loop index.

Now, you use DirectoryExists to check for the existence of your target. If it does not exist, <cfdirectory> creates it. You then append the directory to your CreateList for tracking purposes.

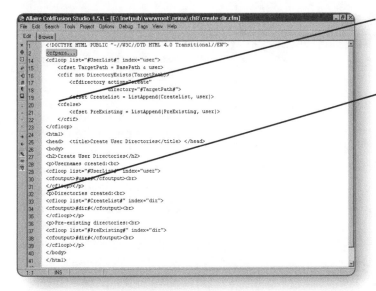

If the directory does exist, you record that fact in PreExisting and take no further action.

You need ColdFusion to report what happened to the users. To create such a report, simply loop over the username and directories lists and use <cfoutput> to display the values.

To create the directories, load this template in your browser. The lists you built to track which directories were created and which already existed gives you some feedback on the success of the operation.

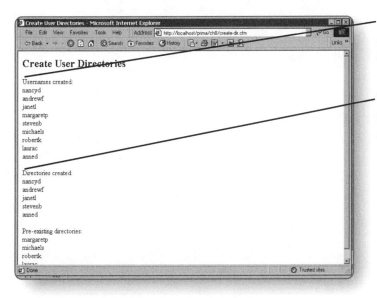

Here is the complete list of usernames upon which the template acted.

With this list displayed, there is no ambiguity about which directories were created.

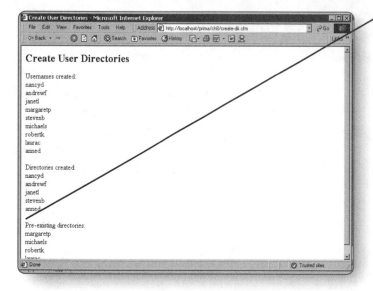

Ah ha! Some of the username directories already existed in your base directory. Good thing you checked first.

In this example, you can see that ColdFusion can be the Web administrator's friend. You don't have to limit yourself to end-user Web applications. You can create a rich set of management and administrative tools with ColdFusion to help you get your job done. Don't overlook the possibility of using ColdFusion to save time in your daily operations.

9

Reading Files

Once you've mastered the act of compiling a directory listing of files, you'll probably need to actually read some of those files. ColdFusion is ready for the next step with the `<cffile>` tag. Your application might need to interact with the file system in order to read in a configuration, search for a log event, or include data from another system. Whatever the task, ColdFusion has the tools you need to get the job done. In this chapter, you learn to:

- Read the contents of a file
- Read and display the contents of a text file
- Read and display the contents of a binary file
- Process the contents of a text file for display

Reading Files with <cffile>

The <cffile> tag is another example of a multi-functional tag because it can perform different tasks, depending on the attributes and values that you pass to it. It has a required action attribute, which defines the operation that <cffile> will perform. The operations that <cffile> can perform are read, write, append, copy, rename, delete, upload, move, and readbinary. This chapter is limited to the read and readbinary operations. The other operations lend themselves to the discussion in Chapter 10, "Writing Files."

You use the read operation to access text files. *Text files* are files that contain only printable and simple formatting characters, such as tabs and carriage returns. HTML files, for example, are plain text files (the HTML directives and tags are themselves ordinary text characters), whereas Microsoft Word and Excel documents are not plain text files because they normally contain styling and layout information in addition to text.

To access nontext (or binary) files, you use the readbinary operation. For ColdFusion's purposes, binary files are all files that are not text files. You use readbinary to access GIFs and JPGs, for example.

When <cffile> reads a file, the contents of the file are stored in a variable specified by the variable attribute. Because the contents of the file now reside in the variable, you have to process the file as a whole, as opposed to line by line. You'll see some examples of how to handle this situation later in the chapter.

In addition to the action and variable attributes, the <cffile> tag requires a file attribute, which specifies the file to read. The file attribute must hold the full path to the file, including the filename. For example, if you wanted to read a log file from your server, you would use the full path enclosed in quotes, such as "e:\apps\cfusion\log\server.log". The action, file, and variable attributes are all required for both read and readbinary.

Reading the Contents of a File

One of the most common uses of the <cffile> tag is for interacting with various server log files. Log files are important for understanding how a server or application is running and for troubleshooting problems when they arise. For the first example, then, you will take a look at one of the ColdFusion server's log files.

This example is simple enough so that you can focus on the operation of the <cffile> tag. The example reads the file and then displays the output as is, using <pre></pre> HTML tags to preserve the formatting.

You first create a variable to hold the filename and path of the file. Notice that the complete path is specified within double quotes.

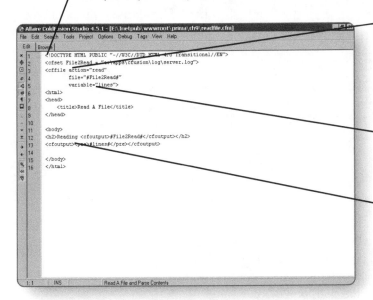

Pass the local variable you just created to the file attribute of the tag. Because you need the value of the local variable, you must use the pound signs.

The lines variable holds the file contents after the *read* operation.

The HTML <pre></pre> tags preserve the formatting of the text as stored in the variable lines.

Once the <cffile> tag is complete, the template will contain a new variable named lines. You can then refer to this variable in order to access the contents of the file, as was done between the <pre></pre> tags.

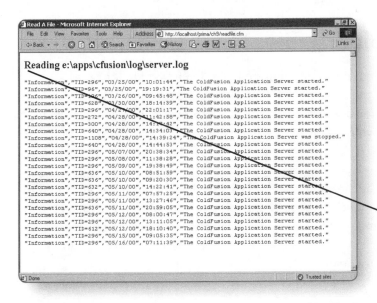

The file you are reading contains a single log entry on each line. Each entry is a list of quoted values, separated by commas.

This header displays the name of the file you are viewing. You can create the header by outputting the local variable File2Read.

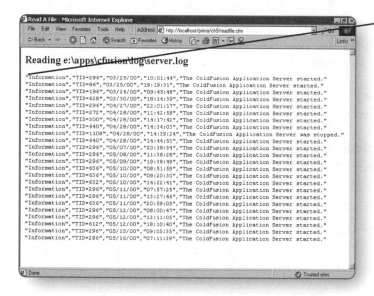

The <pre></pre> tags show you the contents of the file in monospaced font, line by line.

Nothing to it. Of course, you aren't doing much with the file here. Showing the file on a Web page is useful, but you might also want to interact with the information in the file some way. You'll learn about that shortly, but first you need to learn how to read binary files.

NOTE

The file paths in the example scripts are specific to my computer. When you copy scripts from the CD that reference a physical file path, you will need to change the path to match the file path on your computer.

Reading a Binary File

Reading a binary file is not much different from reading a text file. As far as <cffile> is concerned, the syntax is identical; simply change the action attribute value from *read* to *readbinary*. The original binary information contained in the file resides in variable. As with the read operation, the action, file, and variable attributes are required.

Because you can't display binary information very well on a Web page, you need to convert the binary information to base64 encoding so you can see it. Base64 is a popular encoding scheme for sending binary files through e-mail. The conversion retains only printable characters. This encoding is also useful for sending binary information in HTML form fields.

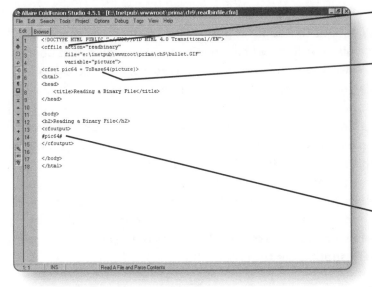

First, you set the action to *readbinary*.

After the *readbinary* operation is complete, you use the ToBase64 ColdFusion function to convert the variable picture into a group of printable characters and then store it in pic64.

Now, you simply use the trusty <cfoutput> to display the value of the converted binary file contents.

Again, nothing tricky here. This is nearly identical to reading and displaying the text file, except for the conversion function call. Of course, looking at a printable version of a binary file might not show you much.

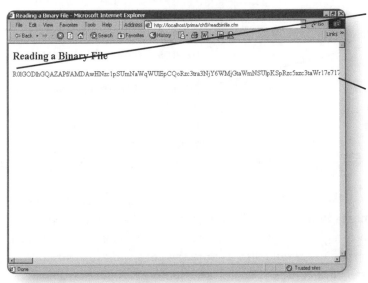

Here's the printable version of the GIF file that was read with <cffile>.

Of course, the converted binary file is just a long string of characters. This string continues way off to the right.

It might be helpful if you could see the whole thing, wouldn't it? Now that you have converted the file contents to a string of printable characters, you can easily manipulate it. You can display the string without ending up in the room next door. Although it is unlikely you will have a need to display this string, it can be a good confirmation that the file you converted actually contained something.

You can break the long string of characters into specified character segments and display each segment on its own line. To do this, you have to loop over the string of characters in steps. In this example, steps of 40 are used. Then using the ColdFusion function Mid, you can display each set of 40 characters in turn. Each iteration of the loop moves you along another 40 characters until you reach the end of the string. This is a good illustration of how you might break up a line of characters into manageable pieces. The converted contents of the binary file in this example are perfect for illustrating this technique.

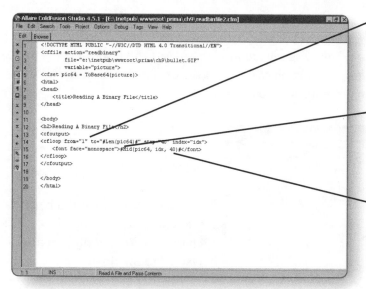

You move from 1 to the length of the string, which is retrieved by the Len function, using a step of 40.

Mid returns a substring from pic64. In this example, Mid starts from position idx and returns the next 40 characters.

Notice that the step amount and the Mid character count are both 40. This way, you ensure that you are not skipping or overlapping characters.

ColdFusion has some very handy functions that deal with strings. These functions are wonderful complements to the list-handling functions you have already seen. Visual Basic programmers might recognize the Mid function; the ColdFusion version operates in a similar fashion. You should also explore the Left and Right string functions, which are also similar to their Visual Basic counterparts, that return a number of characters from the left or right end of a string.

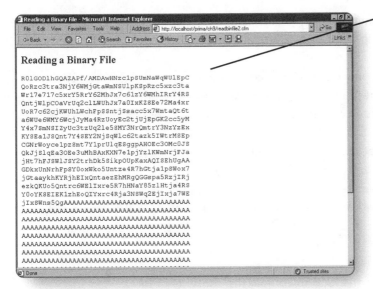

Now you have a binary file that you can inspect a little more easily. Inspecting a binary file in printable form doesn't get you very much, but it does lead to the topic of processing the contents of text files. You will use the techniques outlined here in handling the long single string of characters of the converted binary file throughout your ColdFusion programming career. Processing long character strings is a common task that you will need to master. In case you missed it, you just processed the contents of a converted binary file.

Processing the Contents of a Text File

Before you process the contents of a text file, it helps tremendously to know the format of the text. When displaying the converted binary file earlier in this chapter, you knew that the value of the pic64 variable was simply a long string of seemingly random characters. Because your demands weren't too high about how this string was displayed, it was easy to chop up the string into segments of an arbitrary size.

Most of the text files you will be processing will not be so forgiving. Text files usually have some kind of structure, whether it is fixed length columns, comma-separated values, or sentences in English. It is up to you, as the ColdFusion developer, to know what that format is and to process the text accordingly.

This example uses the most common illustration of data in a text file: comma-separated values with new lines representing a new record. This is a common export format used by Microsoft Excel and Access, as well as many other office applications. Luckily for you, the log files that ColdFusion produces are in this format. That is probably not an accident.

Instead of displaying the file contents as is, the following example, parses each line as a new record and displays it from inside a loop.

You have to remember only one trick to accomplish this feat. What if you could treat the contents of the lines variable as a list of records, or more specifically, as a ColdFusion list? Then you could loop over the list and process each line in turn.

You can. Remember that you can specify the delimiting character for a list using the delimiter attribute of <cfloop>. All you need to know then is how to tell ColdFusion that the delimiter for this list is the carriage return character. The carriage return in a (Windows or DOS-based) text file is the ASCII character 13, while UNIX and Macintosh use ASCII 10 (the newline). You, could therefore, type delimiters="#chr(13)#" in the <cfloop>.

Set the list attribute of the loop to contain the contents of the lines variable.

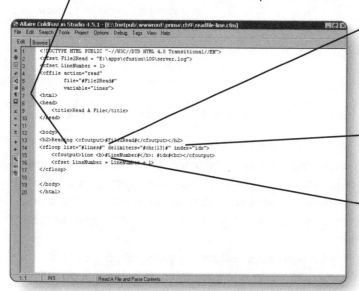

Use the delimiters attribute to set the list item delimiter to the ASCII character 13. To do so, you use the ColdFusion function, Chr.

Through each iteration of the loop, idx holds the contents of one line from the text file.

Set a variable to hold a counter for each time you go through the loop. Here, you display it in front of the line and increment it in the next line.

You have successfully sliced up the value of the file contents variable into lines, just as you sliced up the converted binary file into 40-character segments. You could have specified other delimiters, had you known that some other character was also used to separate records in the text file. For example, the new line character is ASCII 10. If the file contains hard returns after each record, you can add "#chr(10)#" to the delimiter list. This list is a string of characters with no separation between them.

Each new line is prepended with a line number, proving that you have indeed displayed the text file line by line.

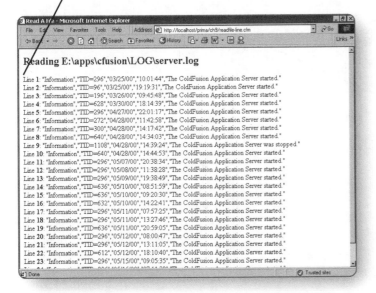

Now that you have sliced up the file contents into lines, you might notice that you have a list within a list. Each line of the log file is a comma-separated list of values. With each line isolated, you can process each line as a list as well.

This structure is very common. You will run across this pattern of data storage again and again. So it is worthwhile to see how you can handle the pattern in ColdFusion.

The basic loop structure of the previous example remains unchanged. All you need to do is add another `<cfloop>` inside the previous example's `<cfloop>`. In this loop, however, you use the default delimiter of a comma (`","`) and use the outside loop's index as the list for the inside loop.

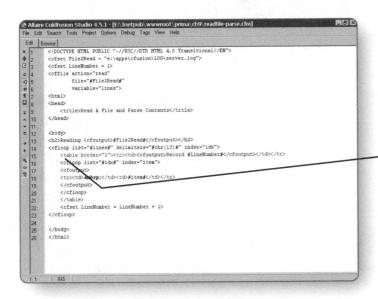

After that point, you treat it as any other loop over a list of values. In fact, for this example, you can completely reformat the information in the log file into data tables.

You can place each line, or record, inside its own `<table>`. Thus, the `<table>` tags are inside the first loop.

To indicate the `list` that the inside loop should loop over, you use the `idx` value of the outside loop.

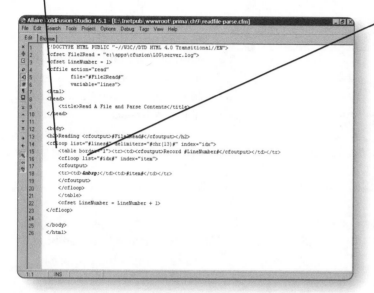

As with any other loop, to display the values of ColdFusion variables, you use `<cfoutput>` tags.

This table layout gives you a different perspective on the log file information. Of course, there is more than one way to format the output of the textual data. You can rearrange the data or change its appearance to emphasize one piece of data over another.

Each line in the log file is numbered and listed as a new record.

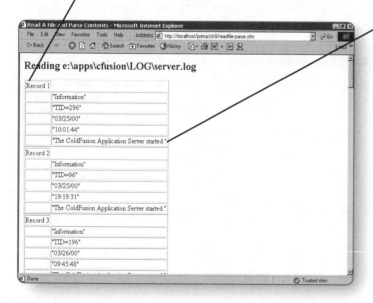

Each comma-separated value from a line in the log file has its own cell in the record's data table.

This output is not necessarily useful. A better method might be to read a log file, parse the values for each log record, and insert the information into a database table. You could then create ColdFusion applications to access the data and query the log tables for trouble-shooting issues, capacity planning, and the like.

However, these exercises are useful for surveying textual data while planning a full-featured application. These short templates are useful as a first step. You can determine where your parsing logic is off or whether you have log entries that need more careful handling.

The exact method for displaying textual data from a file using `<cffile>` depends on the format of the data. Each circumstance will be unique. However, the basic techniques discussed in this chapter provide you with the tools you need to read and use files from inside your ColdFusion applications.

Filtering Log Files for Display

You can take the lessons learned in the last section a step further and try your hand at a generic log file display filter for the ColdFusion log files. This situation is interesting because the log files are a similar—but not the same—format, and ColdFusion writes unusual characters in a single log entry that must be manipulated in some way. This example shows why it is important to understand the format of the text before you code it.

You have two problems to tackle when handling these log files with the same template. First, ColdFusion errors sometimes write carriage returns in the middle of a log entry line, so you cannot assume that the log file contains a list separated by carriage returns. If you do, you might end up chopping some log entries in the middle of the line because of these embedded carriage returns.

Second, the log files don't have exactly the same value lists. To make this a generic log file filter, you have to accommodate a flexible value list on each line of the file.

You can start with the embedded carriage return problem. You can attack this problem by studying the log file entries in the `application.log`. Notice in this log that there are embedded carriage returns in the report of database errors and that a space always follows an embedded carriage return. You can replace this combination (a carriage return followed by a space) with something else so that it won't interfere when you are defining your list of entries.

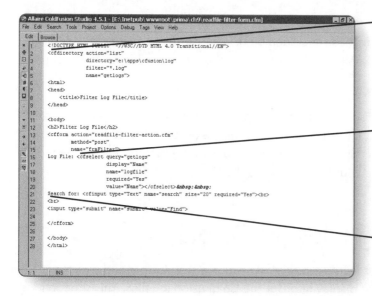

You need a list of the log files, so use <cfdirectory> with the filter set to *.log to get a listing of the files in the ColdFusion log directory.

You can use a <cfselect> with the query attribute set to the <cfdirectory> query name in order to provide a drop-down list of the available log files.

Because this will be a filter (that is, a search), you need a field to gather the search term from the users.

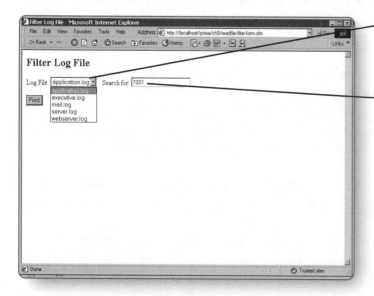

The <cfdirectory> tag found five log files in the log file directory.

Notice how many ODBC errors with code 7001 appear in the log.

Now the hard part begins. The users have selected the log file to filter and the term to find. Your first task is to read in the contents of the selected log file and remove any carriage return/space combinations.

From a study of the existing entries in the log file, the clean up of the embedded carriage return enables you to break the file contents into discrete lines for processing. When handling volatile data, you need to be prepared to revisit this type of text-processing code.

After reassigning the form variables, you set a variable to track the line numbers in the log file for display later. Then you use the <cffile> tag to read in the contents of the log file.

To weed out the problem characters, use the regular expression replace function, REReplace. You reassign the results to the lines variable.

Note the expression you are matching: a carriage return (ASCII 13) followed by a space. The null string ("") is the replacement for the match, and All tells ColdFusion to replace all occurrences of the match in the string.

This code loops over lines with the carriage return as the delimiter.

Here is where you use the REFindNoCase function to look for the search term. If you find a match, you build an HTML table with the LineNumber.

Before you leave the loop, but after the search term check, you need to increment the value of LineNumber to track your progress through the file.

You have one other quirk of the log files to handle. The values are quoted and separated by commas. You need to use the commas as delimiters and drop the quotes, which mess up the display. An easy way to do both tasks at once is to replace quote-comma-quote combinations with a new delimiter, "~~". Anywhere you find a quote-comma-quote in the line, just replace it with a "~~". The resulting line will be a list of values, delimited by "~~".

You also need to handle the differences in the log file entry values. From a study of the log files, you will find that the first four values in an entry are always the same: type, thread ID, date, and time. Therefore, you can display the first four elements of any line in the same way.

If more than five values are on the line, you have extra values beyond the log entry description itself. Therefore, you should check the length of the line after the first four values to determine whether you need to display another row of values. Because the last value on a log entry line is always the entry description, you should always end with a row just for that value.

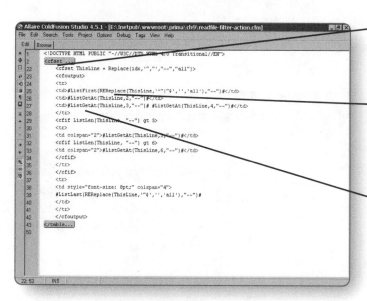

Here, you replace the awkward quote-comma-quote with the new delimiter.

This regular expression replacement finds any leftover quotes at the beginning or end of a value and removes them.

You can use the ListGetAt function to retrieve values from specific positions in the list. Note also that you need to specify the new delimiter with every list-related function.

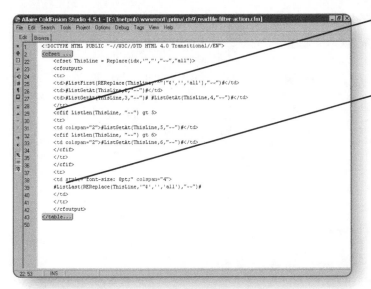

Here is where you decide whether the line needs an additional row.

You can use the ListLast function to retrieve the log entry description. Note that this example uses a regular expression search to remove trailing quotes from the value.

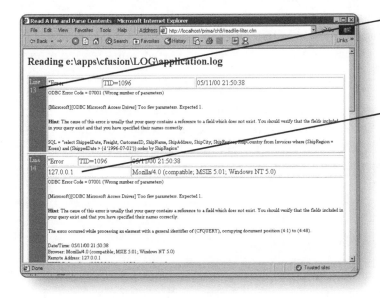

The line number is useful when the users need to go directly to the log file to look at the information.

This entry has extra values—the remote IP address and the user agent string. The template gives them their own row in the table.

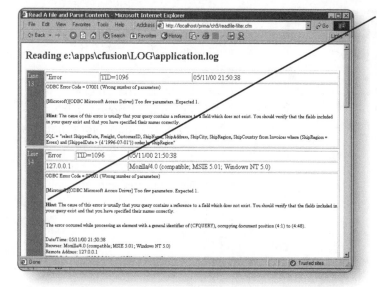

These error descriptions contain the actual text that ColdFusion displays to the browser, including the HTML. You therefore get the same formatting in your log filter display.

Again, a lot is going on in this short amount of code. The details of the code are important, but only because they serve to point out that there is no substitute for understanding the format of the text before you process it. This is the only way you can be confident about processing the text correctly and avoid embarrassing errors in the users' browsers.

The exact method for displaying textual data from a file using <cffile> depends on the format of the data. Each circumstance will be unique. However, the basic techniques discussed in this chapter provide you with the tools you need to read and use files from inside your ColdFusion applications.

10

Writing Files

Writing files is one of the basic operations that programming languages offer. You will need to create content to write a file on disk in your application, or you may need to append new information to an existing file. ColdFusion provides you with a convenient way to interact with files—using the `<cffile>` tag. Although database operations may be your first concern when writing ColdFusion applications, simply by using text files and interacting with the server's file system you can design a robust and maintainable Web application.

In this chapter, you learn to:

- Write a new text file
- Append to an existing text file
- Check for the existence of a file
- Move an existing file
- Upload a file from a Web form

Writing a New Text File

The write operation of the <cffile> tag requires the file attribute, just like the read operation requires the output attribute. The output attribute holds the string that's written to the file designated in the file attribute. For example, "The time is 3:20pm" might be a string to write to a log file.

The default behavior of the write operation is to overwrite a file; it is, in fact, the only behavior of the write operation in the example below. You'll look at why this might be problem a little later. For now, you can try writing a file.

First, set a variable to hold the full pathname of the file to which you want to add the new data.

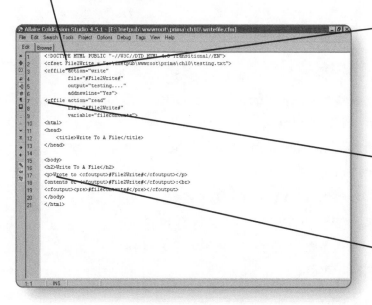

Next, you write the file. To do so, you set the action to "write", place the string you want to write in the output attribute, and specify the file in the File2Write variable.

Just to prove that the information was added, you can read the file contents back into the variable "filecontents".

In the body of the Web page, you can display the name of the file you wrote as well as what was written in <pre></pre> tags.

Writing to a file is just as easy as reading a file. Once the end of the <cffile> tag is reached, the file operation is done. So when the second <cffile> is called with the read operation, the write operation is complete. You now have a test file with the string "testing..." in it.

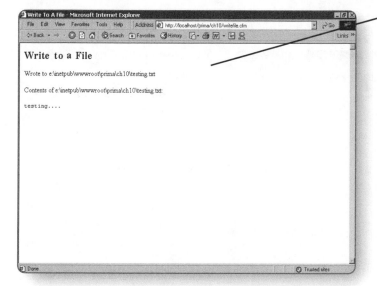

This output shows the contents of the file that you have written.

If you refresh this page, it will look the same. Why? Because the write operation writes over the file each time this template is called. If the operation were appending lines to the file, a refresh would show a new line. Using the write operation of the <cffile> tag is therefore very dangerous; you should always consider the implications before using this operation. It is useful to think of the write operation as *new* to distinguish it from the append operation, which is discussed next.

Appending Data to a File

Appending data to a file is a safer operation. Although you are writing data to a file, you do not actually *overwrite* the file. A common use of the append operation of the <cffile> tag is to write log files from your application to track application usage, inserts, logins, and so on. Log files are a great way to track application use, application errors, and the like. With <cffile> and the append operation, creating log files becomes quite easy.

In this example, you are creating the beginnings of a real logging feature that you can add to your applications. It is often useful to know when an entry was made to a log file. The log file's *timestamp* provides such information. So now, instead of just writing "testing…" in the log file, you can timestamp it as well.

This variable holds the string that's passed as the output attribute.

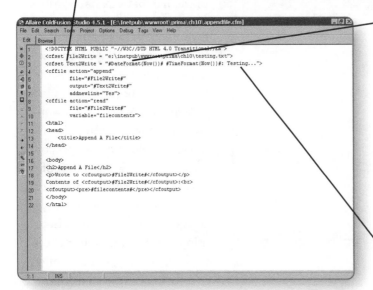

You use the ColdFusion functions DateFormat and TimeFormat with the Now function to create a datestamp and timestamp. Note the pound signs around the function calls. Because these functions are inside a string, you need to use the pound signs to tell ColdFusion to evaluate these functions before assigning the string to the Text2Write variable.

After the timestamp, you place a colon and then your logging information.

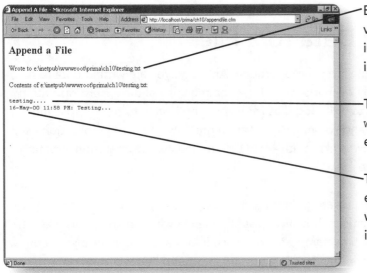

By checking the File2Write variable, you can see this is indeed the same file you wrote in the last example.

This line was written by the write operation in the last example.

The appended timestamp and event information that you just wrote with the append operation is shown here.

You can prove to yourself that the file is being appended by refreshing the page a few times. More timestamps will be added, and the first "testing..." line will remain.

Checking for File Existence

One problem with the operation in the first example is that the file is always overwritten. A better application would first determine whether the file existed and then use the appropriate operation with the `<cffile>` tag. For example, if the file exists, you might want to move the file to another location before you proceed.

You can now combine what you have learned in the first two examples. First, you can determine whether the file exists using the ColdFusion function `FileExists`. Then based on the result of that function call, you either write the file (if it does not exist) or append to the file (if it does exist).

The `FileAction` variable has a default value of `"write"`. This means the file will be, by default, written.

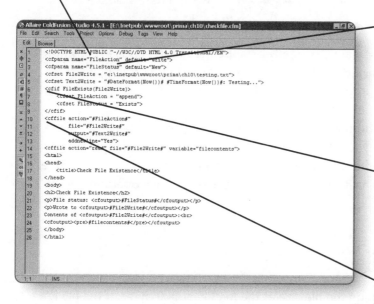

The `FileStatus` variable holds the state of the file. Its default value is `"New"`. Note that this is consistent with the default action in `FileAction`. (A new file is always written, not appended to.)

Now, you can test for file existence. `FileExists` evaluates to yes or no, which satisfies the expression requirement of the `<cfif>` tag.

Simply fill in the attribute values of the `<cffile>` tag with the appropriate local page variables.

The output of the template is very similar to the previous examples, but this time it also indicates whether the file was appended or newly created. In this example, the decision code is actually built into the `<cffile>` tag and the `FileAction` variable. You use the `FileExists` function to decide whether you need to change the value of `FileAction`.

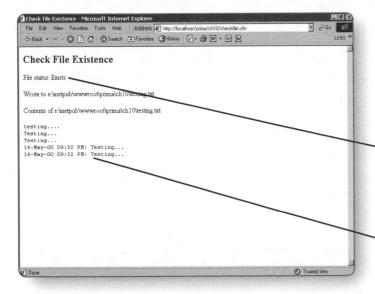

Note also that the append operation of the `<cffile>` tag requires the same attributes as the `write` operation. This enables you to use the same call to `<cffile>` for both operations.

Notice that the code has determined that the file exists. This means the data will be appended to the file.

This line is appended to the file. The previous lines are also written to the file.

Now if the file exists, the data can simply be appended to it. This is exactly how a log file would be maintained. Each line in the log file has a timestamp, which enables you to see the progression of logging activity.

But ColdFusion can do better still. If you leave this logging code as it is, the file will grow without end, until you intervene manually. But can't the file simply be archived and a new file created after a certain date or after it reaches a certain size? Sure. You can add this functionality and, in the process, use the `move` operation of the `<cffile>` tag.

Moving a File

As an example, try capping the file size of the log file at 500 bytes. If the file is larger than 500 bytes when you try to write to it, you can have ColdFusion move it to an archive directory and create a new file instead. You can use the `<cfdirectory>` tag to get the needed file size information. If the file does not exist, the result set of this tag is empty.

The `FileSizeThreshold` variable sets the threshold of the file size for the *move* operation.

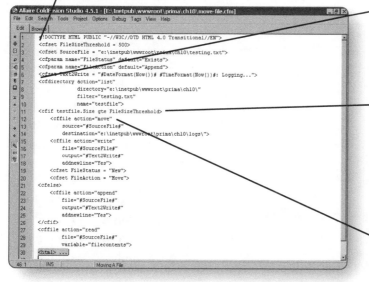

You can use the `filter` attribute of the `<cfdirectory>` tag to list only the information about your log file.

Now, you check the file size of the file against the threshold value. If it is greater than or equal to the threshold, ColdFusion will move the file and write a new one.

The *move* operation requires the `source` and `destination` attributes. The destination path has been hardcoded for brevity. The `source` attribute must contain a full physical path to an existing file; otherwise, ColdFusion will return an error.

You can again track the file status and the file operation for display on the results page. You can also read back the file after the `append` or `write` operation is over.

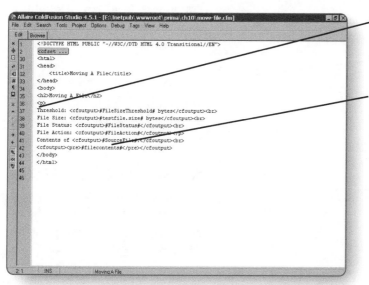

You can display the threshold and other tracking variable values to report your work.

For additional visual confirmation, display the contents of the file.

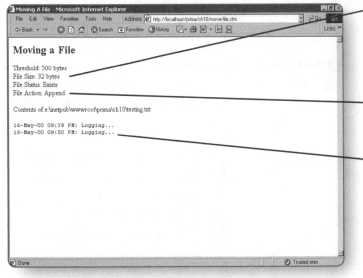

Here, you see the size of the file on disk, prior to appending to it. It is still under the threshold of `500 bytes`.

As you would expect, then, the file operation was an `append`.

This line is appended to the file from this template. It provides another confirmation that the operation was `append`.

The file grows fairly quickly. If you refresh this page several times, you can watch the file size grow until you reach the threshold.

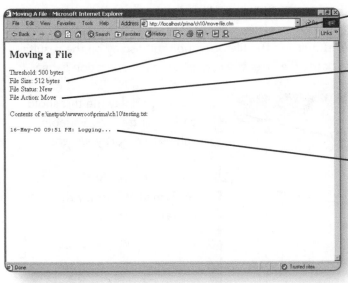

The file size is now `512 bytes`, larger than the threshold value.

The file status is `New` and the action was `Move`, as you would expect if the threshold had been surpassed.

Only one line of output appears when this file is read back, also expected because it is a new log file.

The file has been moved to a subdirectory for archiving, and a new log file is created. You have successfully capped the growth of the log file.

You have used quite a few of the lessons from the previous chapters in this template, and you have created a fairly complete logging solution you can use in your Web applications. You could make one improvement to this logging template. The file that is moved is not renamed, so the move will overwrite any preexisting files of the same name. Try renaming this file as an exercise on your own. You can use the `rename` operation of the `<cffile>` tag to accomplish this.

Uploading Files from a Browser

To round out the discussion on writing files from ColdFusion applications, you need to learn about the `upload` operation of the `<cffile>` tag. Uploading files via a Web browser has become a popular way of submitting files for file-sharing applications and file archives.

The `upload` operation requires that an HTML form encoded as multipart/form-data be used to submit the file. This means that the browser must encode the uploaded file and send the entire form with demarcated sections. The browser handles all this work, so the user doesn't need to know how to do anything more than click the form button.

The `upload` operation also requires the `filefield` (the name of the field in your upload form) and `destination` (a full pathname that indicates where the file will be uploaded) attributes.

The `nameconflict` attribute is not required, but I recommend specifying this attribute for safety. This attribute checks for any conflicts between the filename of the file being uploaded and other files in that path. The default value for `nameconflict` is `"error"`, which stops the execution of the current template and returns an error to the browser when a conflict is found.

You have to build the form necessary for the upload first.

You must set the `enctype` attribute of the `<cfform>` tag to `"multipart/form-data"` if you are uploading files from the form. By specifying this attribute, you ensure that the browser will send the file and form information in the correct format.

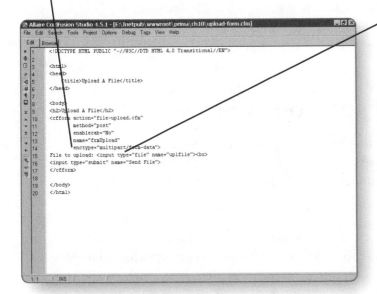

The input element for the file being uploaded is an `<input>` tag with the `type` attribute set to `"file"`. This tells the browser to display a file Browse button along with a text field, so the user can browse to the file location or type it in directly to the text box.

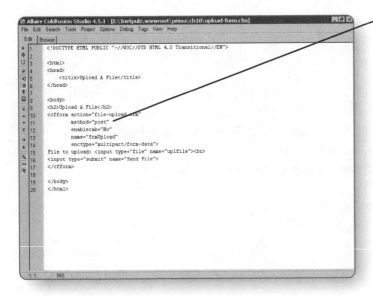

The `method` must be set to `"post"` for a multipart form.

When it sees that an `<input>` tag is of type `"file"`, the browser generates the Browse button. The interface will vary slightly between browsers and operating systems, but the basic functionality should be similar on all platforms.

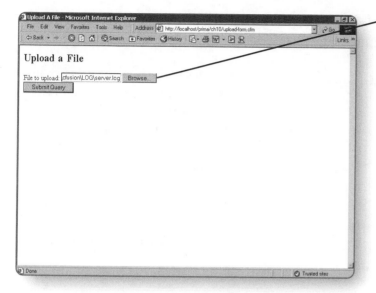

With the type attribute of the `<input>` tag set to `"file"`, the Browse button enables you to locate the file to upload.

The syntax for the upload operation of the `<cffile>` tag is simple. The execution of the tag generates a new variable scope called file. You can access this scope in order to obtain information about the upload operation. You can then use these file scope variables to display feedback about the operation to the Web page.

Use the upload operation to retrieve the file specified by the form.

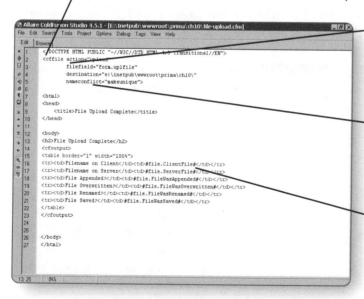

Specify the name of the form field that contains the uploaded file. Note that you do not use the pound signs in this instance.

The "makeunique" value tells `<cffile>` to make the filename unique when a file with the same name already exists.

The file scope variables are created by the upload operation of the `<cffile>` tag.

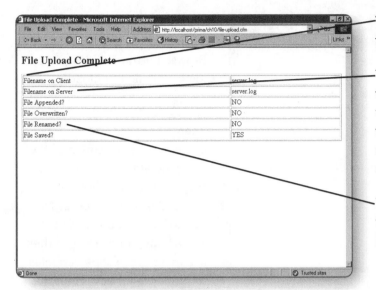

This is the name of the file as the client knew it.

This filename is the name that the upload operation used to write the file. This is the first time for this file, so the name matches the filename on the client.

The upload operation reports that the file was not renamed before being written to the disk.

In the previous example, you didn't bother to determine whether the file existed. If it does, the upload operation will produce an error. A more useful application would check this first and change the name-conflict behavior accordingly, or even take some action with respect to the preexisting file on the server.

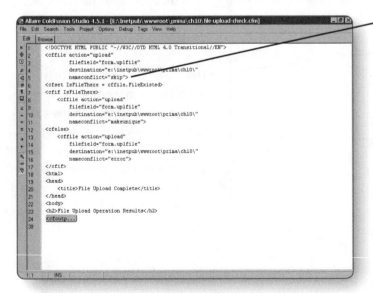

You can use the "skip" value of the nameconflict attribute to populate the file scope variables.

NOTE

The <cffile> tag is used to create a scope called cffile. But Allaire has changed the name of the scope to file. I've included a reference to the old scope name here because it is still valid; Allaire has maintained the old cffile name for compatibility.

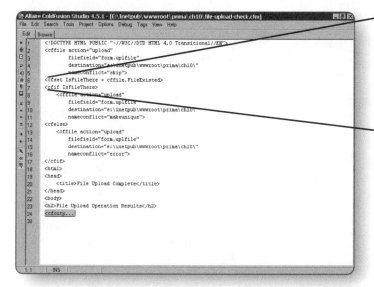

You create a local page variable to hold the status of the file named in the upload. Set the variable to the file scope variable FileExisted.

Check for the existence of the file. If it is there, you instruct the upload operation to make the name unique. The upload operation produces an error if it cannot write the file for some other reason.

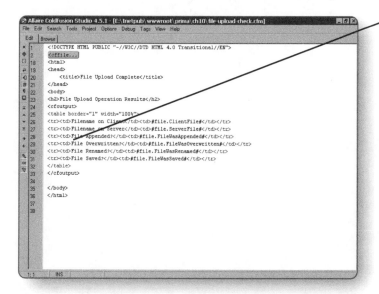

Note that with the logic you have used, the file should never be overwritten.

You could use the file scope operation result variables to customize a response to the users about the upload attempt. Alternatively, you could have attempted some other action to resolve the problem and then tried it again.

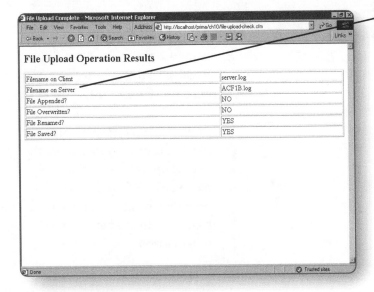

The file existed, so the `upload` operation saved the file with a new, unique name.

The `<cffile>` tag, with its multiple operations, gives you a very powerful tool for handling file operations on the server. Although ColdFusion's real strength is working with databases, using files in creative ways can give your applications a lot of flexibility.

11

Including Files and Templates

You might have noticed in writing Web pages that you spend a lot of time repeating yourself. You often use the same table on several pages, or your page banner is the same across the entire site. With ColdFusion, you can write the code once and include it on as many pages as you need, thus saving yourself time and reducing the chance of inconsistencies or error. In this chapter, you learn to:

- Include standard HTML code in a ColdFusion template
- Include CFML code in a ColdFusion template
- Create standard page headers and footers
- Include a standard search form on a page

Using <cfinclude> to Insert a File into a Template

The <cfinclude> tag inserts the contents of the referenced file in the current template. The contents of the file are inserted at the point in the current template where the <cfinclude> tag is referenced. This allows you to maintain text or code that is repeated in a single file; when you need it, you just <cfinclude> it.

One circumstance this technique is great for is placing a standard title banner on all your Web pages for a given site or application. Instead of repeating the banner in every template you write, you simply include it. If you need to make a change to the title banner, you no longer have to change every single page; you just change the one included file, and all your pages are automatically updated.

First, you need to create your included file. This file can hold anything that you can type directly into the parent template. Any code that you will use over and over again (like a banner or a page footer, or a company address) on more than a few pages would be a good candidate for an include file. Note that this file is not a complete HTML document.

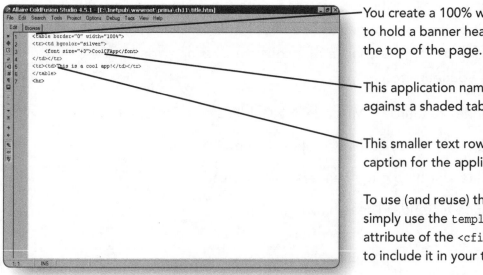

You create a 100% width table to hold a banner header across the top of the page.

This application name will be set against a shaded table cell.

This smaller text row becomes a caption for the application.

To use (and reuse) this code, simply use the template attribute of the <cfinclude> tag to include it in your templates.

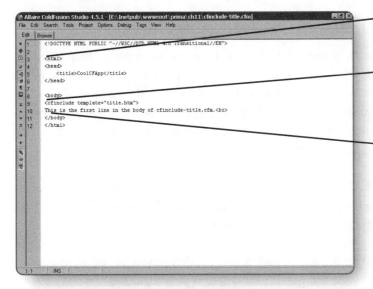

The HTML header tags are in the main page template.

This line brings the contents of the file title.htm into this template.

This text will appear directly after the <table> laid out in the title.htm file.

The resulting Web page is indistinguishable from one in which the title banner code has been manually typed. Your users need never know that you are cutting corners.

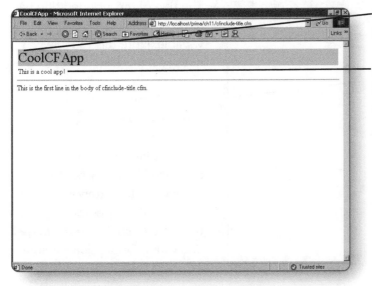

This banner can now appear on the top of any page as needed.

If you change the caption in the included title.htm, it changes everywhere it is used.

Including Files with CFML Tags and Variables

You are not limited to using plain text and HTML tags in your included files. You can also use <cfinclude> to include CFML code in your templates. When you include CFML in this way, the variables in the included template have the same scope as the parent template, and vice-versa. That is, you can reference variables from the parent template in the included template, and you can reference variables from the included template in the parent template.

This means, for example, that you can write a <cfquery> in an included template and reference the query result set in the parent template. This technique is great to use with a query that is commonly reused in your template.

Another common use is to set generic page layout variables to specific values on each page and then reference the generic variables in your included templates. A specific example is the page title. You can convert the previous example from a static HTML title banner to a dynamic CFML title banner.

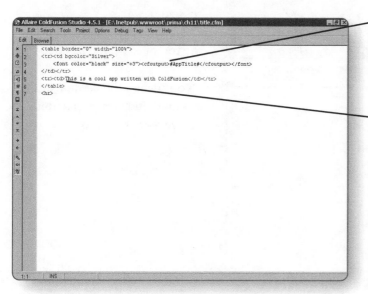

The title of the included title bar now references a ColdFusion variable. Note this variable was not set in this file.

You can make the caption a variable as well.

With the included template converted (don't forget to change the file extension to cfm), you now alter the parent template to configure the page title with a ColdFusion variable.

Create a variable to hold the application name.

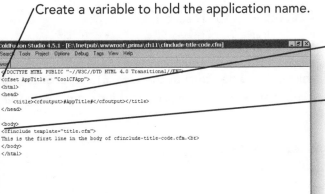

You might as well make the HTML page title dynamic, too.

The only thing that has changed here is the template value. It now points to the ColdFusion version of the title bar file.

Again, the output will be indistinguishable from a template in which the code was actually typed in the parent template. With this technique, you can standardize your page layouts without sacrificing the dynamic nature of the application.

Looks pretty much the same, doesn't it?

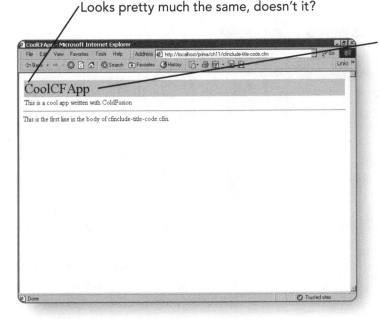

Note that in order to display this banner, the title.cfm template file references the variable in the cfinclude-title-code.cfm template. In previous examples, you have referenced only variables that exist in the same file (or template). When you use ColdFusion variables in an included file that are defined elsewhere, you are assuming that the parent template will define those variables. If it doesn't, ColdFusion will return an error.

Using <cfmodule> to Insert a File into a Template

The <cfmodule> tag can achieve the same effect as the <cfinclude> tag. To prove the point, try using <cfmodule> instead of <cfinclude> in the example with the static HTML title banner.

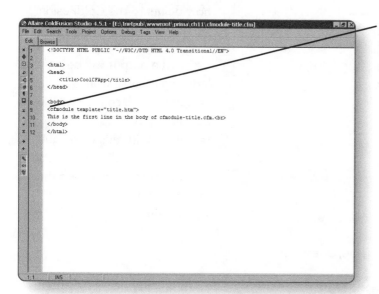

Use the template attribute to include a file by specifying a relative path, just as you did with <cfinclude>.

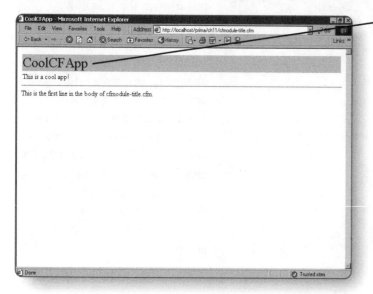

The result of <cfmodule> used in this way is exactly the same as using <cfinclude>.

If they do the same thing, why are there two tags? The <cfmodule> tag has additional properties that you don't learn about until Chapter 23, "Building Your Own Tags." However, the scoping behavior of the <cfmodule> tag is very different from the <cfinclude> tag when you include CFML code.

The <cfmodule> tag creates a new scope for the variables in the included file. Variables created in the included file do not exist outside the included file. Thus, a parent template that includes a ColdFusion template with the <cfmodule> tag cannot reference variables created in that included template.

The included template can reference only variables from the parent template by referencing them with the caller scope. The caller scope is defined in the included template as any variable created in the parent template. You see examples of using the <cfmodule> tag in this way in Chapter 23.

Creating Standard HTML Headers and Footers

You don't have to stop at title banners. You might also note that you repeat the HTML document blocking tags and header tags in your pages. You can put those tags in the include files as well and save yourself even more typing. To do this, you create files that contain all the necessary HTML tags to start and end a Web page and then include them in your parent template.

You can go back to your title banner code, beef it up, and add the HTML tags to start the page.

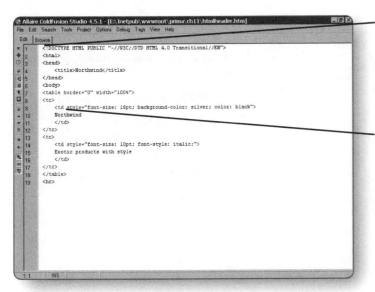

You can include all the standard document tags in the header so that you don't have to remember to put them in each template.

Notice the inline style sheet in the banner table. This gives you greater control over the display. Inline style sheets enable you to change the formatting of an HTML element on the fly, overriding all other style sheets associated with the page.

You can have a nice footer on every page. Because you don't have to type it in again and again, you can be sure that the consistency of your pages won't suffer from the extra code.

A horizontal rule separates the main page content from the `<table>` footer.

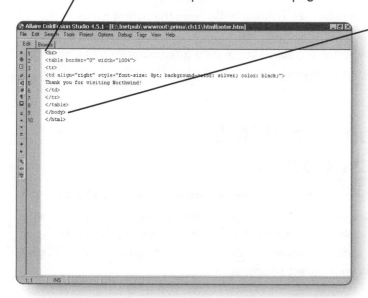

The final `</body>` and `</html>` tags are included in this file to match the starting `<html>` and `<body>` tags in the included header file.

Now your parent template looks quite a bit different. Note that the parent template (in this simplistic example) has fewer lines than the HTML header include file. Making a change in the header of a Web site with several hundred pages would be a tedious task. But with `<cfinclude>`, an update is simple.

The entire HTML document start tags and header tags are brought in from this include file.

With the `<cfinclude>` tags handling the technical details of starting and setting up the HTML page, this template contains only the page content.

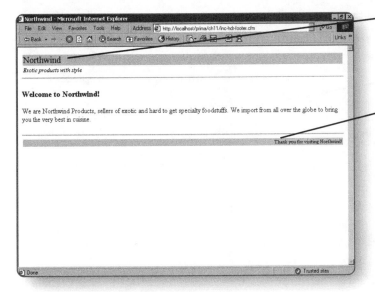

You can now have a consistent page banner on every page by maintaining just the included header file.

The footer provides a clean finish to the page layout. You can also place site navigation hyperlinks in the footer file for easy maintenance.

Wow! That's a lot of page for very little code, relatively speaking.

Another benefit of using the <cfinclude> tag to build Web pages is that new pages can be quickly and easily added to your Web site or application. With a little planning and forethought, you can design page layouts that make developing new Web applications a breeze.

Including a Search Form on Your Page

Another common use of an included template is to add a search form to a Web page. Perhaps you have seen sites with quick search forms on every page of the Web site as a convenience to the visitor? With <cfinclude>, this is an easy thing to add.

This example creates a very simple form—a text box and a Submit button—to be included in a file. The goals of this form are to be as small as possible (so you don't soak up too much Web page real estate) and obvious (the purpose of the form should be clear).

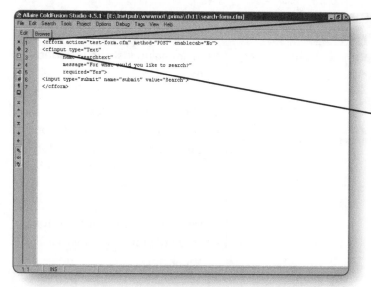

Note that this form does not have HTML page header tags because you will include this form in another template.

To make this form as small as possible, use a small text field with no label.

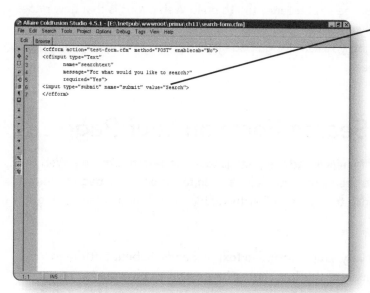

The Submit button of the form describes the form's purpose without the required static text labels.

Consider again the parent template from the previous example, which included the HTML header and footer. You can add to this template the simple Web search form you just created as an included file.

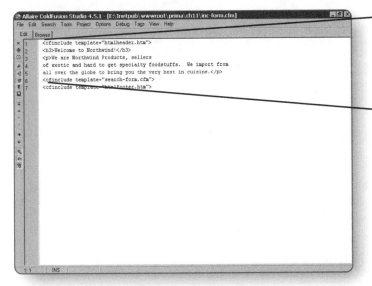

This is the same parent template from the last example, with the same header and footer includes.

Here is the <cfinclude> for the form. The form will appear just before the footer on the page.

Not bad. With the addition of one line of code in the parent template, you have added a quick search form on the Web page. You can add this to every Web page on the site with little impact on code maintenance.

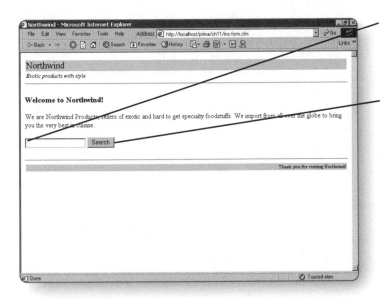

Here is the search form, a convenient tool for visitors of the Web site.

The positioning of the form elements is a direct result of the order of the <cfinclude> tag.

The <cfinclude> tag is a powerful tool and helps you streamline your development efforts. You don't need to repeat code that is used again and again when you can include and maintain a single file. Why reinvent the search form? The <cfmodule> tag is even more powerful, as you will see in Chapter 23.

PART III

Working Outside the Box

12

Sending Mail

If one service has popularized the Internet above any other, it is e-mail. Businesses run on communications more than anything else, and people love to talk to one another. The coupling of e-mail with the Web has caused an explosion of free e-mail accounts for all. ColdFusion contributes its part with the `<cfmail>` tag. In this chapter, you learn to:

- Send a single e-mail message
- Send a form letter to a list of e-mail addresses
- Send a customized form letter to a list
- Attach a file to an e-mail message
- Add additional headers to an e-mail message
- Use a form to create and send an e-mail message
- Validate e-mail addresses for proper form

Understanding How <cfmail> Sends Mail

The <cfmail> tag is ColdFusion's way of sending e-mail on the Internet via the Simple Mail Transport Protocol (SMTP). SMTP is the standard way in which e-mail servers exchange and deliver messages. Before you learn about the <cfmail> tag, a short discussion of how ColdFusion sends e-mail is in order.

Up to this point, all ColdFusion operations have been instigated by a request from the Web browser or some other Web client. Although this is true for the <cfmail> tag as well, it is not how ColdFusion actually delivers the e-mail message generated by the tag.

The <cfmail> tag generates an e-mail message in standard SMTP format as a file that is placed in a directory called the *spool* on the ColdFusion server. Every few minutes, the ColdFusion companion service called the *ColdFusion Executive* checks the spool directory. If messages are waiting, the ColdFusion Executive service handles the actual delivery of the e-mail messages based on the configuration of the mail services. If the messages cannot be delivered for some reason, they are moved to the *undelivr* directory and an error message is logged.

It is important, then, to check the mail log file every so often to make sure that the e-mail is moving. After a mail delivery problem is resolved, you can move the undelivered message from the *undelivr* directory to the spool. ColdFusion will attempt to resend it.

Understanding this process is important because there is no feedback to the template containing the <cfmail> tag when the mail message cannot be delivered. Usually, when the users submit a message to be delivered through a Web page, they feel that it is indeed delivered. It is up to you, as the developer, to inform the users of the result of the <cfmail> tag. This chapter shows examples that respond with text similar to "the message has been queued for delivery."

Sending a Single E-Mail

The <cfmail> tag's required attributes are to, from, and subject. If the ColdFusion server has not been configured with a global mail server for delivering mail, the tag also requires the server attribute. Generally, you should configure a default mail server for the ColdFusion server. Refer to Appendix A, "Installing ColdFusion," for details.

The body of the e-mail message is placed between the <cfmail> and </cfmail> tags.

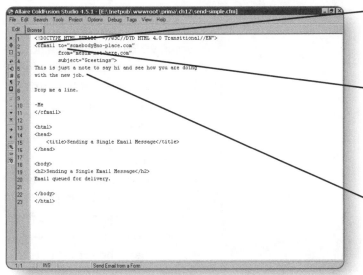

You supply the <cfmail> tag with the to, from, and subject attributes.

You can specify multiple recipients in the to attribute by separating the e-mail addresses with commas. Extra spaces between addresses are ignored.

The text of the e-mail message is sent as is, with new lines and carriage returns intact.

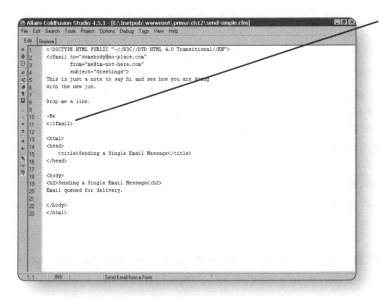

The </cfmail> tag signifies the end of the e-mail message.

NOTE

In case you are wondering, this message ends up in the *undelivr* directory on the ColdFusion server. These Internet addresses are nonexistent (at least at the time of this writing), so the ColdFusion Executive cannot deliver them.

Note that the message claims only to have queued the e-mail.

Sending a Single Email Message

Email queued for delivery.

That's it. The syntax for a simple message like this is itself simple. Of course, this is rarely the way in which you might send a mail message from ColdFusion. Ordinarily, you fill in the attributes and body by using variables defined from a form or a database query. Noticeably absent from this example are references to dynamic elements, such as a mailing list derived from a database query or a form letter filled in from a database. This is where the `<cfmail>` tag shines.

Sending a Form Letter to a List

Consider a situation where you have a list of clients or customers in a database, with e-mail addresses, and you want to send them all a note about a new product or service. The `<cfmail>` tag is your answer. When you want to send e-mail messages in this way, you need to specify the query attribute of the `<cfmail>` tag. Doing so, of course, means that you have to execute a `<cfquery>` prior to calling the `<cfmail>` tag. As an example, consider again the Northwind database.

The shipping department is in hot water about shipping costs. It is auditing all the shippers used in the past, and it needs some feedback from the customers to determine the level of services received.

You, therefore, need to send an identical form letter to all the Northwind customers who placed an order during the month of July 1996. You can query the database for the e-mail addresses of all the customers who fit this description and use the results as the basis for your e-mail list.

Start with the query so the `<cfmail>` tag has something to work with.

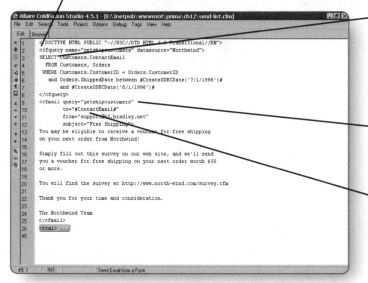

To get the e-mail addresses from the Customers table, you need to join it with the Orders table, from which you can filter for the ship dates.

You use the query attribute to tell the `<cfmail>` tag where to find the values for the to field.

Specify the to field as the e-mail address of the customer from the query. An e-mail message is generated for each row in the query.

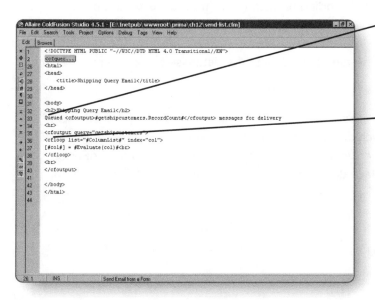

You can report the number of messages generated by referencing the RecordCount from the query.

Loop over the query to display the e-mail address that will receive the message.

When you request this template from the Web server, the e-mail messages are generated and queued. In other words, once the page is requested, you will not have a chance to bring those e-mail messages back. Make sure that you have it right the first time.

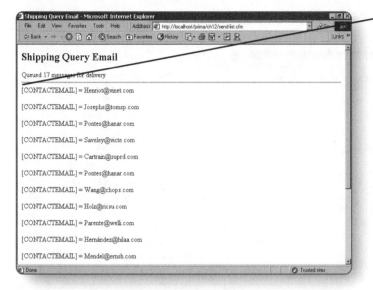

This page can be saved as a record of the mail operation.

The information displayed in the body of the Web page is for reference only. Because this template is more for administrative use, it simply displays the e-mail addresses of all the recipients. This feature is wonderful. It certainly beats the old mail-merge operations done in your word processor.

Sending a Customized Letter to a List

You can do better than just sending to a static list. You can customize each message to the individual customer and the individual order.

To do so, you need to fine-tune the query to the database to include more information.

This time, you join the Customers table with the Orders table and the Shippers table so that you can include information about the shipping company. Then you can place the record-specific data in the body of the message as a ColdFusion variable, just like you place data inside a <cfoutput> using the query attribute.

The Shippers table is added to the query by joining the Orders.ShipVia column with the Shippers.ShipperID column. Note that a few more columns have been added to the SELECT list.

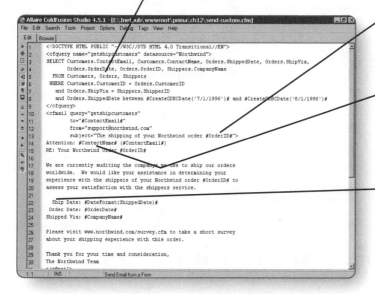

You customized the subject attribute value by including the OrderID.

Note the addition of the customer's contact name as a memo header, along with the OrderID again.

You include the particulars of the shipment to give the customer a reference for communicating with Northwind.

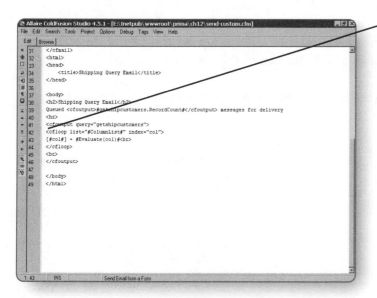

You repeat the same display code from the previous example, again so that you have a copy of the mail operation.

Don't forget! Once you load this template in your browser, the mail is gone. You don't want to be accused of spamming your customers with errant and incorrect information.

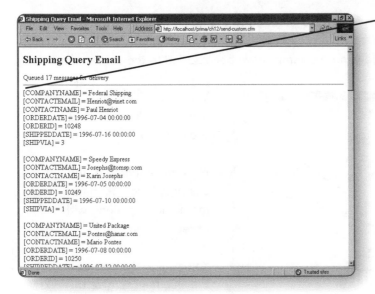

This turns out to be a useful record of the customer orders for the period in question. You should send this to the shipping department!

Excellent. This should generate some great feedback about how the shipping partners are doing. You've also saved somebody an afternoon of merging mail.

Attaching a File to an E-Mail

Now it is time to give the marketing and sales folks a hand. They want to send out a new catalog to all the customers who ordered a particular product.

You use the child tag <cfmailparam> to include an attachment to the e-mail. You place this tag inside the <cfmail></cfmail> tags, typically below the message, and use the file attribute with a full pathname to the file to be attached.

You first need to query the database for all the customers who purchased the product in question.

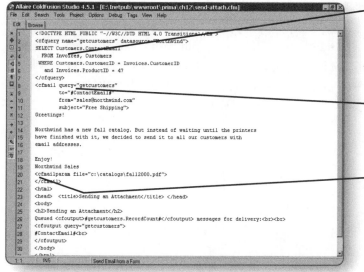

This time, you need to join the `Invoices` table with the `Customers` table and filter for `ProductID` 47.

Specify the `query` in order to generate the e-mail list from the `Customers` table.

The `<cfmailparam>` tag instructs the `<cfmail>` tag to attach the indicated file to the mail message.

The display code of this template is nearly identical to the previous example. It also includes a loop to output the list generated by the query.

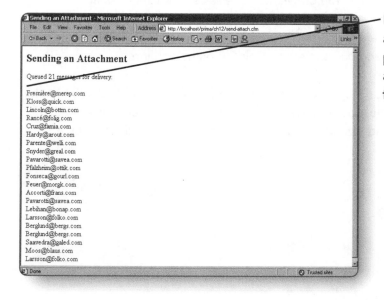

Because this output is useful as a record of the mail operation, perhaps you should consider adding some kind of file-logging feature to this template.

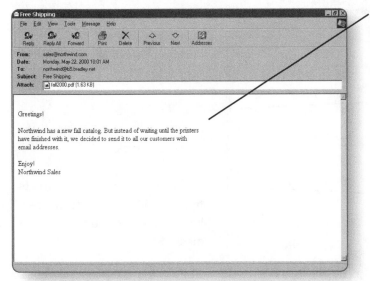

Attachments are easy. But just to prove that the mail did go out with an attachment, take a look at how this message will appear to the customers.

Adding New Headers to an E-Mail

This mailing was big success. Too big, in fact. The sales department wants to change how customers reply to the catalog messages so that the sales mail account doesn't fill up with catalog requests. They have set up a new e-mail account to handle these requests and questions. Can ColdFusion help them?

Yes it can. You can add a "Reply-To" header to the e-mail message so that when the customers press the Reply button, the address in the Reply-To field is used rather than the sales e-mail address. The <cfmailparam> tag can handle this for you.

The product that determines the list of customers has changed, per instructions from the sales department.

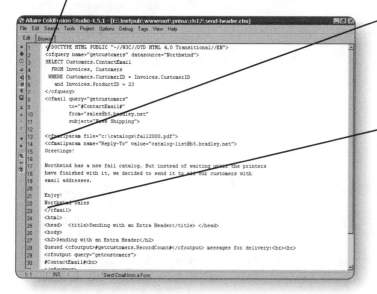

Here you add a second <cfmailparam> tag, this time containing the name and value attributes to describe the additional header for the e-mail.

The additional <cfmailparam> tag is the only change made to this template, other than previously noted.

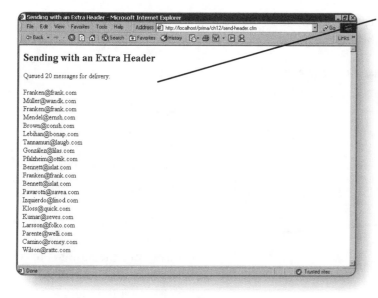

Out it goes! The sales staff is ecstatic with this new e-mail functionality. They are already predicting an increase in sales for the quarter based on the e-mail responses they have received.

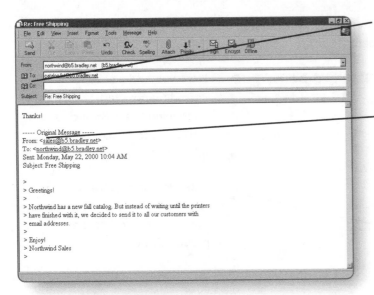

Note that the reply field is populated with the e-mail address specified in the extra header.

The origin of the note is the sales account, but the reply address is the catalog-list account.

Using a Form to Write E-Mail

These examples have been sending canned e-mail messages up to this point. How about allowing the Web users to generate the e-mail message? How would you go about doing that? You can use a form to get the e-mail information from the users and then submit the information to a form processor that uses the <cfmail> tag.

On the form, you need to provide the user with a way to enter the destination address, subject, and who the mail is from. To do so, create three text fields to hold the to, from, and subject values of the e-mail.

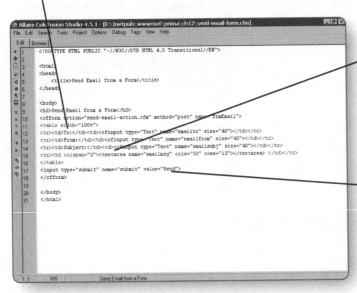

Because an e-mail can be long, use a <textarea> form element to hold the body of the e-mail message. This enables the user to enter as lengthy an e-mail as she likes.

The Submit button is a little misleading, but the intent is to send the message, isn't it? Remember that the message is queued for delivery in the spool, not actually sent.

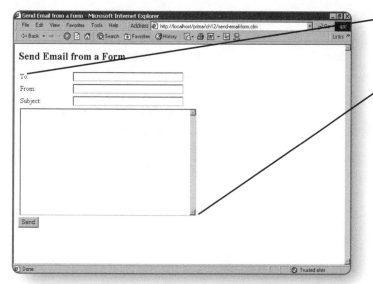

You now have a very familiar form, resembling many e-mail interfaces.

The `<textarea>` can be scrolled when the message runs too long for the size of the box.

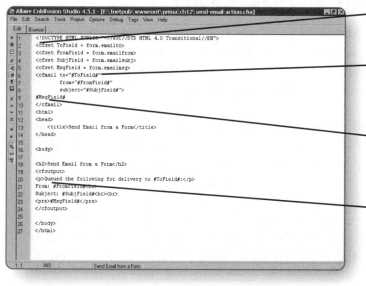

You reassign the form variables for use in the `<cfmail>` tag.

Use the reassigned local variables in the to, from, and subject attributes.

Simply place the MsgField variable inside the `<cfmail></cfmail>` tags.

On the display, you provide a report of what has happened and a summary of the e-mail message.

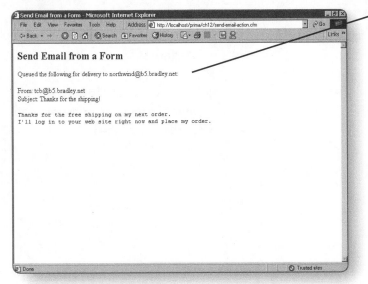

The output shows the users what was sent. Of course, perhaps a confirmation form between the initial form and the action template would be more appropriate. This form would allow the users to correct mistakes they make before sending the message.

Validating E-Mail Addresses

One of the most common reasons e-mail messages end up in the *undelivr* directory is the presence of badly formatted e-mail addresses in the `to` attribute of the `<cfmail>` tag. You can perform a simple check on the recipient address that the users enter and prevent a lot of these errors from happening.

You can use ColdFusion's regular expression functions to do the checking. Regular expressions are a powerful way to match or search textual information. A full discussion of regular expressions is beyond the scope of this book, but you can learn a lot from the discussion of the one in this example.

The basic tasks here are to check the `ToField` variable to determine whether it contains a list of addresses and then check each address in the list to determine whether each conforms to an Internet-style e-mail address. The address format should be `something@somewhere.someletters`. If not, you abort the template processing and explain to the users that a badly formatted e-mail address exists.

This regular expression function returns a number greater than zero if either a comma or a semicolon appears in ToField. If either a comma or a semicolon appears there, you have a list of addresses.

You loop over the list and specify that either a comma or a semicolon can be the delimiter.

The first part of this regular expression, [a-zA-Z0-9_-]+@, translates as "match any one or more alphanumeric characters, underscores, or dashes, followed by an @ sign." This expression is checking the validity of the first part of the e-mail address.

Because the REFind function returns a positive integer when it finds a match, a zero means it didn't find a match. In this case, no match means the address is badly formatted, so you abort the template and show an error.

Notice the Replace function just outside the <cfloop>. Here, you replace all semicolons with commas because the <cfmail> tag uses commas to separate e-mail addresses in the to attribute.

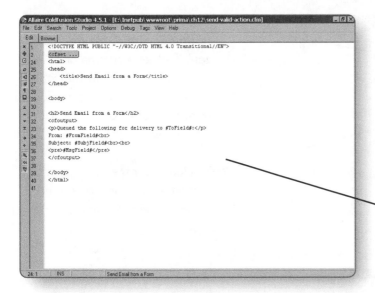

Regular expressions are pretty difficult to read, but you might want to spend some time learning about them. You can create highly complex matching patterns. The ColdFusion documentation has a short section on regular expressions that I recommend as a starting point.

The display code of the template is identical to the previous example. It displays the changed delimiters of the recipient list.

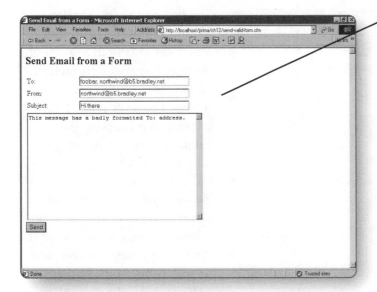

This person is mixed up about those delimiters! The reason these examples used the comma and semicolon is that they are the two most common address delimiters used. By expecting either of the two delimiters in the code, you eliminate the problem of guessing which one the users are using.

This display is not very user-friendly. But until you've learned a little more about handling errors in Chapter 24, "Handling Errors," you will have to stick with this. At least this does explain exactly why there is an error.

13

Retrieving Mail from a POP Server

Sending mail is only half of the story. Most people like to receive mail, too. You can accommodate those folks by interacting with the mail server using the `<cfpop>` tag. Although this chapter only scratches the surface of this powerful tag, you can still use the code in this chapter to construct a useful mail client. Everything you need to get started is covered here. In this chapter, you learn to:

- Check for new e-mail
- Retrieve message headers
- Retrieve messages with attachments
- View messages in a Web page

Using <cfpop> to Retrieve Mail Messages

ColdFusion enables you to retrieve mail messages with the <cfpop> tag. This tag interacts with a mail server known as a *Post Office Protocol*, or POP, server. POP servers are very common for holding and delivering e-mail on the Internet. POP services are often offered on e-mail servers that are primarily used in other ways, such as Microsoft Exchange, which is used to retrieve mail.

POP mail services enable you to retrieve e-mail only from the e-mail account's inbox. That is, you cannot interact with mail folders on the POP server. From the standpoint of writing a Web interface for reading e-mail with <cfpop>, this approach is actually easier. You don't have to worry about specifying or creating folders on the server.

The <cfpop> tag provides two retrieve actions, getheaderonly and getall, as well as one delete action. Because messages can be very large, especially when they have attachments, the getheaderonly operation is more efficient when retrieving the messages. You use getheaderonly when you need to see only the subject, who sent it, and when. You use this operation to implement an inbox view for the POP account. When you need to see the actual body of the message, use the getall operation. You use this operation to implement a message view for an e-mail message in the inbox. By creating templates for these two basic views , you will implement a rudimentary POP mail client in this chapter.

Checking for Mail

The basic mail operation involves determining how many mail messages you have in your inbox. You can do so using the getheaderonly action of the <cfpop> tag. The <cfpop> tag returns a result set, much like <cfquery> does. As such, you can check the RecordCount variable of the result returned so that users can see the number of messages in the inbox.

The `<cfpop>` tag requires the server (the name or IP address of the POP server), username (the account name on the POP server), and password (the POP account's password) attributes to connect to the POP server, as well as the action attribute.

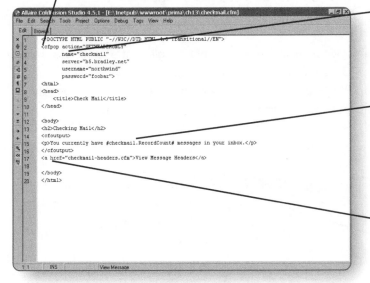

You also need the name attribute so that you can reference the result from the getheaderonly action.

You display the RecordCount variable of the `<cfpop>` operation result in order to report the number of messages waiting.

This links to the next example template so that you can view the headers.

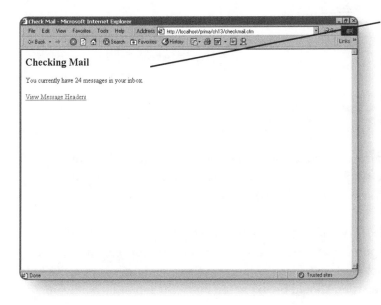

This example is a pretty simple one for connecting to the POP server. Notice that the password is shown in plain text. In a more complete implementation of a production application, you request the users to supply the usernames and passwords in a login form and use the form variables for authentication. Doing so will be easier when you learn about sessions and state maintenance in Chapter 17, "Using Applications in ColdFusion," and Chapter 18, "Tracking Sessions."

Retrieving Headers

Now that the users know they have mail waiting, they probably want to read it. You can use the same operation to retrieve the messages' headers and therefore display the senders, subjects, and dates sent.

As you can see from the previous example, the <cfpop> tag's syntax is simple. The complexity of creating a POP e-mail client in a Web page is displaying the information returned from the POP server in a useful way. In this example, you use the HTML tables to create an interface to display the headers in a Web page.

Use the tag's getheaderonly action.

Create a table with a row of column headers to describe the column contents.

Loop over the result of checkmail to display each message in a row on the table.

The POP server sends the date as a string. You need to convert the date to a ColdFusion date object so you can manipulate it.

You convert the parsed date to the ColdFusion server's local time using the DateConvert function. Doing so is necessary because the POP server timestamps messages in Universal Time Coordinates (UTC) format.

As you can see, the POP server likes to do things its way. ColdFusion is ready, though, with the pop argument of the ParseDateTime and DateConvert functions. This argument, when included, instructs the function that the date is from a POP server and that the date string should be expected in a POP server format when parsing.

Note that the example has passed the From and Subject variables to the HTMLEditFormat function to escape special characters. This function converts them to HTML encoded characters, such as < for a less-than symbol.

The ID numbers are hyperlinks to the example template. They enable the users to view individual mail messages.

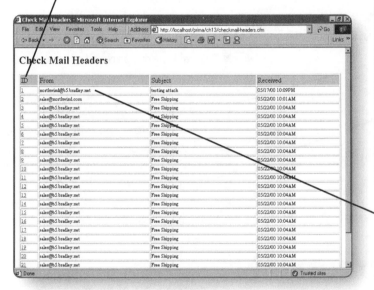

NOTE

The ID numbers are of significance mostly to the POP server. The server uses these numbers to track the status of messages with respect to the client accessing them. You can use these numbers to retrieve and delete messages from the POP server.

Notice that the font in the table body is smaller so that more information can fit in the Web page.

You now have created a familiar interface for previewing e-mail messages. You also have a way, using the hyperlinked ID numbers, to view the individual messages.

Retrieving Attachments

You can send attachments along with messages, and the POP server hangs on to them until they are requested or deleted. Because they are files, they need to be stored somewhere when the ColdFusion server retrieves them using the <cfpop> tag. You need to tell the <cfpop> tag where it can store these files. In this section, you learn how to use the attachmentpath attribute in conjunction with the generateuniquefilenames attribute to instruct the tag how to handle these files.

TIP

If you want the users to be able to download an attachment as a hyperlink from the Web server, you need to store the files in a location that is accessible from the Web server as a virtual path or as a path from the document root.

```
Allaire ColdFusion Studio 4.5.1 - [E:\Inetpub\wwwroot\prima\ch13\checkmail-attach.cfm]
File  Edit  Search  Tools  Project  Options  Debug  Tags  View  Help
Edit   Browse
1   <!DOCTYPE HTML PUBLIC "-//W3C//DTD HTML 4.0 Transitional//EN">
2   <cfpop action="GETALL"
3          name="checkmail"
4          attachmentpath="e:\inetpub\wwwroot\prima\ch13\"
5          generateuniquefilenames="Yes"
6          server="b5.Bradley.net"
7          username="northwind"
8          password="foobar">
9   <html>
10  <head>
11      <title>Check Mail</title>
12  </head>
13
14  <body>
15  <h2>Check Mail with Attachments</h2>
16  <table width="100%" border="1">
17  <tr style="background-color: silver;">
18  <td>ID</td><td>Att?</td>
19  <td>From</td><td>Subject</td><td>Received</td>
20  </tr>
21  <cfoutp...
37
37:1   INS       View Message
```

You now use the `<cfpop>` tag's `getall` action to retrieve the attachments and the message body.

Set the `attachmentpath` to a location under the Web server's document root.

It is recommended that you set `generateuniquefilenames` to `yes` so that files will not be overwritten when a name conflict occurs.

Note that you are retrieving all components of the messages for this display. This operation is not very efficient, but if you want to determine whether a message has an attachment before showing it, you must use this operation.

This code adds a column to show an "X" if the message has an attachment.

If the value of `Attachments` is an empty string, no attachments are with this message.

```
Allaire ColdFusion Studio 4.5.1 - [E:\Inetpub\wwwroot\prima\ch13\checkmail-attach.cfm]
File  Edit  Search  Tools  Project  Options  Debug  Tags  View  Help
Edit   Browse
1   <!DOCTYPE HTML PUBLIC "-//W3C//DTD HTML 4.0 Transitional//EN">
20  <cfpop ...
21  <cfoutput query="checkmail">
22  <cfset Received = DateConvert("utc2local", ParseDateTime(Date, "pop"))>
23  <tr>
24      <td style="font-size: 8pt;"><a href="checkmail-view.cfm?id=#MessageNumber#">#MessageNumber#</a></td>
25      <td style="font-size: 8pt;"><cfif Attachments is not "">X</cfif></td>
26      <td style="font-size: 8pt;">#HTMLEditFormat(From)#</td>
27      <td style="font-size: 8pt;">#HTMLEditFormat(Subject)#</td>
28      <td style="font-size: 8pt;">
29      #DateFormat(Received, "mm/dd/yy")# #TimeFormat(Received, "hh:mmtt")#
30      </td>
31  </tr>
32  </cfoutput>
33  </table>
34
35  </body>
36  </html>
37
21:1   INS       View Message
```

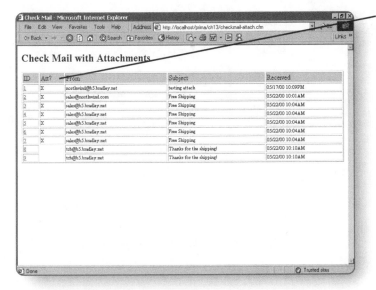

Messages with an "X" in this column have an attachment.

This page loaded much slower. Perhaps this overhead is not worth the benefit of knowing the attachment status of a message before actually viewing it. This is a decision you'll have to make.

Retrieving and Viewing Messages

Now your users want to actually read their messages. No problem. The <cfpop> tag's syntax in this case is nearly the same as in the last example. You need to add one more attribute to the tag: the messagenumber attribute. This attribute instructs the <cfpop> tag to retrieve only the message with this number.

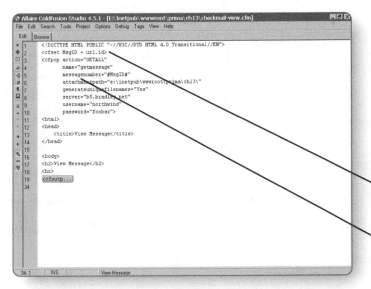

You can pass the message number in using a url variable. Remember the hyperlink on the ID number from the previous examples? Beyond specifying the message number, this template simply displays the message retrieval results.

You reassign the url variable to a local page variable.

You add the messagenumber attribute to the <cfpop> tag, using MsgID as the value.

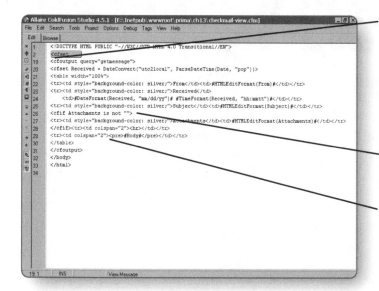

Because you know that this result has only one row (the message), you can move the `<table>` inside the `<cfoutput></cfoutput>` tags for the display.

If the message has attachments, display the list here.

Use the `<pre></pre>` tags to preserve text formatting in the body of the message.

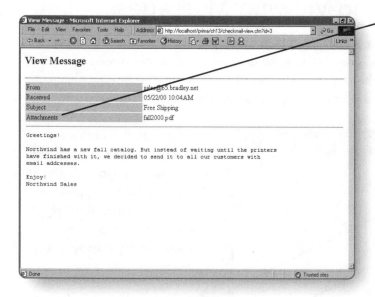

This message has one attachment. If the message included more than one, this line would include a comma-delimited list of filenames.

You have a clean, simple interface for reading an e-mail message. The missing elements here are links to the attachments for download and a way to reply or send new mail. Wait a minute! Didn't you just do that? Hmm.

These examples should be taken as starting points for building your e-mail client interfaces. I've pointed out some of the bigger omissions to be addressed; you will undoubtedly find others.

14

Connecting to an FTP Server

Even though other protocols have popped up, the venerable File Transfer Protocol (FTP) server still has life in this new Web age. The protocol remains a popular method for sending and receiving files across the Internet. Even Web browsers know how to connect to an FTP server to retrieve files. ColdFusion hasn't forgotten about FTP either—it uses the `<cfftp>` tag to interact with FTP. In this chapter, you learn to:

- Connect to an FTP server
- Get a directory listing
- Traverse a directory tree
- Retrieve a file from an FTP server
- Send a file to an FTP server

Using <cfftp>

The <cfftp> tag is another example of a multi-functional tag. The different operations that it supports require different attributes. The action operations supported by the <cfftp> tag are open, close, getcurrentdir, changedir, createdir, listdir, existsdir, existsfile, getfile, putfile, rename, remove, exists, and getcurrenturl. I don't think "multi-functional" quite covers it.

This chapter covers only a few of these operations to familiarize you with the <cfftp> tag. However, once you know how to use the operations covered in this chapter, you can easily modify your knowledge to use the others. With this long list of operations, you can build a rich interface to the FTP protocol.

Connecting to an FTP Server

The basic operation that you can perform with the <cfftp> tag is to connect to the server. The <cfftp> tag requires the server, username, and password attributes when opening a connection to the FTP server. Unless you use the connection attribute, the <cfftp> tag authenticates to the FTP server each time it is called. Each authentication operation takes time. You can eliminate this overhead by telling ColdFusion to remember the connection from call to call by giving the connection a name in the connection attribute. This technique is called *caching*. Caching improves the performance of your calls to <cfftp> by keeping the connection to the FTP server open.

You can take advantage of caching in a single template by using the server, username, and password, along with the connection attributes, with the first call to <cfftp> in a template. You then use just the connection attribute with the subsequent calls to the tag. You will be able to extend this caching technique across templates when you learn about session and state management in Chapter 17, "Using Applications in ColdFusion," and Chapter 18, "Tracking Sessions."

In the meantime, though, you can start by opening an FTP connection.

You set the `action` attribute to `open` and tell the tag what the server is and what username and password to use. The `connection` attribute names the connection for reuse, though we aren't reusing the connection in this example. The `stoponerror` attribute tells ColdFusion to stop processing the template immediately if there is an error. You see how to handle `stoponerror` set to `no` later in this chapter.

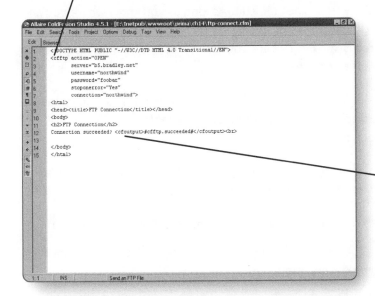

The `<cfftp>` tag generates some standard variables you can access, such as `succeeded`. These variables exist in the `cfftp` scope. You use these variables later in the chapter to handle FTP errors.

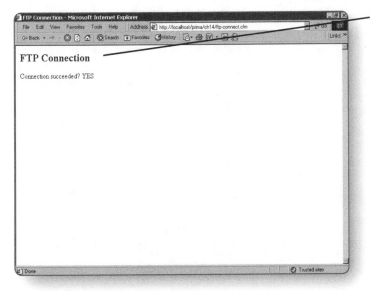

This template simply connects to the FTP server and determines whether the connection attempt was successful. This operation is not very interesting, but it's a necessary one, as you will see later.

Navigating the Directory Tree

Navigating an FTP directory tree is not difficult. As long as you know where you are and where you want to go, there's no problem. So the first order of business in traversing a directory tree is knowing where you are. It becomes a matter of telling the server where you want to go after that.

This example builds a Web interface into an FTP server directory tree. You connect, find out where you are, display the current directory's contents, and display the hyperlinks to navigate out of it.

You can reuse this template as a general-purpose navigation tool. Therefore, it's wise to use a url variable to track your progress through the directory tree.

Set the base directory to the ftp directory in the home directory of your target FTP account.

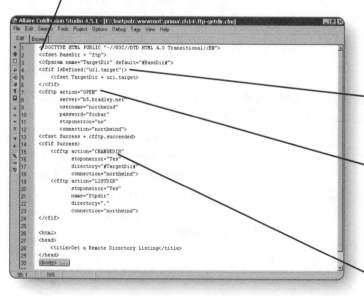

Set a default value for the TargetDir of your directory listing.

Next, determine whether the template has been called using a new url base directory.

Now, you open a connection and determine whether it succeeded. If it did connect properly, you proceed with your directory operations.

Set the operation to changedir and move to the TargetDir directory. You'll get your directory listing in the next call to <cfftp>.

Notice that the connection attribute accesses the cached connection from the previous open operation. This operation alleviates the need to authenticate to the FTP server each time.

In the body of the HTML page, you first check for the success of the open operation. If it failed, you display the error and abort the template.

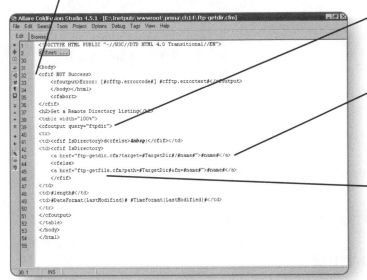

You loop over the results of from the <cfftp> operation and display the results in a table.

This hyperlink uses the url variable target. It is set to the current TargetDir, plus the name of the directory from the result.

This code jumps ahead to the next section, "Retrieving a File." You'll learn about this then.

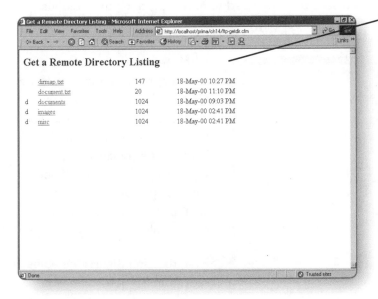

The display is plain, but efficient. It lists the contents of the current directory on the FTP server. The directories are hyperlinked back to this template, with the target variable displaying the new base directory.

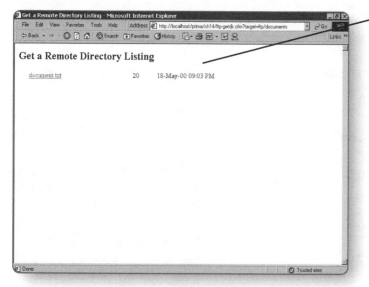

To prove that it works, you can follow a directory down one level. The display is the directory listing for the *documents* subdirectory. You can see that only one file, document.txt, is in the directory.

Retrieving a File

Retrieving a file when the ColdFusion server is performing an FTP operation means that the file will be copied from the remote FTP server to the ColdFusion server, not to the Web client. This means that you need to have a place on the ColdFusion server to store the file, at least temporarily.

In this template, you create a directory to store the files. If the file already exists in the download location, the operation will fail. You can configure this behavior by specifying the failifexists attribute. If you set this attribute to no, the <cfftp> tag will overwrite an existing file.

First, reassign the url variables sent from ftp-getdir.cfm. You can also create variables to hold the names of the local download directories.

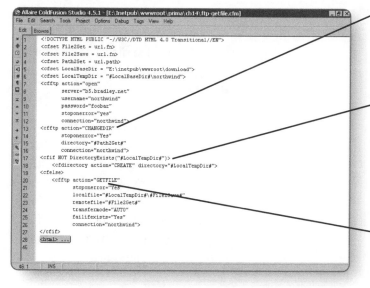

After the connection succeeds, you change to the file's directory, as specified by `Path2Get`.

Next, determine whether the local download directory exists using the ColdFusion function `DirectoryExists`. If it doesn't exist, you create it using `<cfdirectory>`.

Now, you retrieve the file using the `getfile` operation. You need to specify the `<cfftp>` tag's `localfile` and `remotefile` attributes for this operation. The `localfile` is the destination filename on the ColdFusion server, and the `remotefile` is the source file on the FTP server.

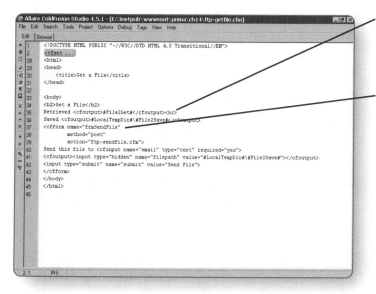

In the display code, you show the operation's results using the local page variables.

This form is also jumping ahead a bit. This is how you retrieve the newly downloaded file.

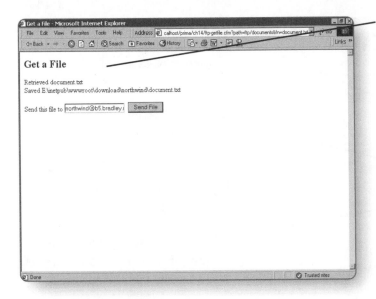

Now you have the FTP file operation's results. If all has gone well, a file is waiting for you in the download directory. All you do is retrieve it.

Because you created the download directory under the Web server's document root, you can simply create a link on this results page by translating the physical location of the file to a virtual path suitable for a hyperlink reference.

But consider this option instead. You can have the file mailed to the users. This method is widely used to retrieve files from FTP servers and e-mail list servers all over the world. As an example, return to the form on the results page.

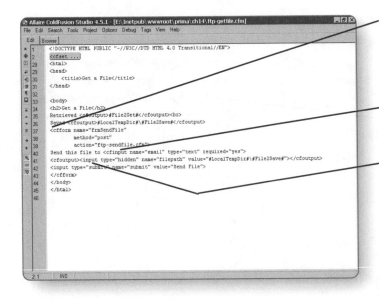

You need to create a form on the results page first. This form must require that the users provide their e-mail addresses.

A simple text form field gathers the e-mail address you need.

You can also create a hidden form field that holds the location of the file to be mailed.

Now, all you need is a form-processing template to handle the mailing of the file as an attachment. You probably remember how that was done in Chapter 12, "Sending Mail."

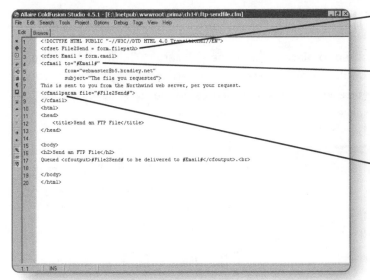

You reassign the form variables to local page variables.

Now, you generate an e-mail message with <cfmail>, using the e-mail address provided by the form.

Attach the file retrieved from the FTP server using a <cfmailparam> tag.

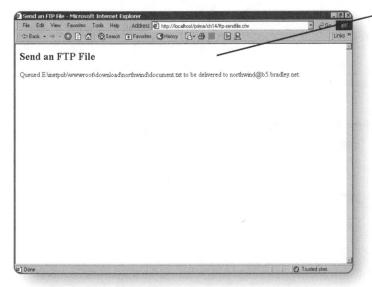

Mission accomplished. The file has been retrieved from the remote FTP server to the ColdFusion server and delivered via e-mail to the user. A little old-fashioned, certainly, but sometimes the old ways are the best.

Another approach is to use a download directory on the Web server to store files retrieved from the FTP server. You can then create a Web page with links to these files for download to the user's browser.

Sending a File

At some point, you will need to place a file on the FTP server. ColdFusion can help you do that, too. Because this book has already covered uploading files from your Web browser to the Web server, this section focuses on the steps necessary to place a file on the FTP server from the ColdFusion server.

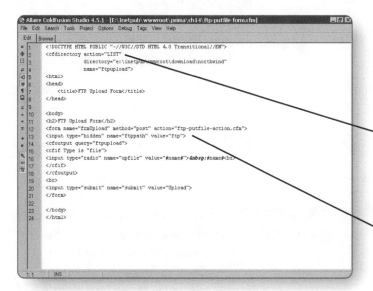

First, you need to create a form that displays the files currently on the Web server in case you want to send one of them to the FTP server.

Use `<cfdirectory>` with the `list` attribute to obtain the file list from the Web server directory.

You can cheat here a little and send the FTP target directory in a hidden form field.

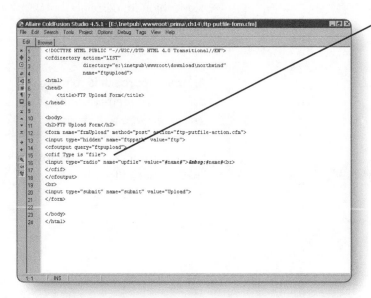

If the listing is a file, you display a radio button and its name, with the button's value containing the filename as well.

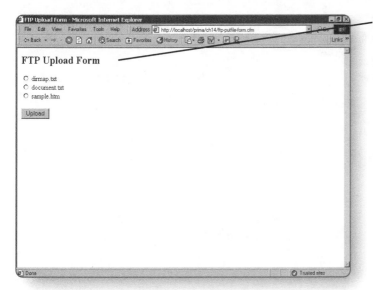

You have a few files to choose from in this listing. Now consider how you handle the FTP upload in the form-processing template.

After reassigning the form variables, you set the `LocalTempDir` variable to the same path that the `<cfdirectory>` tag uses to list the files.

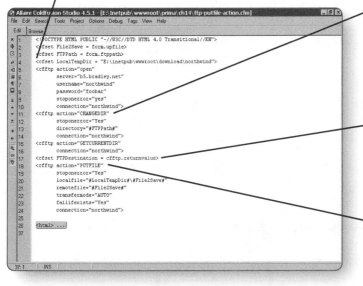

After connecting to the FTP server, you change to the directory specified in the `hidden` form field. This directory will be the destination of the file upload.

After the directory change, ask the FTP server what the current directory is and store it in `FTPConnection`.

The call to the `<cfftp>` with the `putfile` operation is identical to the call with the `getfile` operation. You just reverse the remote and local file locations. With `getfile`, you are retrieving a file from the FTP server; with `putfile`, you are sending a file to the FTP server.

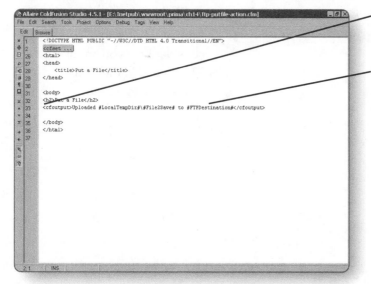

Here, you report the results of what you've done.

Now, use the target directory's stored value to show the users where the file went.

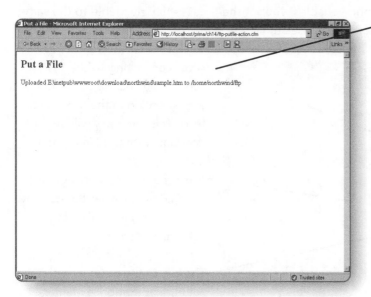

There is no reason why you cannot combine this putfile operation with a file-upload form from Chapter 10, "Writing Files." You still need a directory to hold the file temporarily on the ColdFusion server, but this technique would obviate the need to display a directory listing from which to choose a file to upload.

15

Retrieving Other Web Pages

The amount of information on the Web is staggering, and people search for information in this vast arena almost daily. Some of that searching is often repetitive because it's for updated data. The vastness of the Web also makes these searches complex. With ColdFusion and the `<cfhttp>` tag, you can make searching for and retrieving information a little less strenuous. In this chapter, you learn to:

- Retrieve a Web page with `<cfhttp>`
- Submit a Web form
- Process the contents of a retrieved Web page
- Put the power of the big Web search engines in your application

Using <cfhttp> to Retrieve a Web Page

The <cfhttp> tag retrieves a Web page specified in the url attribute of the tag via a get or post operation. It then stores the entire contents of the page in a variable named filecontent with a cfhttp scope, so when you reference the filecontent variable, you need to prefix it with cfhttp. Alternatively, you can specify the path and file attributes to store the Web page in a file. If the Web page requires authentication, you can specify the username and password attributes.

The <cfhttp> tag acts like a Web browser. Of course, it is not a fully featured Web browser, so it does not run Java applets or render graphics. However, it can retrieve files and HTML documents from the Web for inclusion in or processing by your Web application. The <cfhttp> tag is yet another way in which ColdFusion enables you to bring disparate data formats into your Web application.

The simplest example of using <cfhttp> is to perform a get operation, which retrieves a Web page. The <cfhttp> tag requires the action and url attributes. You can retrieve a simple Web page and then display it in the browser. The resolveurl attribute translates relative URL paths in the retrieved document to absolute paths. To translate the URLs, set this attribute to true.

Start the template with the <cfhttp> tag using the *get* method.

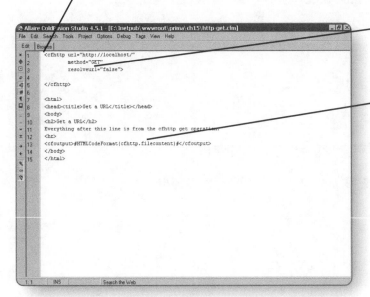

Setting resolveurl to false leaves the hyperlinks in the retrieved document intact.

The cfhttp.filecontent variable holds the contents of the file. You output this variable using the HTMLCodeFormat to prevent the browser from attempting to parse HTML tags in the file.

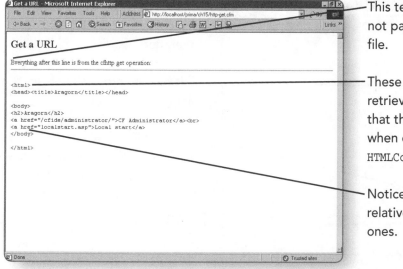

This text is part of the template, not part of the retrieved HTML file.

These are the contents of the retrieved file. It is easy to see that this is the entire HTML file when displayed with the HTMLCodeFormat function.

Notice that the anchor links are relative paths, not absolute ones.

The <cfhttp> tag is also used to retrieve a Web page and extract links from the text. But you need the full, absolute path on each link to access them. So you should get the same page and resolve those links to absolute paths.

You can display more information about the operation. The <cfhttp> tag populates more variables in the cfhttp scope than filecontent. You can also get statuscode, mimetype, responseheader, and header.

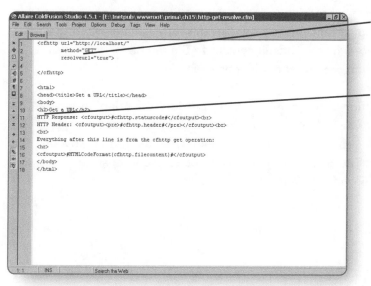

This time, you set the resolveurl attribute to true to translate the links.

As a report of the operation, you can output the statuscode and header of the get operation.

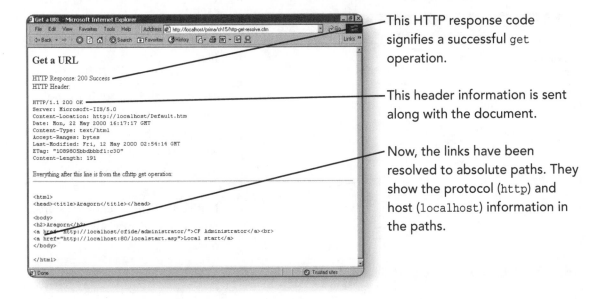

This HTTP response code signifies a successful get operation.

This header information is sent along with the document.

Now, the links have been resolved to absolute paths. They show the protocol (http) and host (localhost) information in the paths.

The header lines displayed in this example can be processed to make decisions on how to handle the contents of the variable cfhttp.filecontent.

Submitting a Form

You can use the <cfhttp> tag to submit forms. You need to know what form fields are expected by the form-processing script on the remote server. Then you need to fill them in. The child tag, <cfhttpparam>, handles this for you. The <cfhttpparam> also enables you to upload files or submit cookies to the remote server. This section uses a simple form post operation for an example.

You will submit information to a dynamic query to produce the shipping report in Chapter 7, "Dynamic Query Building." You need to supply values for region, regoperator, shipdate, dateoperator, and sort fields from the form that you created for that report. The <cfhttp> tag requires you to use a separate <cfhttpparam> tag for each form field value to be sent.

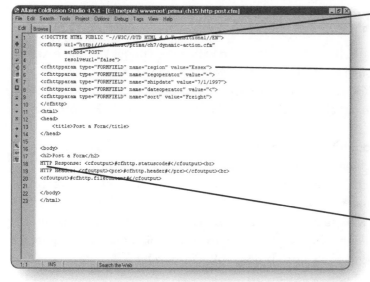

To submit this form, you use the post operation.

You need to set the type for each parameter to formfield in the <cfhttpparam> tags because the parameters are form fields. Give each tag a name that matches the form field names, and give each tag a value.

You can display the results and then display the return page as is.

Here is the shipping invoice report, complete with the table display.

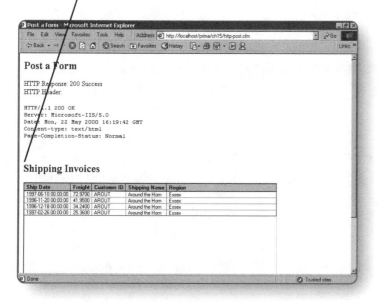

With the <cfhttp> and <cfhttpparam> tags, you can automate form submissions to commonly submitted forms on the Web. Alternatively, you can traverse a Web site by navigating links and submitting forms with these tags. This can be an automatic way of testing user navigation paths. But you also need to extract the links from the pages you retrieve to traverse them.

Processing the Contents of a Web Page

Once you retrieve it, you can do almost anything with a Web page. You can extract strings from the page, such as stock quotes or weather reports. You can extract all the URLs from a page. You can use a regular expression again to assemble the URLs on the Web page. This example looks only for URLs that use the HTTP protocol.

The trick to moving through the file contents is that you need to have the program restart the find operation each time it finds a match, and do so at least one character past that match. To track where the search is in the file, you can create a pointer variable and have the program update the pointer as it finds matches. To control the search, you will use a conditional loop that checks whether the pointer is smaller than the file's length but larger than zero. If the pointer is zero or greater than or equal to the length, the search is done—it exits the loop.

To keep track of the URLs that it finds, the program adds them to a list as it finds them. You can use the Mid function to extract the actual link string from the file contents.

First, you get the page. Then you set defaults for the URLList and ptr variables.

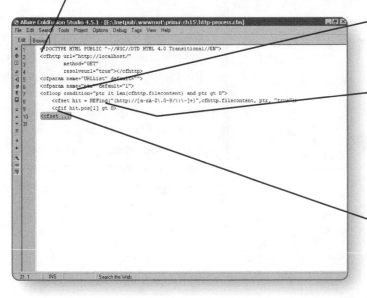

Start the loop with the condition as described in the opening of this section.

The REFind function returns a ColdFusion structure (named hit) that tells you the position and length of the matching string from the regular expression.

This says, "if the position returned from REFind is greater than zero, you've found a match. If not, there is no match, so set the pointer ptr to zero."

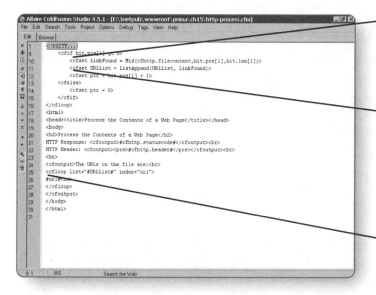

When a match is found, the program extracts it with the Mid function and saves it in LinkFound.

The program appends the link to the URLList list, using the ListAppend function. Then it moves the pointer (ptr) along by one so that it doesn't match the same link again.

Here, it loops over the URLList to display the links that were found on the page.

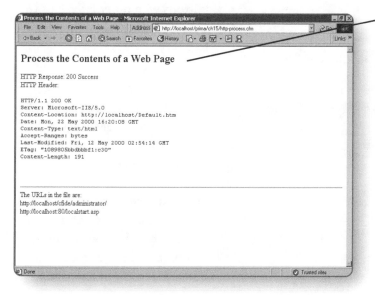

You can take this list of URLs and traverse all the links on the site or store these links in the database to check later. Compare this list with the output from the previous example to confirm the list of links.

Interacting with Search Engines

With all your newfound skill, you can add search capabilities to your Web applications. To access these search engines in your ColdFusion templates, you need to know the format of the form fields submitted to the engines from the engines' own forms. Just browse to the search form on the search engine site and view the form's source code. Look for the <input> tags and note their names.

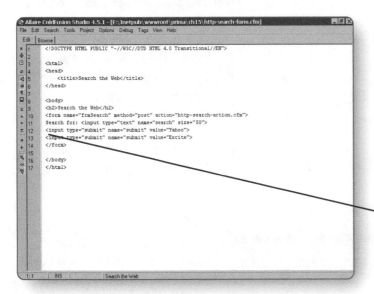

Start with a simple HTML form containing a single text field and two Submit buttons.

Here, you use multiple Submit buttons with different values to determine which search engine to query.

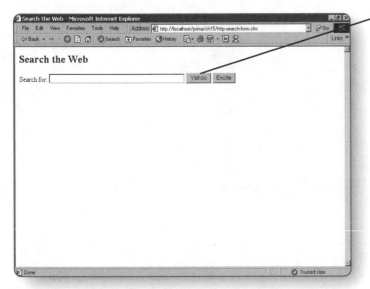

Using the value attributes of the Submit buttons gives you a clean way to enable users to choose a search engine.

This interface works well when you have limited search engine choices, but if you add others, you probably need to use radio buttons or a drop-down list.

By reviewing the source code of the Web forms on Yahoo and Excite, you learn that the search forms used by the big engines submit queries using a `get` action, so you don't have to use the `<cfhttpparam>` tags.

Because this search term is going to be added to a URL address, you need to encode the search terms from the form using the `URLEncodedFormat` function.

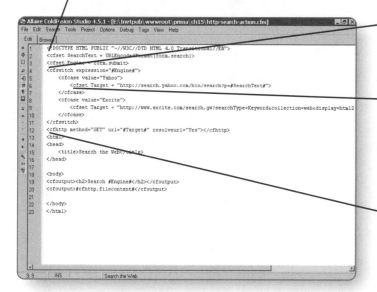

You can use a `<cfswitch>` tag to determine which search engine the users want to use.

Now, you just build the URL used by the `<cfhttp>` tag. This example builds the Yahoo search URL and stores it in the `Target` variable.

A call to the `<cfhttp>` tag with the `Target` URL compiles the search results.

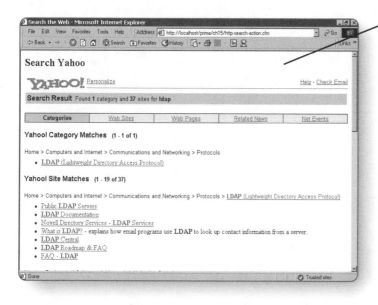

Here is the result of a search sent to Yahoo! on ldap (Lightweight Directory Access Protocol, a method of looking up information in a hierarchical database on the Internet). I've included the entire page to show you that this indeed comes from Yahoo! You can process the file contents returned to extract the links, for example.

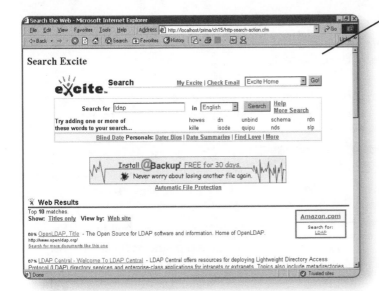

Here are the results of the same search from the Excite search engine. This kind of search option can be a nice service to add to your users' applications.

16

Performing Text Searches

Searching for a bit of text within pages of data is one of the most common search functions. You can approach this type of search in many ways. ColdFusion offers several ways in which you can search for text. It even includes a robust indexing engine for creating high performance text searches. In this chapter, you learn to:

- Search for text using SQL queries
- Search data with dynamic SQL queries
- Search text files with the Verity search engine
- Search text in databases with the Verity search engine
- Maintain your Verity indexes

Searching Your Databases with SQL

Before you get fancy with indexing engines and collections, consider the basics. SQL can be your search language, and your database can be your engine. After all, one of the main reasons for using a database to store information is that it can index that information for quick retrieval.

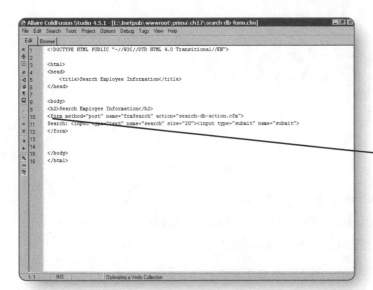

First, you create a simple form to request a search term from the users. Then you create a form-processing template to search the database for the requested information.

Another simple form that retrieves a search term from the users. Nothing special here.

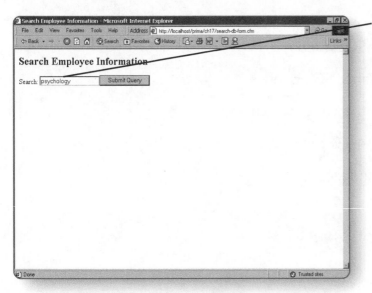

You can search for anyone with experience or training in psychology, as specified in the employee notes.

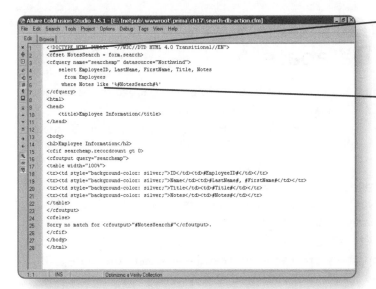

You reassign the form variable to a local page variable, NotesSearch.

Use the like SQL keyword with the % wildcard character to match columns anywhere in the text.

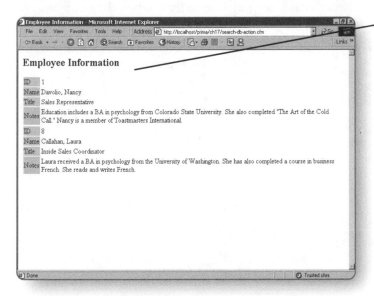

The output is clear and concise with no ambiguity. An extension of this search might be to provide a link where users can view the entire employee record.

Using Dynamic Queries to Search a Database

You can take the previous example a little further. Referring back to the techniques you learned in Chapter 7, "Dynamic Query Building," you can extend the search parameters to include more than text values by creating a dynamic query to search the database.

You can extend the previous example by enabling the users to specify an earliest hire date for the employee information search. Of course, you could extend this even further, but this example illustrates the point.

Here is your trusty friend, the <cfform> tag. You set the action to the form-processing template and set the method to post.

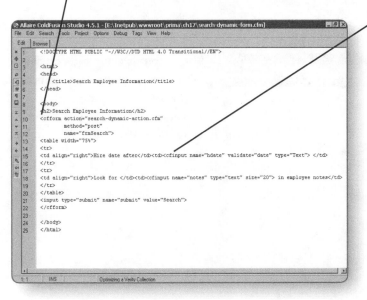

You then create two form fields, one for the hire date and one for the search term that searches the Notes column of the Employees table.

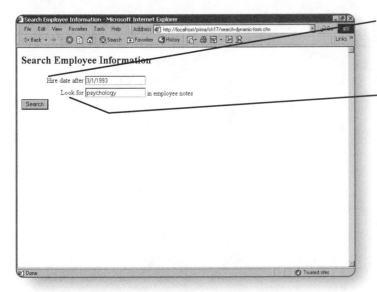

Inform the users that the date entered here will be the earliest hire date.

Tell the users how this search term will be used in the search.

This form is plain enough. As with any form requesting information from the users, this form's intent and the purpose of the information provided should be clear to the users.

You reassign the form variables and, in the process, create an ODBC-compliant date from the hire date parameter.

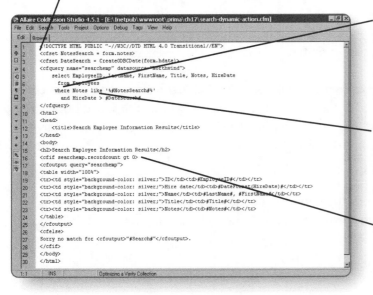

This where clause is a simple dynamic query filter. It uses the NotesSearch and DateSearch variables to search the database.

Use the like SQL keyword with the % wildcard characters to search the Notes column for the search term.

As in the previous example, the program checks for a result and if it gets a hit, displays the information in a table.

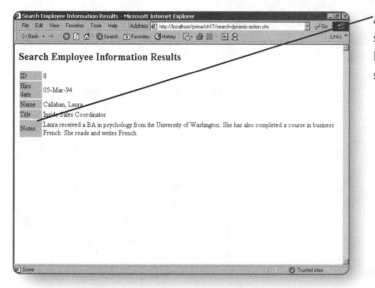

As you can see from the results set display, this employee has a BA in psychology, which was the search term.

Using the Verity Search Engine

ColdFusion ships with a search engine called Verity that you can use to index your Web files and text databases. The Verity engine creates indexes on custom data sources, such as documents or text fields in a database, which you can then search using the <cfsearch> ColdFusion tag.

To use Verity, you need to create a collection that holds the indexes to be searched. Then you create indexes for the collection by specifying keys, titles, and bodies of text to index. These indexes can be modified, updated, or deleted, either inter-actively in the ColdFusion Administrator Web pages or by using the <cfindex> tag in code.

First, you learn how to use the Verity collections and the <cfsearch> tag to find information, and then you learn how to use the <cfindex> tag for maintaining your indexes.

Using Verity to Search Web Files

You can use Verity collections to index and search files on your Web server. In fact, Verity understands several file formats that you can index: Adobe Acrobat, Microsoft Word, Microsoft Write, Corel WordPerfect, Lotus Ami Pro, and so on. Of course, it also indexes plain text files like HTML and ColdFusion templates.

This example includes a collection containing an index of some of this book's example code. You can use this collection as the first example of the <cfsearch> tag.

The search form code is much like the other forms in this chapter, so I'll dispense with the exposition of that code.

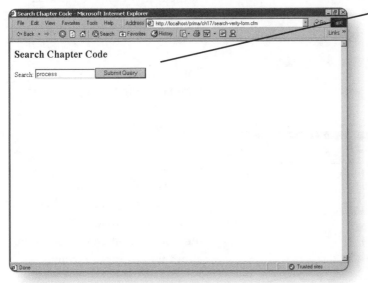

You can search the templates indexed for the term *process*. Before you see the results, take a look at how the form-processing template uses the <cfsearch> tag.

The `<cfsearch>` tag requires the `collection` attribute, which contains the name of the collection to search.

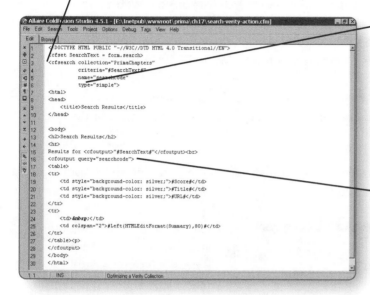

The `type` attribute specifies the type of search to be performed. The search can be `simple` or `explicit`. With `explicit` searches, you can use the full power of Verity's search language in the `criteria` attribute.

As with other ColdFusion tags, `<cfsearch>` returns a results set that you can display using `<cfoutput>`.

The results of a `<cfsearch>` contain the following columns for display: `key`, `title`, `score`, `summary`, `url`, `custom1`, `custom2`, `currentrow`, `recordssearched`, `currentrow`, and `columnlist`. This example uses the `score`, `title`, `summary`, and `url` columns to display the results. Consult the documentation to learn more about these output columns.

The score is a numerical representation of the strength of the hit on the index.

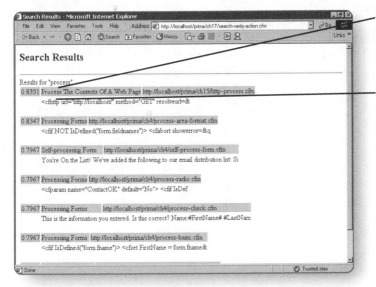

The title is extracted from the `<title></title>` tags of the indexed files.

The `summary` column is a short summary of the indexed material, up to the first 500 characters.

Using Verity to Search Databases

You can also use Verity to index database fields. This results in faster searching and reduces the performance hits on your database. First, you need to create an index on the data based upon a query. You learn how to create such an index in the next section.

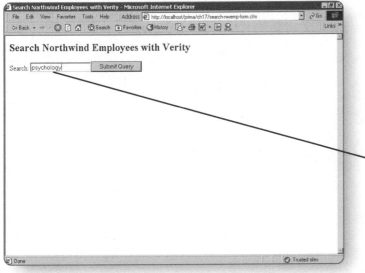

This example includes a collection called NWEmployees, which contains an index on the Notes column of the Employees table. Again, the search form is not remarkable; you can cut to the chase.

You can search once again for the psychologists in the company.

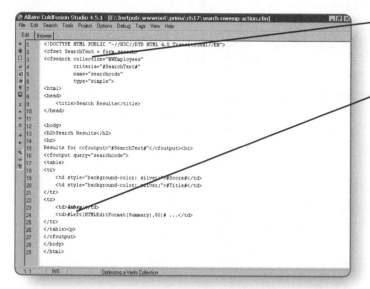

You use a simple search once again, but this time, you specify the NWEmployees collection.

You want only the first 80 characters of the summary, so you use the Left function to trim the summary. Note this value is also escaped with the HTMLEditFormat function.

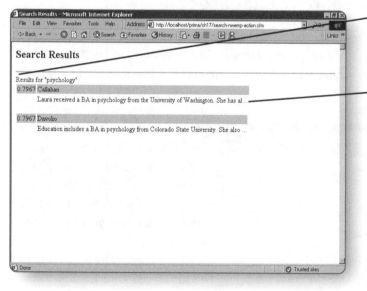

You can display the search criteria as a reminder to the users.

You use an ellipsis to denote that the text continues. The users are viewing a reduced portion of the text.

Maintaining Your Verity Collections

Data changes and files are deleted or added. With this basic fact in mind, you need to periodically maintain those Verity indexes to keep them fresh and accurate. You can maintain your collections manually with the ColdFusion Administrator interface to Verity (except your database-derived indexes). Alternatively, you can use the <cfindex> tag to maintain your indexes.

The <cfindex> tag is yet another example of a multi-functional tag. You can refresh, update, purge, or delete your Verity collection indexes with this tag. You learn only about the update operation in this chapter.

You have to create a query to generate the information you want to index.

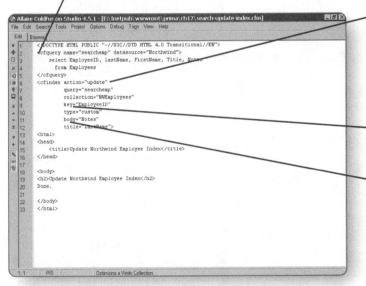

You call <cfindex> with the query attribute specifying the query name and the action set to update. Set the collection to NWEmployees.

Here, you use the EmployeeID as the index's key.

The main body of data to index is the Notes column of the Employees table.

That's it. Once this template is requested, the index operation begins. If this is a large result set, the template might take a long time to complete. You might receive a request timeout error in your browser. Don't panic. The indexing operation will still be completed.

To clean up a collection for better performance, you should optimize it after several update or purge index operations. You can use the <cfcollection> tag to perform the optimize operation. Although most operations with the <cfcollection> tag are usually best handled in the ColdFusion Administrator utility, it is often desirable to automate the optimize operation on your Verity collections. You investigate ColdFusion scheduled tasks in Chapter 21, "Generating Static Web Pages."

The <cfcollection> tag has two required attributes, collection and action.

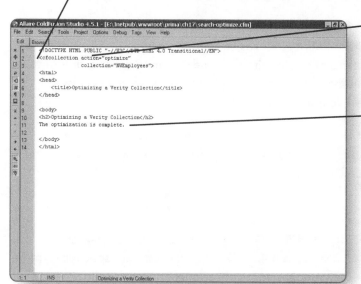

You set the action to optimize and the collection to the name of the collection you want to optimize.

The <cfcollection> tag has no output, like the <cfindex> tag, so you have nothing more to report to the users.

Many of the operations necessary to maintain your Verity collections can be accomplished from the Verity utility in the ColdFusion Administrator. Because most maintenance operations are irregular, the Administrator interface is often the most efficient way to handle those chores.

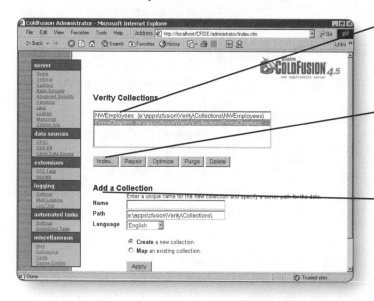

The Verity utility has two sections. This top section displays the existing Verity collections on this ColdFusion server.

The row of buttons along the bottom of this list enables you to perform the indicated operations on the selected collection.

The second section provides an interface to add new collections to the list. You specify the name, location, language, and type of collection and click the Apply button.

Verity collections are powerful text search tools when simple database searches don't fit the bill. However, these indexes need to be maintained. Begin with careful database and index planning, and use ColdFusion code to automate the task.

PART IV

Building Applications

17

Using Applications in ColdFusion

You can build serviceable applications in ColdFusion with what you have learned up to this point. But ColdFusion takes you even further. You can build Web applications that maintain state across requests, track sessions, and use application-level variables. This functionality enables you to create truly dynamic Web applications with all the features of a traditional desktop application. In this chapter, you learn to:

- Create and configure a ColdFusion application
- Use `<cfapplication>` to define an application
- Use the special application.cfm file
- Create custom error-handling templates
- Use cookies for state maintenance

Establishing Global Application Settings

A traditional application has a consistent look and feel in its interface and across application operations. To create consistency in an application, the developer must be able to access the *state* (the continuity of the relationships between transactions) of the application at any given point. Additionally, the developer will almost certainly require and use global settings or functions available in every component of the application.

On the Web, each transaction between a client and a server is self-contained and does not rely on or relate to any other transaction. To maintain a state, the transactions must have a way to relate to one another so that the state can be passed from one transaction to the next.

To relate these transactions, you create a session between the client and the server. A *session* is a collection of related transactions with a shared state. After you establish a session with a changeable state, you can create an application that gives the users the same features as a typical desktop application.

ColdFusion tracks a client's state with a unique ID and token, stored in cookies. It also stores these objects in a database on the ColdFusion server. With these unique identifiers, ColdFusion can track unique client transactions.

Using <cfapplication> to Define an Application

ColdFusion provides you with the `<cfapplication>` tag to define the client and session management to use for a given template. The `name` attribute of this tag contains the application's name and defines a new scope maintained by the application server. You can access this scope by using the `application` scope name prepended to a variable name, such as `application.MyTitle`.

To enable client state management for an application, set the `clientmanagement` attribute to `Yes`. When a new client connects to the server, the ID and token values are generated and stored in a new scope called `client`. These `client` variables are stored in the default client storage area.

To enable session management for an application, set the sessionmanagement attribute to Yes. You must also enable client state management in order to use session management. When a client connects to the server, a new scope called session becomes available.

You can set timeouts for the session and application variable scopes. Use the sessiontimeout and the applicationtimeout attributes of the <cfapplication> tag. You use the CreateTimeSpan function to generate a value for these attributes.

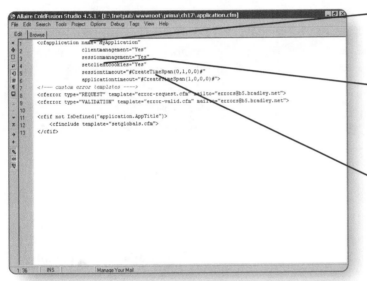

The name attribute informs ColdFusion as to which application this template belongs.

Setting setclientcookies to Yes tells ColdFusion to automatically send a cookie containing the ID and token values to the client.

The four arguments of the CreateTimeSpan function are days, hours, minutes, and seconds, respectively. This example sets the session to time out in one hour.

To maintain client state in a template, the template must contain the <cfapplication> tag. ColdFusion makes this easy with a special file named application.cfm.

Using Application.cfm to Define a ColdFusion Application

When ColdFusion receives a request for a CFML template, it looks for a file named application.cfm. The program searches in the current directory and then moves up the directory tree until it reaches the root of the disk. When ColdFusion finds the file, it includes said file at the top of the requested template and executes it prior to executing any of the directives in the requested template.

Using this behavior, you can create a set of actions that will be executed in every template in your application, thus creating a consistent configuration between template requests.

This file is the ideal location for the `<cfapplication>` tag. This file also becomes the obvious choice for setting default variables or for application-level constants.

Here is the application name. This name associates the application with any template on the ColdFusion server in which this file is included.

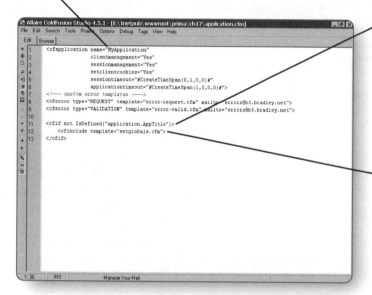

This example has moved all the global settings to another template called setglobals.cfm. If the `application` scope variables don't exist yet, you include this template to set them.

Because you are using `<cfinclude>` here, you must use a relative path to the setglobals.cfm file. This path will be relative to the parent template, not to the application.cfm file.

By moving the default variables and application constants to a separate file, you can alter them without disturbing the application.cfm file. This also enables you to swap out the setglobals.cfm template without affecting the `<cfapplication>` settings.

Controlling Access to Shared Variables

Multiple transactions can access variables in the application and session scopes. Without some control over how these scopes are accessed, you run the risk of corrupting the variable values stored there.

ColdFusion therefore provides the <cflock> tag to lock access to these variables. You can use this tag whenever you need to read or write session or application scope variables. The <cflock> tag requires either the name or scope attribute, along with the timeout attribute. The following examples use the scope attribute. The type of lock can be readonly or exclusive. Use exclusive locks when writing to these variables.

You can wrap the entire contents of this file with a <cflock> using the application scope.

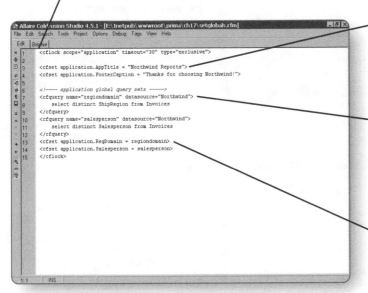

You need to create the application variables— AppTitle and FooterCaption— and set their values.

You can then perform queries and save their result sets as application variables. Doing so is a great performance enhancement for queries used frequently.

You then create the application variables to hold the query result sets and set them to the names of the queries you just performed.

By calling the setglobals.cfm template only when the application level variables do not exist, you ensure that the queries in that template are not run every time the application.cfm template is run. Saving the query result sets also limits the hits on the database, which increases the performance of your application.

Using the Application Defaults and Constants

Now, all you have to do is take advantage of these defaults and constants. This example uses the included header and footer templates as the first benefactors of these variables.

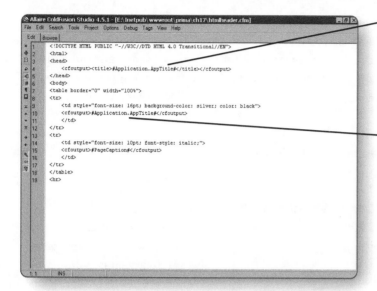

Use the `application.AppTitle` variable to set the title of the Web page. This variable gives you a consistent way to label all the pages of your application.

You can use the same variable to set the header on the page. Again, you have consistency between pages and within the same page.

The `application.FooterCaption` variable in the footer reinforces the consistency of the application.

Note that by using these application defaults and constants, you can change the entire application simply by editing the setglobals.cfm template. Doing so will change every page of the application. This is a huge shortcut to code maintenance.

But you don't have to stop with headers and footers.

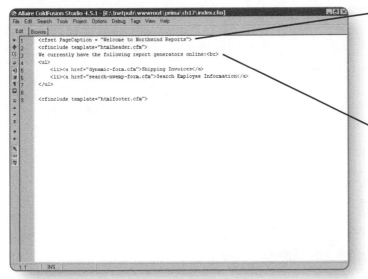

Because you don't want every page to be identical, you can set a new caption for the header here, before the header template is included.

This demonstration application contains a set of report generators from previous chapters.

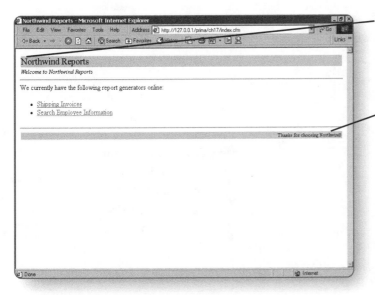

Here, you have the application.AppTitle. This title appears on every template in this directory.

The application.FooterCaption provides a nice finish to the page.

Now, take a closer look at the Shipping Invoices report. You might be able to put those application-level queries to good use here as well.

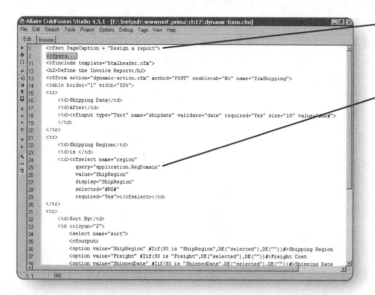

You need to set the page caption and some default values for the form here.

For the select list, use the `application.RegDomain` query result set to provide the options.

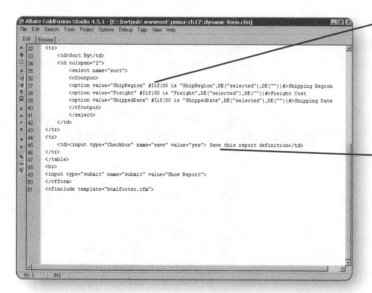

For each <option> of the <select> tag, check the SO variable for a match. If it matches, you output the selected attribute to the <option> tag.

Give the users the option of saving this report. The form-processing template uses this field to decide whether to write a cookie to the browser.

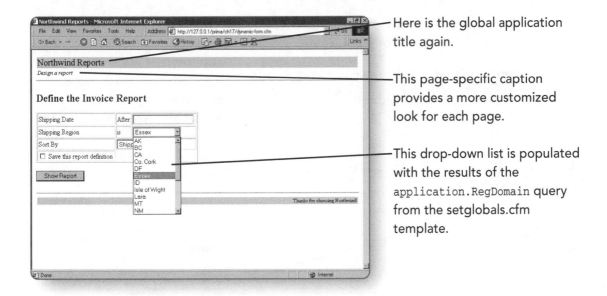

Here is the global application title again.

This page-specific caption provides a more customized look for each page.

This drop-down list is populated with the results of the application.RegDomain query from the setglobals.cfm template.

Defining Custom Error Pages with <cferror>

Another feature most desktop applications have is error handling. When used in conjunction with the application.cfm template, the <cferror> tag enables you to specify a template that's executed when an error is encountered. This enables you to maintain a relatively consistent look for your application even when errors occur.

The <cferror> tag can specify error templates for different types of errors. Use the type attribute to specify request, validation, monitor, or exception. This section covers the request, exception, and validation types.

The validation type is triggered when a form validation error occurs. This operation overrides the default validation error pages discussed in Chapter 4, "Processing and Validating Forms." The request type is triggered when any other error is encountered on the template. The exception type is triggered when it encounters any exception generated by the ColdFusion language processor, much like the request type is.

Here's one caveat to consider. Error templates for the validation and request types can use only HTML and the <cfoutput> tag. When the <cferror> invokes the error template, ColdFusion creates a scope called error, which is populated with information about the error that occurred. You can display these error variables with the <cfoutput> tag in the error template.

The exception error template, however, has access to all the ColdFusion tags and functions. It therefore offers you more options when handling errors. The example application is using the request type, but I have included a sample template to use as an exception error template.

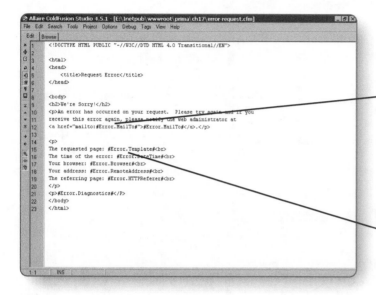

You can pass an e-mail address using the mailto attribute of the <cferror> tag. You can display the value of the mailto attribute using the error.MailTo variable.

The template variable provides the name of the template that produced the error.

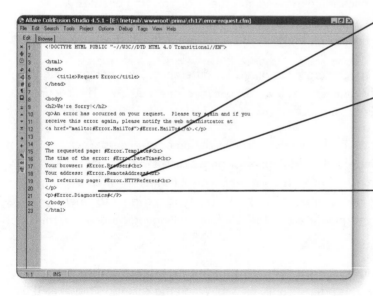

The RemoteAddress variable contains the IP address of the client that received the error.

The HTTPReferer variable holds the name of the page that led to the page that generated the error.

The Diagnostics variable contains the details of the error, including what the ColdFusion server believes to be the cause of the error.

This example purposely introduced an error into the dynamic-form.cfm template so that ColdFusion will invoke the `request` error template. The error template is not pretty, but it is a little more informative than the typical ColdFusion error page.

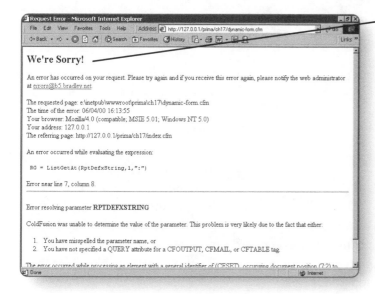

The heading at least admits that the error is not the user's fault.

The `validation` error template is invoked only when you use the hidden validation fields on standard HTML forms. This error template is not used when you are validating form data with the `validate` attribute of the form elements in a `<cfform>`; that validation takes place on the client browser using JavaScript.

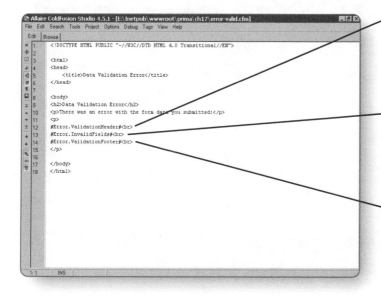

The `ValidationHeader` variable contains boilerplate text for the beginning of a text block describing the validation error.

The `InvalidFields` variable contains a bulleted list of fields that failed their validation checks.

The `ValidationFooter` variable contains more boilerplate text, this time for the end of the text block.

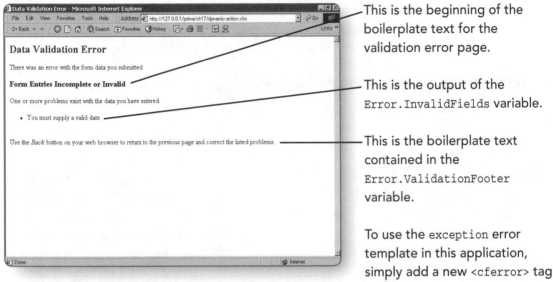

This is the beginning of the boilerplate text for the validation error page.

This is the output of the `Error.InvalidFields` variable.

This is the boilerplate text contained in the `Error.ValidationFooter` variable.

To use the `exception` error template in this application, simply add a new `<cferror>` tag to the application.cfm file and comment out the `request` type `<cferror>` tag. In the new `<cferror>` tag, specify the error-exception.cfm template. This sample error template writes the generated exception to a log file, thus creating an audit of the errors generated in the application.

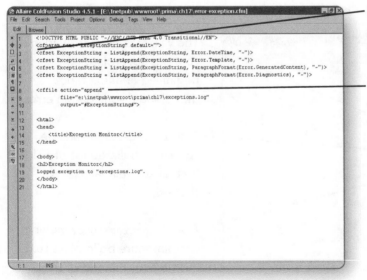

Here, you are building a delimited string with the `error` variables.

Using `<cffile>`, you can append the `ExceptionString` to a log file for error-tracking purposes.

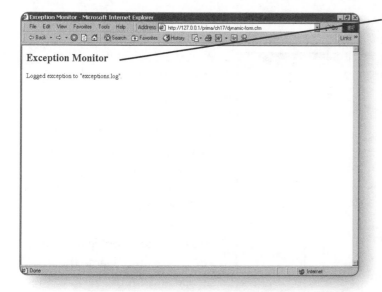

This output is pretty sparse but still helpful. You might want to provide more information about the problem to the users using a real exception error template.

Using Cookies for State Maintenance

You can do your own state management by writing cookies to the client browser. This strategy is useful, for example, when you want to save the state of a particular page or operation for reuse. The following example enables the users to save the report configuration for later use.

Note that the check box on the previous report definition form enables the users to save the report configuration they are about to submit. The form-processing template checks for the check box and writes a cookie to the browser if the users have selected it.

Here, you can determine whether a cookie on the client browser is storing a report format.

The cookie is saved as a list delimited by colons. You can extract the three values with ListGetAt and set the local page variables appropriately.

Next, determine whether the users selected the Save check box.

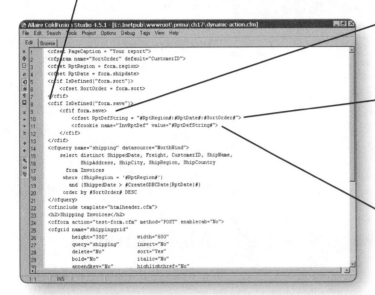

If they did select it and the value is true, you need to write a cookie.

You then create a string variable that contains a list of the three local page variables that define the report. Use the colon as the list delimiter.

Next, create a cookie using the `<cfcookie>` tag. Name the cookie and set the value to the `RptDefString`.

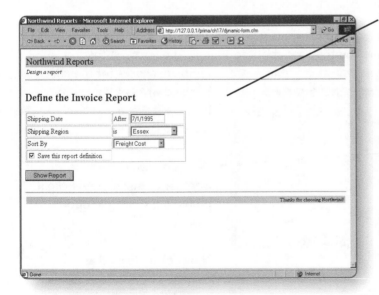

This form contains a client with the cookie. The cookie holds a previous report definition. Save it again.

Remember the following restrictions on cookies. Netscape allows a maximum of 20 cookies to be saved on the client browser from the same server. ColdFusion requires three cookies for client management when it is enabled. Netscape also allows a maximum of 4KB to be stored per cookie. ColdFusion encodes non-alphanumeric data at a three to one ratio, and it throws an error when you try to store more than 4000 encoded bytes in a cookie.

18

Tracking Sessions

You know how to create applications in ColdFusion and can track clients and maintain application-level defaults and constants. Now you need to use session management in your ColdFusion applications. Again, ColdFusion makes it easy for you. After you enable session management in your application.cfm template, you are on your way. But you will need to understand a few details. In this chapter, you learn to:

- Use session management in ColdFusion applications
- Set session variables
- Use session variables for state management
- Use session variables for customization
- Write cookies in conjunction with session management

Using Session Management

A session starts with the first connection to the server by the client. ColdFusion creates the client variables, cfid and cftoken, and updates its client variable storage. A session ends sometime after the last transaction of the client with the application on the server. ColdFusion gives you the ability to time out a session after a period of inactivity. This timeout value can be set as a default value for the entire ColdFusion server; alternatively, you can set the session timeout in the <cfapplication> tag using the sessiontimeout variable.

To illustrate the use of session variables for maintaining a session in a ColdFusion application, this example uses the POP e-mail client from Chapter 13, "Retrieving Mail from a POP Server." You will add a login form to log in to the POP server. You will also use session variables to store the user's return address and cookies to store the login information.

You need to enable client and session management using the <cfapplication> tag.

Don't forget to enable client management (by setting the clientmanagement attribute to Yes in the <cfapplication> tag) if you want to use session management. Session management requires client management to be enabled.

Setting Session Variables

Session variables must follow the same rules for naming that other ColdFusion variables do: begin with a letter, follow with letters or number, no non-alphanumeric characters other than the underscore allowed. To designate a variable as a session variable, you must prefix the name with session and a period.

You use the POP client built in Chapter 13 for this example. You add session variables to track the login information to the POP server. Doing so enables you to reuse this information on each subsequent call to the <cfpop> tag.

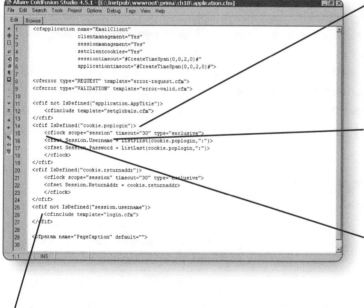

You need to check for the existence of the cookie that holds the POP login information. If it is there, you use it to set the username and password for the session.

When you enable session management, you gain access to a new session scope. Here, you create two session variables—username and password.

Don't forget to lock access to the session variables using a <cflock> tag with the scope attribute set to *session*.

To ensure that you get the username and password for the POP logins, check for the existence of the session.username variable. If it is absent, include the login form.

So far, you have handled all the authentication-related tasks for the POP login in the application.cfm template. Because the template is included with every template loaded from this directory, you can make sure that the session is still current and collect the necessary information from the users. This technique is common when working with applications that require authentication of some kind.

This example also combines the state management strategy of using cookies with session management. This way, the users have the option of bypassing the authentication step when they are interested in saving their login information in a cookie.

Using Session Variables for State Maintenance

The `<cfpop>` tag requires the `server`, `username`, and `password` attributes for every trip to the POP server. This means you need access to these values each time you call the `<cfpop>` tag. Saving these values and reusing them as needed is solution. In other words, you want to save the state of the POP login between the client browser and the server.

You first need to get the username and password information from the users. In this example, you get the usernames and passwords from the login form. You also ask the users for the name of the POP server and whether they want to save the login information in a cookie.

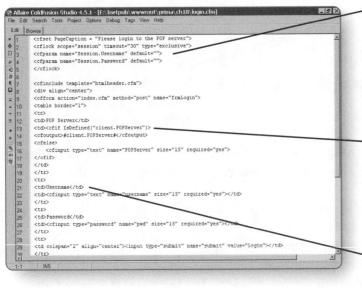

You need to set the `session.username` and `session.password` defaults here. Notice that an `exclusive` lock is appropriate here because you are writing to the variables.

Next, determine whether this client already has a variable for the POP server. If not, you include a form field so the users can provide it.

You need to provide required text fields for the username and password.

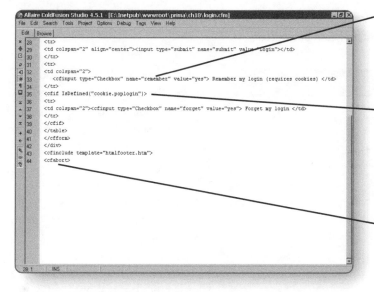

Here, you provide a check box so that users can decide whether to store this form's login information in a cookie.

As a bonus, the example determines whether the poplogin cookie exists. If so, you offer to "forget" the login information that it stores.

You stop processing additional CFML with the <cfabort> tag.

Note that the login form template is included from the application.cfm. Therefore, another template was actually requested from the browser, not the login form. If you don't abort the processing at the end of the login template, the requested template will also be processed and displayed. You definitely don't want this behavior.

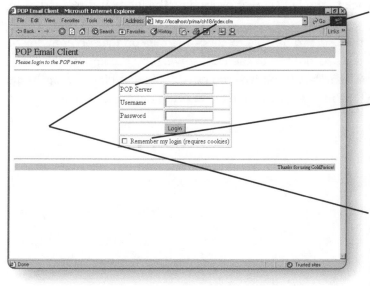

This client has not connected to the server before, so the program prompts for the POP server name.

This client also does not have a cookie with the login information, so the program offers to store this username and password.

Because you included the login form from application.cfm, the originally requested template is listed in the address, not in login.cfm.

Because this template is the action of the login form, you need to determine whether the login form has been submitted.

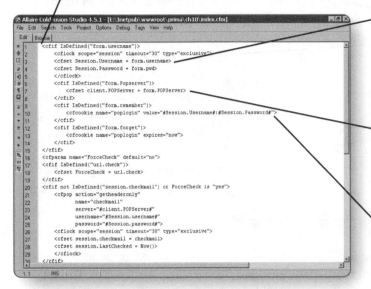

If it has been submitted, you assign the form.username and form.pwd values to their session counterparts. You then pass these to the <cfpop> tag.

If the form is sending you the popserver field, you set the client variable, popserver, to that value.

If the remember or forget form fields have been submitted, you need to process the cookies.

To improve the performance of this application, save the query result set from the <cfpop> tag when the mail is checked. By saving the query as a session variable, you don't have to go back to the POP server every time the inbox is displayed.

However, you do want the users to be able to check the mail on the server at any time, so you need to force a return trip to the POP server. You accomplish this with a url variable. When this template is loaded, you need to execute the <cfpop> tag if the session.checkmail result set does not exist or if the url.check variable exists and is positive.

You set a default value for the ForceCheck variable, which holds the value of the url.check variable.

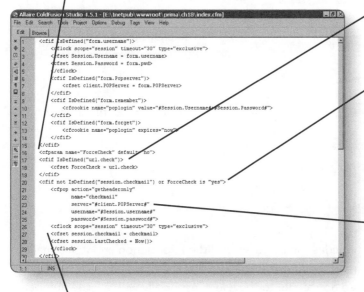

If the url.check variable exists, set the ForceCheck local page variable.

Check for the existence of the saved result set and the status of the ForceCheck variable to determine whether you should execute the <cfpop> getheaderonly operation.

You then pass the appropriate client and session variables to the <cfpop> tag.

Now, you save the result set in a session variable. You also set session.LastChecked to track when you last checked the POP server.

Because session.checkmail is like any other query result set, you can tell the users how many messages they have by displaying the RecordCount variable.

Here, you note the date and time that the inbox was last checked by displaying the session.LastChecked variable.

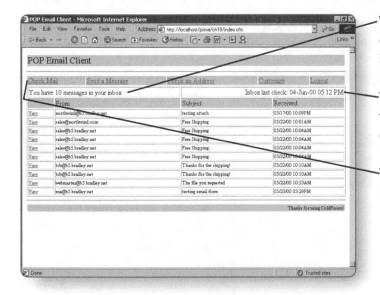

With a quick glance, the users can see how many messages are in the inbox.

The LastChecked variable tells the users when they last checked the inbox.

This link checks the inbox on the POP server for new messages.

The inbox display now provides the users with all the information and functionality necessary to check and read their e-mail. The performance gain attained by saving the query result set will be noticeable to the users, especially with a large number of messages in the inbox.

Now that you have created session variables to hold the authentication information of the user's POP account, you can reuse these variables on each template that uses the `<cfpop>` tag to communicate with the POP server.

Here, you are reusing the client variable. It is passed to the `<cfpop>` tag for the message retrieval operation.

You also can reuse the username and password variables in the session scope to authenticate to the POP server.

In addition to simply timing out a session, you can provide a pseudo-logout function for the POP e-mail client. The `session` scope is actually a ColdFusion data type called a *structure,* an array of values, indexed by a set of keys. These keys can be any value, including strings. The `session` scope is a structure, and the variable names in the scope are keys to the values. ColdFusion provides a set of functions specifically for manipulating structures.

For the logout function, then, you simply delete the `session.username`, `session.password`, and `session.checkmail` variables. With these variables gone, you have effectively logged the users out.

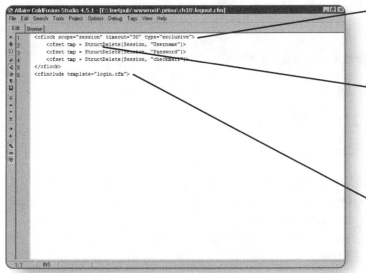

You need to lock the `session` scope because you are altering variables in the scope.

Delete a variable in the scope by specifying `Session` as the structure name and the variable name as the key to delete in the `StructDelete` function.

When you are done, you should include the login form so that the users can log in again.

TIP

Structures are a powerful data type in ColdFusion. You can use structures to organize complex data for easy retrieval in your templates. With good template planning, the proper use of structures can save you many lines of code. Please refer to the ColdFusion documentation for more on how to use structures to the best advantage.

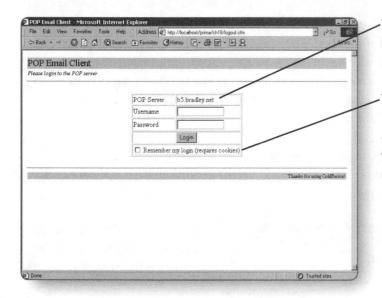

The ColdFusion server remembers this client, so it fills in the POP server.

The login form offers both "remember" and "forget" options to provide the most flexible cookie options to the users.

Using Session Variables for Customization

You can use session variables to customize the Web application during a specific session. You took the first step toward customization when you saved the `checkmail` operation's query set. Most customizations are for the convenience of the users rather than for performance. You can also consider storing the authentication information as a customization.

You can extend this fundamental customization by allowing the application to save the users' return addresses in a session variable. You also can add a customization form so that the users can change the username, password, server, or return address information during the session.

NOTE

ColdFusion never writes the values of session variables to disk, unless you write code to do so. Therefore, storing passwords or other sensitive information in session variables is quite safe. These variables exist only in the memory of the ColdFusion server, and they disappear when the session timeouts or when the ColdFusion server is restarted.

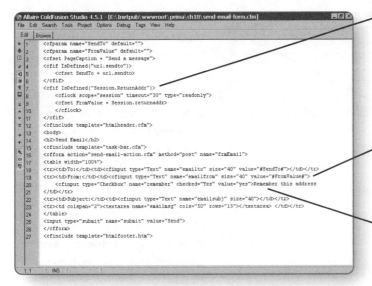

First, you have to check for the existence of the `Session.ReturnAddr` variable. If it exists, you set the local page variable, `FromValue`, to that value.

Use the `FromValue` stored in the value attribute of the `<cfinput>` tag for the "From" field.

Here, you offer to store this return address with a check box.

Because you offer to store the return address, you need a mechanism to save it. This example uses a cookie to save the value to the user's client browser. You need to check for the existence of the cookie in the application.cfm template so that you can set the session.ReturnAddr variable when you set the other cookie information.

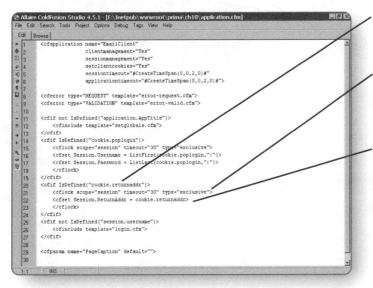

First, check for the existence of the cookie.

Don't forget to lock the session scope when setting or changing session variable values.

Next, read in the value from the cookie in order to use this return address for the duration of the session.

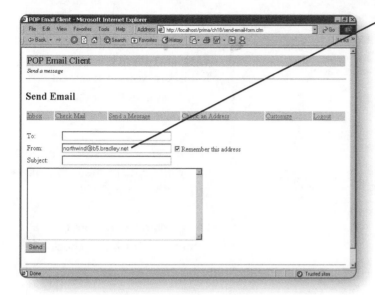

With the session variable set, the "From" field is automatically filled in.

You can give the users a form to change the session variables currently in use. If the users have more than one POP e-mail account on different servers, they can use this form to change the values and check their other account. You can also offer to store this new authentication information in the `poplogin` cookie.

This simple form includes the `popserver`, `popuser`, `poppwd`, and `return` variables.

The save option is a direct parallel to the code in the login form.

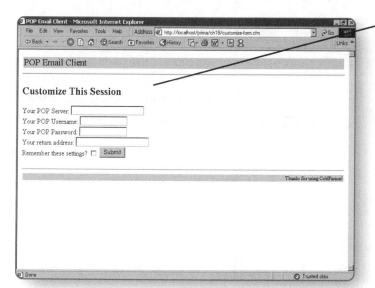

Try to keep forms like this one as simple for the user as possible. Customization is a popular feature, but over-customization will chase your users away.

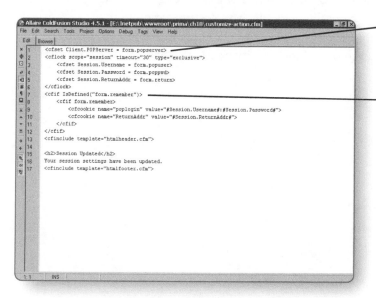

You then save the appropriate form field values in the appropriate scope variables.

Check for the remember form field. If it is set to yes, you set the cookies poplogin and returnaddr to the new values.

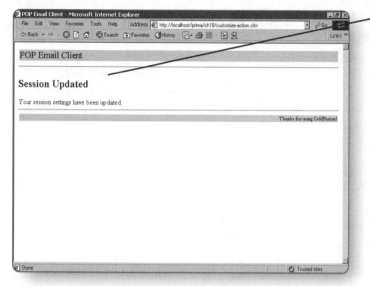

The user has updated the session information. From this point on (unless the user changes the values again), the new values of the session variables set by the customization form will be used in all templates.

The e-mail client is now a fairly good facsimile of a basic desktop e-mail client. With the performance-enhancing session variables and customization of the authentication information, you are providing your users with a flexible Web application that includes the basic functionality needed to handle POP e-mail.

19

Handling Authentication and Security

The Web is a great way to collect information anonymously. The HTTP protocol, with its stateless nature, lends itself to an open access network. But as a provider of information and application services, you often need to know who is accessing your Web site. You need to authenticate users in order to provide appropriate services and to protect your data. In this chapter, you learn to:

- Decide among authentication options for your Web site
- Use your Web server's authentication mechanisms
- Use a database to authenticate users
- Review ColdFusion's advanced authentication features
- Review alternative authentication options

Choosing an Authentication Option

As soon as people realized that the Web was a place to share information and do work, security became an issue for Web developers. Security concerns can be broken into two areas: authentication and access control.

Authentication deals with the not-so-simple process of proving that you are who you say you are. The username/password combination is one familiar authentication structure. Users have a secret string of keystrokes that (supposedly) only they know. The program compares the username/password pair against a username/password database of some kind; if they match, the user is authenticated to the database. This is a simplistic view of most login processes, but it suffices to illustrate the most common mechanism of authentication.

Access control deals with the issue of who can access which resources. In the simplest form, access is open once authentication is established; if you have access to a set of resources, such as a Web site, you have access to everything on it. Access control can be granular as well. You can limit access to certain pages on a site. You can even limit access to certain functions in your application.

This chapter focuses on authentication, as opposed to access control. There are many authentication mechanisms for your Web applications. The choice before you is basically what source of username/password pairs to use to authenticate your users. This chapter covers Web server authentication and custom database authentication as the easiest forms of authentication to implement. The chapter also introduces you to the ColdFusion server's advanced security features. In a final note, you will read about alternative strategies for authentication.

Using Web Server Authentication

Most modern Web server software can handle authentication of some variety. In fact, authentication mechanisms are part the specifications for HTTP produced by the *World Wide Web Consortium*, the standards body that tends to the health and well being of the Web. You will find some authentication mechanisms in Internet Information Server (IIS), WebSite Professional, and Apache Web servers, to name a few. Generally, these Web servers either enable you to set up your own username/password database on the Web server or leverage the underlying operating system's authentication mechanisms for use on your Web site.

The following example uses IIS. If you are using a different Web server, check your documentation for the steps necessary to configure your server authentication.

This example configures IIS so that it provides authentication services for a subdirectory of this chapter's folder on the local Web server.

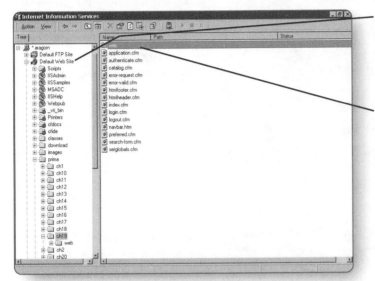

In Internet Services Manager, open the Default Web Site folder located in the left navigation panel.

Navigate to the folder you want to protect. This example establishes security for the Web folder in the Ch19 folder.

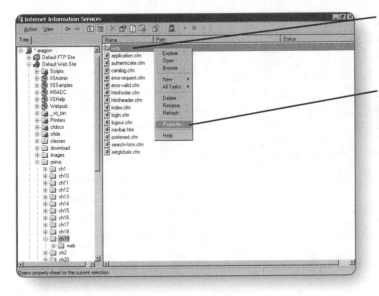

Right-click the Web folder to access the pop-up menu. Select Properties from this menu.

Alternatively, you can click the Properties button on the toolbar.

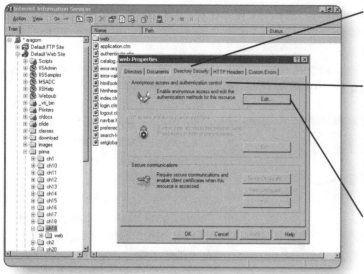

Select the Directory Security tab from the Web Properties dialog box.

From the Directory Security tab, you configure different types of security services for this Web directory. For this example, choose Anonymous access and authentication control.

Click the Edit button.

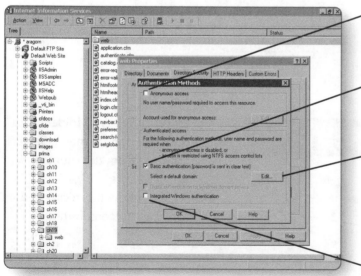

The Anonymous access check box is filled by default. Clear this check box as I have here.

Select the Basic authentication check box to use HTTP basic authentication.

Click the Edit button to change the Windows NT domain that the Web server uses as the username/password database to authenticate against.

Make sure the Integrated Windows authentication check box is clear. This is a Microsoft extension for tighter integration with Windows.

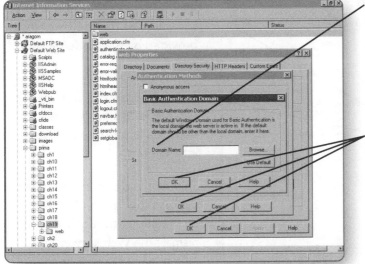

If you want to use another Windows NT domain to authenticate against, specify it here. To use the default domain (the local server), you leave this blank.

Now, just click the OK buttons until you are back to the Internet Services Manager window. You're done.

Handling Basic Authentication

With the authentication domain set for your Web directory, you can build your application. Basic authentication is the standard authentication mechanism for Web servers. The process that the Web server uses is simple.

When a client requests a page in a protected directory, the Web server responds with "you need authentication for this page." The client then displays a dialog box to the users so they can enter a username and password. The users supply this information, and the Web client then requests the page again, this time with the authentication information included in the request.

The Web server uses this information to authenticate the users. If the credentials are good, the requested page is returned to the client. If not, the Web server starts the process over with an "authentication required" response.

You can access this authentication information from the cgi variables called auth_user and auth_password. Another cgi variable is also included, auth_type, which contains the type of authentication that the server used. Currently, the only supported value for this variable is Basic.

Take a look at a demonstration template before you jump into an application using this form of authentication.

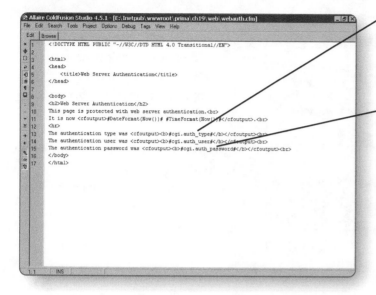

On this page, you simply display the values of the `cgi` variables provided by the authentication attempt.

The `auth_password` variable, by default, is displayed in clear text. You'll return to this issue a little later.

This simple demonstration page displays the variable provided by the authentication mechanism of the Web server. Take a look at what happens when you request this page.

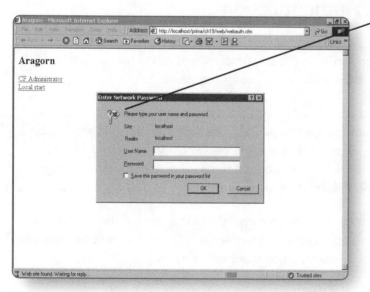

Internet Explorer displays a dialog box that asks for your username and password when you request the demonstration template.

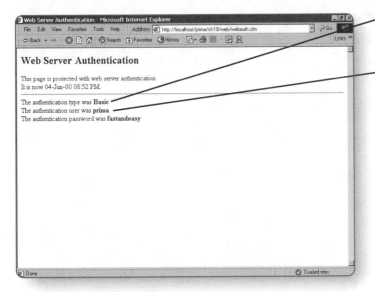

The authentication type is Basic.

This display demonstrates that you have access to the username and password provided by the users.

Accessing Basic Authentication Information with ColdFusion

Take a look at how you might use this information in a ColdFusion application with session management. Note the parallels to the state management code in the POP e-mail client discussed in Chapter 18, "Tracking Sessions."

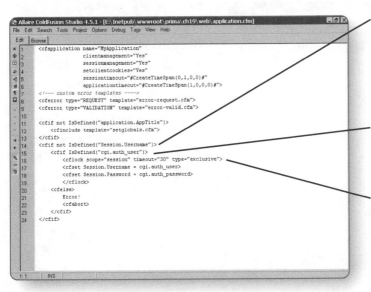

First, check for the existence of the session variable, Username. If it doesn't exist, the users are in the process of authenticating to the Web server.

Next, you check for the auth_user variable in the cgi scope.

If this variable is there, you lock the session scope and assign the cgi.auth_user and cgi.auth_password variables to their session counterparts.

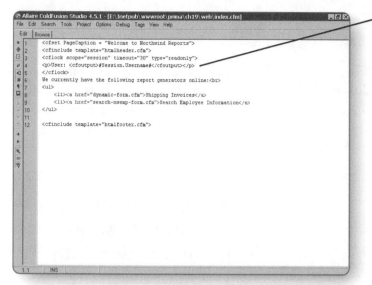

You can display the session.username on the index page as a confirmation of who has logged in.

Notice that the prima user is currently logged in to view some reports.

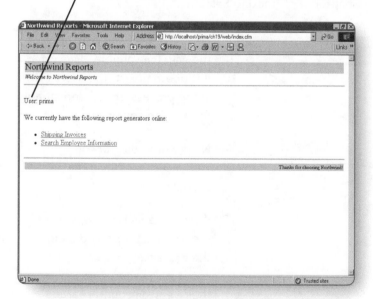

There is one problem with this method of authentication. The password field in these examples has been in clear text. Security officers will have seizures if you implement your authentication this way. Clear text passwords sent over the Internet are a serious security risk that you want to avoid.

You can still use Web server basic authentication mechanisms, but you need to add an encryption technique between the client and the server. The most popular and widespread encryption scheme used on the Internet is Secure Socket Layers (SSL), mentioned in Chapter 18. SSL requires the purchase of digital certificates from a trusted certificate vendor, such as VeriSign. A discussion of digital certificates and SSL are beyond the scope of this book. If you are interested in using this technology, a good place to start is in your Web server software's documentation.

Providing Database Authentication

You can provide your own source of username/password pairs for your authentication needs. All you need is a database of username and password pairs. You already know how to query a database using ColdFusion. You have the same issues of clear text passwords with this technique, but the same solutions you used for Web server basic authentication can be used for database authentication.

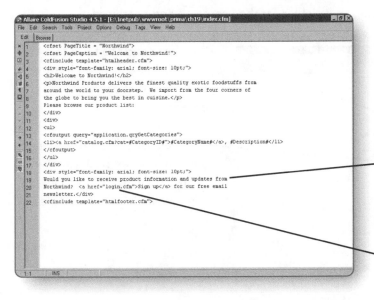

This example provides a Preferred Buyers Club Web page for certain Northwind customers. You need a database with usernames and passwords. You'll find one on the CD in this chapter's directory.

On the new home page of the Northwind Web site, you ask the customers whether they want to join the club.

You then provide a link to a login form so that users can authenticate to the Web server.

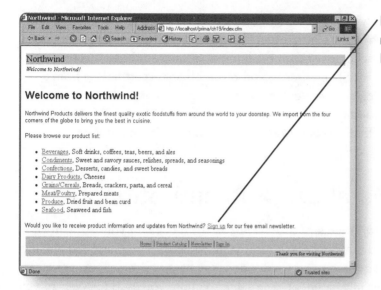

Follow the link to sign up for the newsletter and log in to the Preferred Buyers Club.

First, you set default `session` variables for the username and password.

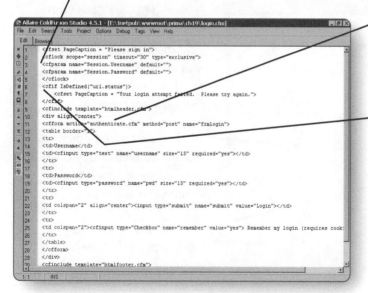

You then send the form to a custom authentication form processor that checks the database.

You then send a failed authentication attempt back to this login form with a `url` variable communicating the failed status.

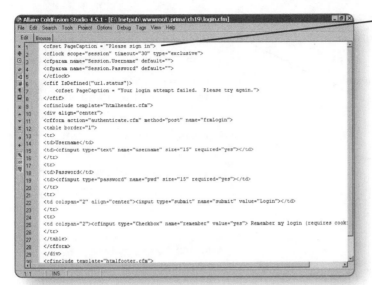

You need to change the caption of the page to inform the users that the authentication attempt failed and that they should try again.

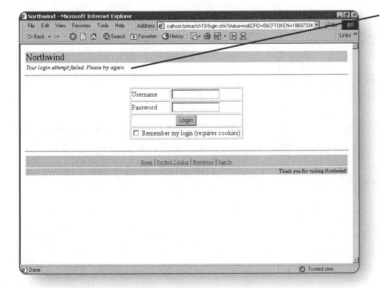

Oops! Wrong password. You'll have to try again.

The authentication process is a simple query to the database, using the provided information from the login form. If the query returns a single row, the authentication attempt succeeds. You send the users on to the special Web page; otherwise you return them to the login form to try again.

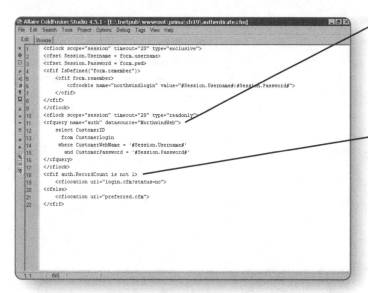

The query selects the CustomerID from the authentication database where the username and password from the form match the database row.

If the RecordCount is not 1, return the user to the login form to try again. Otherwise, send the user to the Preferred Buyers Club page.

With no match, you send the users back to the login form with the url.status set to no to signify a failed authentication attempt.

If the authentication succeeds, you send the users to the preferred.cfm template.

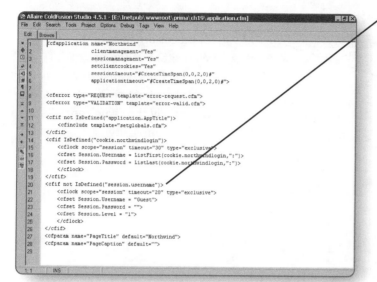

If the `session.username` is not defined, you create it and set it to a guest account.

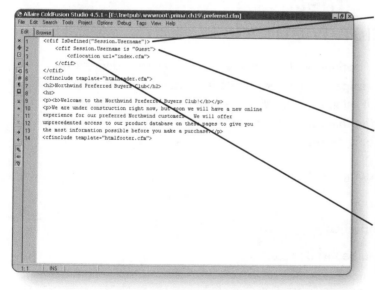

Check for the `session.username` variable as a failsafe, because the `session.username` variable is guaranteed to be set in the application.cfm template.

Because this is a "members only" page, determine whether a guest user is trying to access the page.

If it is a guest, you simply send the guest back to the home page.

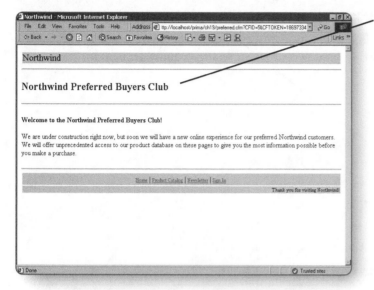

This is a simple example. A lot of pieces are missing to this Web site. But the basic mechanisms required to create an authentication database are essentially the same regardless of the complexity.

Developing Other Authentication Methods

If none of the preceding options work for you, you can always build your own mechanism. ColdFusion ships with libraries that enable developers to create extensions to their ColdFusion servers. With this capability, you can create a custom authentication tag that can be used with whatever authentication source you require. Here are some examples:

- Direct Windows NT domain authentication

- Kerberos authentication

- Radius server authentication

- Direct LDAP server authentication

If you are interested in developing these types of extensions to ColdFusion, refer to the documentation covering the CFX API and creating custom tag extensions.

20

Controlling Template Flow with Switchboards

The majority of the applications you write will use a simple, linear set of templates to accomplish their goals. This linear flow will suffice in most circumstances. However, you can lay out templates in different ways for a more flexible program flow, thus enabling more reuse of code. In this chapter, you learn to:

- Pass information between templates using url variables
- Pass information between templates using form variables
- Pass information between templates using session variables
- Use the <cflocation> tag to redirect program flow

Passing Information between Templates with URL Variables

You're ready to consider how data flows between the templates you've created. One of the easiest ways to pass information between templates is to use URL variables because they work in most circumstances and can preserve the state of a template.

You can use this technique to create a switchboard. A *switchboard* redirects the flow of the application based upon some criteria. You can also use switchboards to hide the structure of your Web site. You can use the switchboard concept in conjunction with the <cfinclude> tag to include different templates in the switchboard template. The result of this technique is that (potentially) every page on your Web site has the same base template name.

You create a home page, a dynamic product catalog, and a Web survey for the Northwind site, all accessible only through the top index page.

You create a TemplateSwitch variable to control the switchboard and set it to default to the home page switch, top.

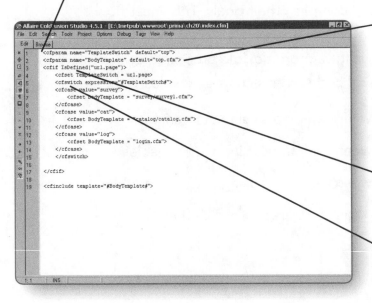

You also need to create a BodyTemplate variable, which holds the name of the template you want to include. Set the BodyTemplate variable to the home page template name, top.cfm.

You then check for the url variable, page, to determine which page should be displayed.

The <cfswitch> tag is the heart of the switchboard. Based on the value of TemplateSwitch, it sets the template included in this page.

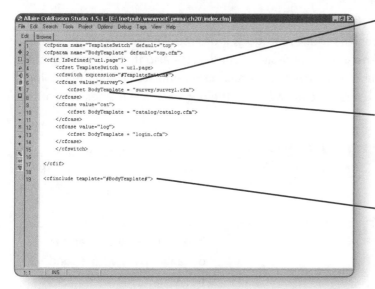

Each `<cfcase>` value represents a page to display. The `value` of `<cfcase>` is an expected value of the `TemplateSwitch` variable.

Inside each `<cfcase>` tag, you set the `BodyTemplate` variable to the name of the template you want to include.

Pass the value of `BodyTemplate` to the `template` attribute of the `<cfinclude>` tag to include the requested page.

Note that the index.cfm switchboard template contains no HTML code. All the code for the page resides in the included templates.

This is the home page template. You begin with the inclusion of the HTML header template to format the page.

Note the link to the product catalog. It references the switchboard template with a different `page` url variable, plus a product category ID that the catalog.cfm template uses to determine which product category to display.

The link to the survey form is also a link to the switchboard template. This time, the `page` is the `survey` switch criteria.

The catalog is also an included template. This template uses an additional url variable to display a specific product category, if desired. The catalog displays the entire product listing if no url.id variable is found. Note also that the catalog.cfm template resides in a subdirectory of the switchboard template. When the catalog page is requested, the users have no idea that the page actually resides in another directory.

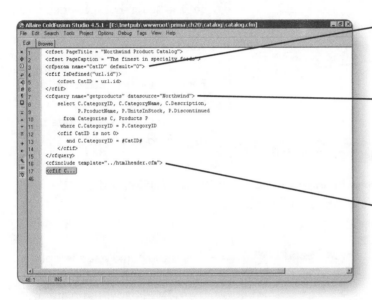

Set a default CatID variable and then check for the url.id. If url.id exists, set the CatID to it.

This query retrieves the product information. Note that it is a dynamic query with a conditional where clause based on CatID.

Note that the included header file is relative to the current template. You need to refer to the parent directory of the htmlheader.cfm template.

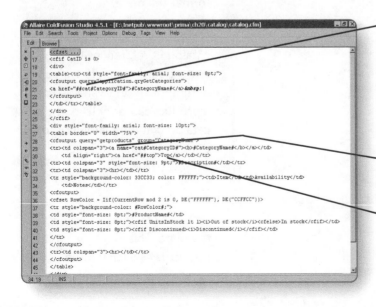

Create anchor names embedded in the page for easier navigation when the entire product catalog is viewed. This loop produces a navigation bar for the page.

The navigation bar uses this anchor.

This link sends the users back to the top of the page.

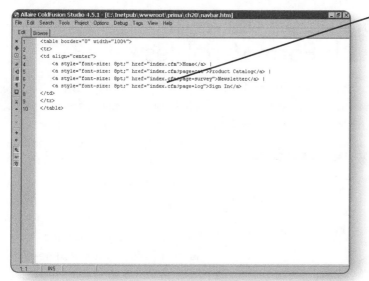

Each link in the site navigation bar is simply a pointer to the switchboard with a different page switch.

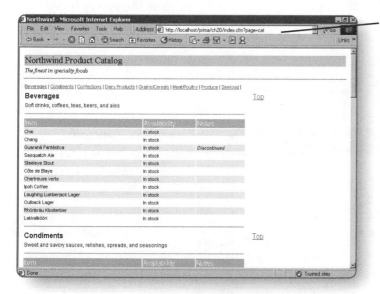

The address line shows only the switchboard URL. Users cannot tell from here that the catalog is in a different directory on the server.

Passing Information between Templates with Form Variables

You can leverage the flow of data between forms and their processing templates in order to build data that's processed at the end of a chain of forms. The forms use form variables to pass the information along the chain to a final form processor.

This final processor is matched not to a single form, but to the chain as a whole.

Here, you create a Northwind Web survey comprised of a series of Web forms. You need to pass along the form fields from one form to the next.

You access the survey form through the switchboard just like the other pages on the Web site.

```
Allaire ColdFusion Studio 4.5.1 - [E:\Inetpub\wwwroot\prima\ch20\index.cfm]
File  Edit  Search  Tools  Project  Options  Debug  Tags  View  Help
Edit  Browse
1    <cfparam name="TemplateSwitch" default="top">
2    <cfparam name="BodyTemplate" default="top.cfm">
3    <cfif IsDefined("url.page")>
4        <cfset TemplateSwitch = url.page>
5        <cfswitch expression="#TemplateSwitch#">
6        <cfcase value="survey">
7            <cfset BodyTemplate = "survey/survey1.cfm">
8        </cfcase>
9        <cfcase value="cat">
10           <cfset BodyTemplate = "catalog/catalog.cfm">
11       </cfcase>
12       <cfcase value="log">
13           <cfset BodyTemplate = "login.cfm">
14       </cfcase>
15       </cfswitch>
16
17   </cfif>
18
19   <cfinclude template="#BodyTemplate#">
```

Because the survey form templates are in a subdirectory, you need to specify a relative path for the header and footer templates.

The action attribute points to the next page on the form.

Each question is named with a "Q" plus the question number.

```
Allaire ColdFusion Studio 4.5.1 - [E:\Inetpub\wwwroot\prima\ch20\survey\survey1.cfm]
File  Edit  Search  Tools  Project  Options  Debug  Tags  View  Help
Edit  Browse
1    <cfinclude template="../htmlheader.cfm">
2
3    <form name="frmSurvey" action="survey/survey2.cfm" method="post">
4        <p>1. How did you hear about us?<br>
5        <input type="checkbox" name="Q1" value="Friend">Friend<br>
6        <input type="checkbox" name="Q1" value="Website">Website<br>
7        <input type="checkbox" name="Q1" value="Email">Email<br>
8        <input type="checkbox" name="Q1" value="Magazine">Magazine<br>
9        </p>
10
11       <p>2. Have you purchased from Northwind before?<br>
12       <input type="radio" name="Q2" value="Yes">Yes<br>
13       <input type="radio" name="Q2" value="No">No<br>
14       </p>
15
16       <p>3. What are your interests?<br>
17       <input type="checkbox" name="Q3" value="Cooking">Cooking<br>
18       <input type="checkbox" name="Q3" value="Dining">Dining<br>
19       <input type="checkbox" name="Q3" value="Travel">Travel<br>
20       <input type="checkbox" name="Q3" value="Golf">Golf<br>
21       <input type="checkbox" name="Q3" value="Reading">Reading<br>
22       <input type="checkbox" name="Q3" value="Gardening">Gardening<br>
23       </p>
24       <input type="submit" name="submit" value="Next">
25   </form>
26
27   <cfinclude template="../htmlfooter.cfm">
```

When you pass this information to the next form, the form fields from the first page must be added as form fields to page two so that they can be passed to the form processor. You can create a separate template to hold the code that rolls over the form fields. You loop over the fields passed in from the first page, make sure that the field is a question, and then output the form field's HTML code.

You need to track the field names from the form so you don't attempt to roll over duplicates.

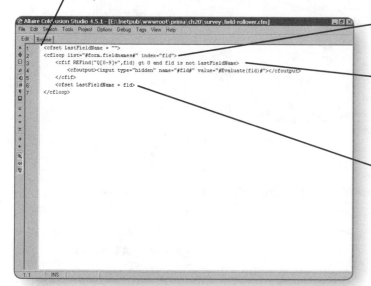

Loop over the form.fieldnames to extract the question fields.

If the current field is a question and it doesn't match the last field (it's not a duplicate), you output the form field code.

Set the LastFieldName variable to the current field name in order to check for duplicates on the next iteration of the loop.

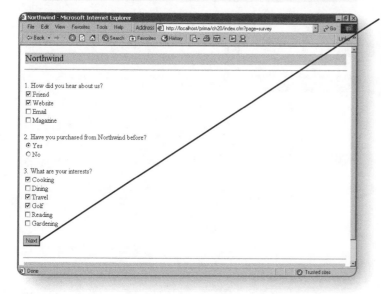

Note the Next button, rather than Submit. This tells the users more is to come.

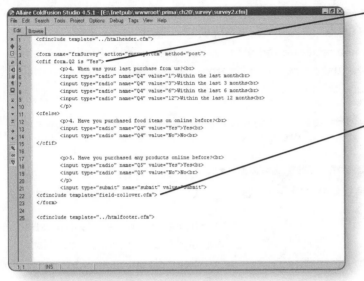

Here's a bonus. You can alter question four based on the answer to question two in order to provide a more targeted survey.

Here, you include the code to roll over the form fields from the first page of the survey.

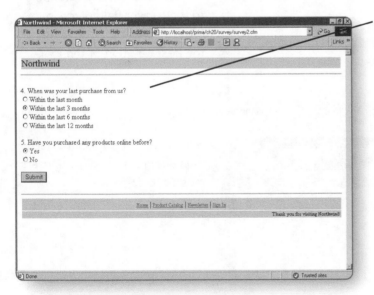

For the form processor, you take all the form fields from the first two pages and output them as a single line in a text file.

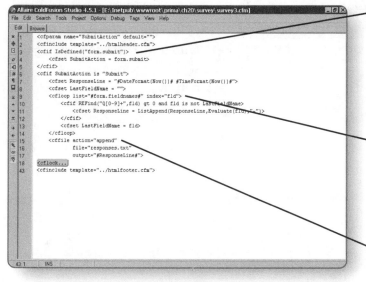

You need to determine whether the form was posted from the previous survey form page. This is a sanity check and prevents unusual errors from unpredictable users.

This loop, which is from the field-rollover.cfm template, parses the field names. Here, you are building the ResponseLine to be placed into the text file.

Use <cffile> to output the ResponseLine to the responses.txt file.

As a bonus, you can track whether the users filled out the survey in this session.

In this form, you use a form action to redirect the users to another page.

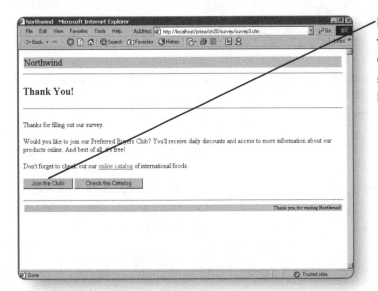

Finally, you can enable the users to join the Preferred Buyers Club or to check the catalog by supplying a form with two buttons.

Passing Information between Templates with Session Variables

State management is not conceptually far from program flow. Your templates can take different courses of action depending on the state of an application or session. An obvious flow control is for login or authentication status. By determining which user is logged on or whether a user is logged on at all, you can direct the flow of the application to the appropriate template or resource.

You will now extend the Northwind Web site to include a Preferred Buyers Club with login and authentication features. To ensure that only club members can access the club's Web page, you need to track the logged-on users with session variables. You can then use these session variables to check the eligibility of users to view the club pages.

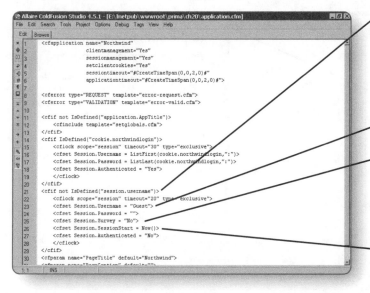

You first check for the existence of the `session.username` variable. If it doesn't exist, you need to set default values for the session.

The default `username` is `Guest`.

For this example, assume that the users have not taken the survey and are not members of the Preferred Buyers Club.

For fun, you can track when the users arrived at the site and initiated this session.

To make the pages more interesting, you can display the name of the current users and the time they logged on.

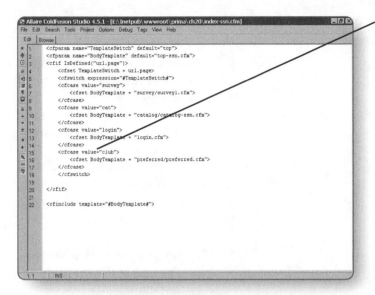

Notice the new switch added to the switchboard. The authentication template sends the users here after a successful authentication.

This tag determines whether the login form has been referenced from the authentication template with an authentication status.

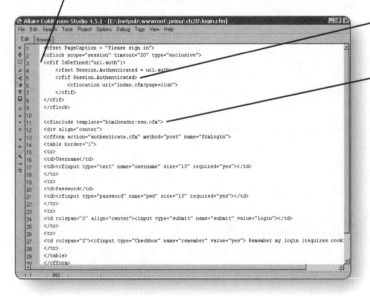

If the users are authenticated, you send them to the club page.

If they are not authenticated, the login form is loaded again, ready for another attempt.

The login form uses the session variable Authenticated to control the flow of the application. You either send the users to the club page or load the login form again, signifying that the previous login attempt failed.

Using <cflocation> to Redirect Program Flow

ColdFusion provides another tag to help with template redirection and program flow. The <cflocation> tag redirects the client browser to the location specified in the url attribute. One major difference here is that the <cflocation> tag does not hide the path of the URL on the server. The destination URL appears in the client browser's address line.

On the survey-processing template, you added a small form to enable the users to select a button to take them to the product catalog or the Preferred Buyers Club. The form's action attribute points to a redirect.cfm template, which handles the form results. This template is nothing more that a tiny, two-way switchboard. It uses the <cflocation> tag for redirection.

First, determine whether the users pressed the Join button.

If the users want to join, you redirect them to the login page via the index.cfm switchboard template.

Next, determine whether the users pressed the Catalog button.

Now, you redirect the users to the product catalog via the switchboard template. Note that the product catalog is loaded with all products.

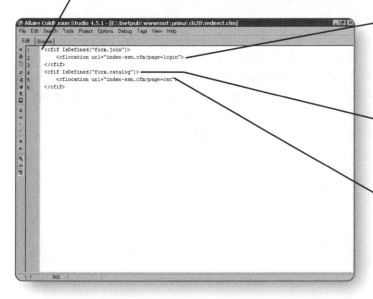

You don't have to limit the use of the `<cflocation>` tag to dedicated switchboards. You can use these tags to make simple decisions like the previous one in almost any template. In fact, you will do that in the authentication processor.

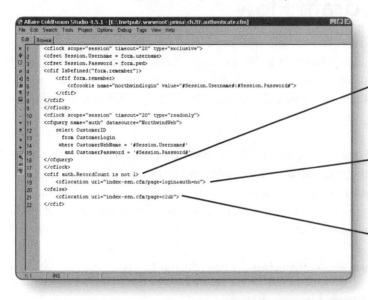

If the authentication query does not return a single record, a problem exists.

If there is a problem, you redirect the users to the login page, via the switchboard.

If the authentication is successful, you redirect the users to the club page.

As you can see from the examples in this chapter, you can design sophisticated program flow into your ColdFusion applications. When designing applications and deciding on the program flow, your guiding principle should be ease of use. If your program flow interferes with the users' abilities to use your application, you can guarantee that the users will stop using it. After you address usability, turn your attention to code-reuse and code-maintenance issues.

21

Generating Static Web Pages

Static Web pages are fast. But to get the speed, do you have to give up the dynamic pages that ColdFusion provides? Not necessarily. ColdFusion enables you to schedule templates to run at specific times of the day. You can use this functionality to build pages that update themselves periodically but are served from your Web server as static HTML pages. This way, you get the best of both worlds. In this chapter, you learn to:

- Decide whether dynamically generated static pages are right for you
- Use `<cfschedule>` to generate static pages
- Create batch schedules to submit to the ColdFusion server

Dynamic Does Not Necessarily Mean On-Demand

To see the pages you've created so far, you must request or load them into your Web browser, thereby invoking ColdFusion to read and process the CFML tags in your templates and then send the HTML output to the requesting browser through the Web server. This is called *on-demand* Web page creation. You can save this output from the browser as a static HTML page for viewing later.

However, with ColdFusion, you can skip the trip to the client Web browser by writing templates to create static Web pages that can be published by the Web server. ColdFusion has a component called the *ColdFusion Executive* that performs scheduled tasks. You can configure these tasks in ColdFusion Administrator or programmatically by using the <cfschedule> tag.

If you request a CFML template from a scheduled task and save the results to a text file, you automatically save the output of a ColdFusion template as a static HTML page.

Take a look at ColdFusion Administrator Web pages that enable you to create these scheduled tasks.

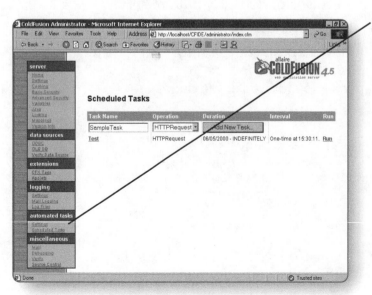

Access the task list by selecting Scheduled Tasks from ColdFusion Administrator's navigation bar.

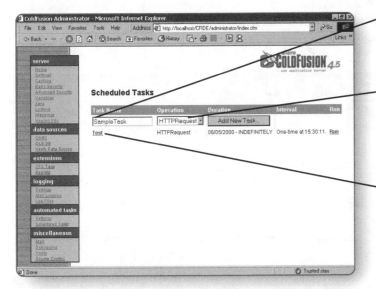

To create a new task, give it a name in the Task Name field and click the Add New Task button.

Only the HTTPRequest operation is currently available. Allaire intends to offer more operations in the future.

Below the add form is the existing task list. Only one task is listed here, Test. Its duration and interval are also specified.

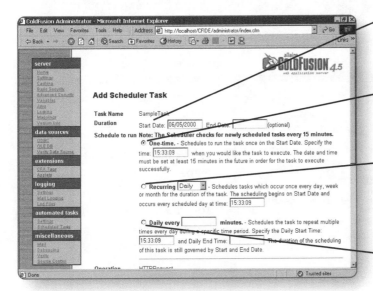

By default, the start date is set to the current day. The end date for the task is optional.

You can schedule the task to run one time only. You simply specify the time to run the task.

You can schedule the task to run on a recurring schedule. This can be daily, weekly, or monthly at a given time of day.

You can also schedule the task to run daily every so many minutes.

The URL specifies the file to retrieve. This can be any valid URL address, not just from the local ColdFusion server.

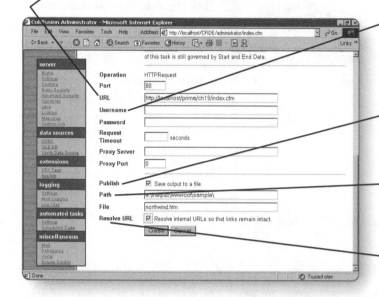

If the page requires basic Web server authentication, you can specify the username and password here.

To save the results of the HTTP request operation, you must select the Publish check box.

Specify the local pathname and filename of the file that holds the result.

To translate relative URLs in the target file to absolute paths, you must select this check box.

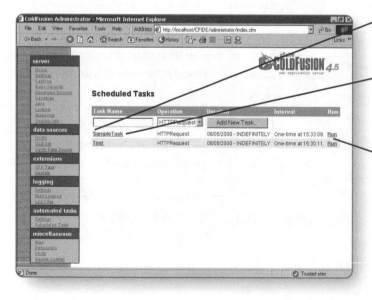

The sample task now appears in the list of scheduled tasks.

You can change the properties of the task by clicking the task name.

You can also invoke the task immediately by clicking the *Run* link.

For most tasks, you will use ColdFusion Administrator to interface with the scheduled tasks. This is the most convenient way to set up a single or repeated task on the ColdFusion server. However, you might find that automating the scheduling process is helpful in some circumstances.

Using <cfschedule> to Generate Static Pages

ColdFusion provides the <cfschedule> tag to create and manage the ColdFusion server's task list. Using the action attribute, which is required, <cfschedule> can update, delete, or run a task. If you perform the update operation on a task that does not exist, ColdFusion creates the task with the properties you specify in the tag.

The action and name attributes are always required. When using the delete and run operations, action and name are the only required attributes. When using the update operation, the operation, startdate, starttime, url, and interval attributes are also required. When publish is true, the file and path attributes are required.

Here, you create a promotional Web page, called special.cfm, for the Northwind online store that changes each month. First, you create the necessary CFML templates to generate the page, with queries, includes, and the like. Then you create the monthly task in a template using the <cfschedule> tag.

The <cfapplication> tag contains a simple specification for the WebSpecial application.

As with other applications, you set a few default values for page display variables.

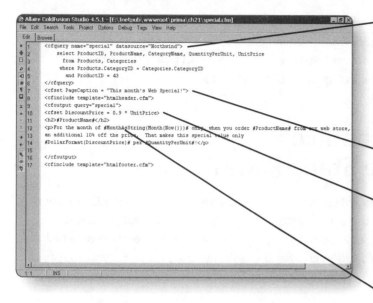

This query retrieves some product information. `ProductID` is hardcoded to the SQL statement for demonstration purposes. In a real application, this value would also be dynamic.

Set the page caption to indicate the purpose of the page.

A simple calculation provides the discount for this product, based on the product's list price.

Using the `MonthAsString` and `Month` functions, you can customize the page to show the month the page is generated.

Because this page doesn't change much (only once a month), it is a perfect candidate for a dynamically generated static page. You can reduce the hits to the database and the ColdFusion server by generating a static page that's regenerated once a month. And by scheduling this process using ColdFusion's task scheduler, you don't have to remember to do it every month.

This is what the page, special.cfm, looks like when invoked directly.

The generated page determines what month it is and fills that information in for you. This provides a slicker look to the promotion.

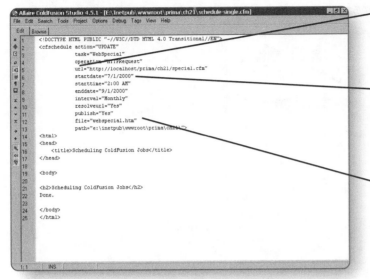

You set the url attribute to the special.cfm template described previously.

You schedule the task to run monthly on the first of the month at 2:00 AM, until 9/1/2000.

Now, you create the webspecial.htm file from the results of the request.

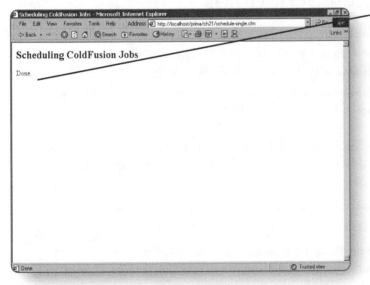

There is no output from the <cfschedule> tag to display to the users, so be sure to tell them when it's done.

That's all there is to it. To prove to yourself that the task was created, take a look at the Scheduled Tasks in ColdFusion Administrator.

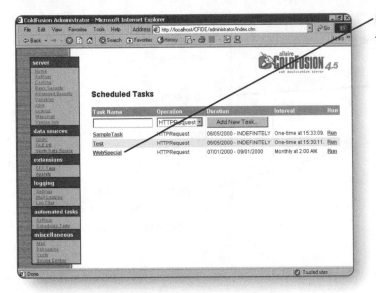

Here is the task, scheduled via the `<cfschedule>` tag.

Creating Batch Schedules

Using ColdFusion Administrator is fine for a new task here and there. But if you frequently generate static pages, you might want to automate scheduling as much as possible. One way to deal with a large number of tasks is to schedule them in batches. You can create a batch schedule text file and read it in via the `<cffile>` tag. Then you can invoke `<cfschedule>` to create the tasks.

First you need a file format for the batch schedule. The file record needs a task name, a start date, a start time, an interval, a URL, a filename, and a path.

TIP

You may not want to give out the password to the ColdFusion Administrator for your users to create their own scheduled tasks. Instead, you can create a ColdFusion application to mimic the ColdFusion Administrator interface to gather scheduling information from your users. You then use the `<cfschedule>` tag to schedule the task on the user's behalf, without compromising your administrator's password. The examples in this chapter will give you a good start on this project.

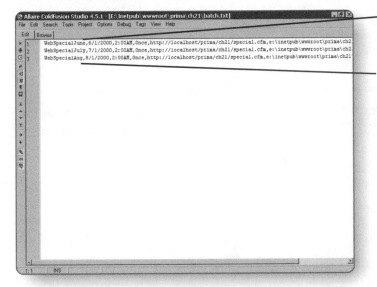

This example uses simple values in the text file with no quotes.

This example uses commas to delimit the values, which makes it easy to parse the file when you read it in.

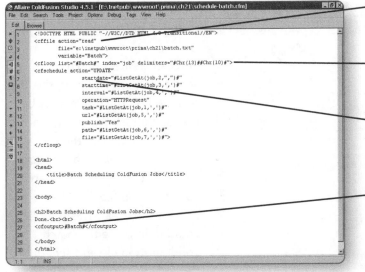

You read the file into a variable named Batch.

You then loop over each line of the file in Batch.

You can access the values of the <cfschedule> attributes by using the ListGetAt function.

You then dump the contents of the file into the browser window. This confirms that the tasks were created.

To create the scheduled tasks from the batch file, all you need to do is request the schedule-batch.cfm template. You then load this template into your browser. Note that you also can invoke this template by requesting it from another scheduled task.

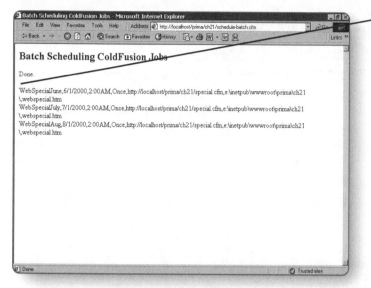

The output of the batch text file confirms to the users what tasks were scheduled.

These tasks are scheduled pretty quickly. Take a look at the scheduled task list to confirm that these were done.

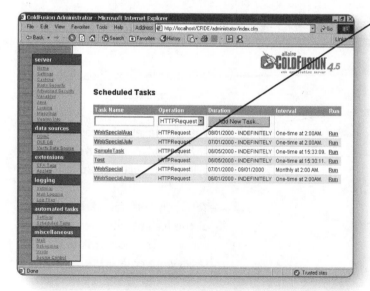

Here are the scheduled tasks from the batch job.

You can create a batch scheduling system using these techniques. You might start by creating a task that runs at a regular interval and then request a template that checks a standard location for a batch configuration file, like the previous text file. This template could then parse the batch configuration file and schedule the jobs that it finds in the file. If no files are found, the template does nothing.

22

Leveraging the Browser

Sometimes, even ColdFusion is not enough to get the job done. But that's okay; you have plenty of other tools to help you. One of the best tools for making your Web application stand out is the client's browser. You can use style sheets for layout and display control, and you can use JavaScript to add dynamic action to a Web page. ColdFusion also enables you to use XML (Extensible Markup Language) to move data around. In this chapter, you learn to:

- Create a dynamically generated style sheet
- Use JavaScript to create dynamic form elements
- Use ColdFusion with JavaScript to create database-driven form elements
- Review the use of WDDX and XML to convert data structures

Creating Style Sheets

Style sheets enable you to specify the physical character of a Web page, such as fonts, font sizes, colors, and indentations of specific HTML elements. By placing all the style directives in a separate file, you can reuse a style sheet across all pages in an application. You can link the style sheet template into each page through the <head> section of the HTML document. When you link a style sheet in this manner, the style sheet file must have a MIME type of text/css associated with it, which indicates to the browser that the file is a style sheet and should be embedded in the parent HTML document.

In this example, you will create a ColdFusion template that produces a style sheet based on a URL variable. You use the variable to specify the style's color scheme. Based on this scheme, you can change a set of colors used in the style sheet for table headers, text, and so on.

You can override the Web server in sending the MIME type by using the <cfcontent> tag. The <cfcontent> tag must appear on the first line of the template and requires the type attribute, which specifies the current template's MIME type.

Check for the scheme variable in the url scope and set the local page variable accordingly.

Now, you simply determine which color scheme you should use for the style sheet.

```
Allaire ColdFusion Studio 4.5.1 - [E:\Inetpub\wwwroot\prima\ch22\style.cfm]
File  Edit  Search  Tools  Project  Options  Debug  Tags  View  Help
Edit | Browse |
1    <cfcontent type="text/css">
2    <cfparam name="scheme" default="gray">
3    <cfif IsDefined("url.scheme")>
4        <cfset scheme = url.scheme>
5    </cfif>
6    <cfif scheme is "gray">
7        <cfscript>
8        AnchorColor = "000033";
9        BaseFontFamily = "Arial, Helvetica, sans-serif";
10       BaseFontSize = "10pt";
11       BaseFontColor = "000000";
12       BaseFontStyle = "normal";
13       BaseFontWeight = "normal";
14       Color_Title_BG = "CCCCCC";
15       Color_Title_FG = "000000";
16       Color_H1_FG = "000066";
17       Color_H2_FG = "000066";
18       Color_H3_FG = "000099";
19       Color_H4_FG = "000099";
20       Color_RowHighlight = "CCCCCC";
21       </cfscript>
22   </cfif>
23   <cfif scheme is "green">
24       <cfscript>
25       AnchorColor = "339999";
26       BaseFontFamily = "Arial, Helvetica, sans-serif";
27       BaseFontSize = "10pt";
28       BaseFontColor = "000000";
29       BaseFontStyle = "normal";
30       BaseFontWeight = "normal";
         Color_Title_BG = "009900";
1:1      INS
```

NOTE

ColdFusion gives you the option to streamline your code using the `<cfscript>` tag. Code within the beginning and end tags can dispense with the bracketed tag syntax and use a syntax much like JavaScript. See the ColdFusion documentation on `<cfscript>` to review the streamlined syntax.

These ColdFusion variables determine the style sheet's colors and font characteristics. The `<cfscript>` tag helps streamline this list of variables.

```
Allaire ColdFusion Studio 4.5.1 - [E:\Inetpub\wwwroot\prima\ch22\style.cfm]
File  Edit  Search  Tools  Project  Options  Debug  Tags  View  Help
Edit | Browse
1   <cfcontent type="text/css">
2   <cfparam name="scheme" default="gray">
3   <cfif IsDefined("url.scheme")>
4       <cfset scheme = url.scheme>
5   </cfif>
6   <cfif scheme is "gray">
7       <cfscript>
8       AnchorColor = "000033";
9       BaseFontFamily = "Arial, Helvetica, sans-serif";
10      BaseFontSize = "10pt";
11      BaseFontColor = "000000";
12      BaseFontStyle = "normal";
13      BaseFontWeight = "normal";
14      Color_Title_BG = "CCCCCC";
15      Color_Title_FG = "000000";
16      Color_H1_FG = "000066";
17      Color_H2_FG = "000066";
18      Color_H3_FG = "000099";
19      Color_H4_FG = "000099";
20      Color_RowHighlight = "CCCCCC";
21      </cfscript>
22  </cfif>
23  <cfif scheme is "green">
24      <cfscript>
25      AnchorColor = "339999";
26      BaseFontFamily = "Arial, Helvetica, sans-serif";
27      BaseFontSize = "10pt";
28      BaseFontColor = "000000";
29      BaseFontStyle = "normal";
30      BaseFontWeight = "normal";
        Color_Title_BG = "0088008";
```

Now, you output the style sheet. The variables set previously are replaced by the selected scheme's values.

You can use the same style sheet and change only the variable values to achieve a new color and font scheme.

```
Allaire ColdFusion Studio 4.5.1 - [E:\Inetpub\wwwroot\prima\ch22\style.cfm]
File  Edit  Search  Tools  Project  Options  Debug  Tags  View  Help
Edit | Browse
36      Color_H4_FG = "003300";
37      Color_RowHighlight = "99FF99";
38      </cfscript>
39  </cfif>
40  <cfoutput>
41  BODY  {
42      font-size : #BaseFontSize#;
43      font-family : #BaseFontFamily#;
44      font-weight : #BaseFontWeight#;
45      font-style : #BaseFontStyle#;
46      color : #BaseFontColor#;
47      text-decoration : none;
48      text-align : left;
49      background-color : White;
50  }
51  H1  {
52      font-size : 24pt;
53      font-family : #BaseFontFamily#;
54      font-weight : normal;
55      font-style : normal;
56      color : #Color_H1_FG#;
57  }
58  H2  {
59      font-size : 20pt;
60      font-family : #BaseFontFamily#;
61      font-weight : bold;
62      font-style : normal;
63      color : #Color_H2_FG#;
64  }
65  LI  {
        font-size : #BaseFontSize#;
```

```
Allaire ColdFusion Studio 4.5.1 - [E:\Inetpub\wwwroot\prima\ch22\style.cfm]
File  Edit  Search  Tools  Project  Options  Debug  Tags  View  Help
Edit  Browse
66        font-size : #BaseFontSize#;
67        font-family : #BaseFontFamily#;
68        font-weight : #BaseFontWeight#;
69        font-style : #BaseFontStyle#;
70        color : #BaseFontColor#;
71        text-indent : 4pt;
72        list-style-type : square;
73    }
74    A  {
75        color : #AnchorColor#;
76    }
77    .banner {
78        font-size : 16pt;
79        font-family : #BaseFontFamily#;
80        font-weight : bold;
81        color : #Color_Title_FG#;
82        background-color : #Color_Title_BG#;
83    }
84    .footer {
85        font-size : 8pt;
86        font-family : #BaseFontFamily#;
87        font-weight : normal;
88        color : #Color_Title_FG#;
89        background-color : #Color_Title_BG#;
90    }
91    .rowhighlight {
92        background-color : #Color_RowHighlight#;
93    }
94    </cfoutput>
```

You create a few style classes for the banner, footer, and highlighted row elements on your pages.

```
Allaire ColdFusion Studio 4.5.1 - [E:\Inetpub\wwwroot\prima\ch22\index.cfm]
File  Edit  Search  Tools  Project  Options  Debug  Tags  View  Help
Edit  Browse
1     <cfparam name="TemplateSwitch" default="top">
2     <cfparam name="BodyTemplate" default="top-js.cfm">
3     <cfset Style = "green">
4     <cfif IsDefined("url.page")>
5        <cfset TemplateSwitch = url.page>
6        <cfswitch expression="#TemplateSwitch#">
7        <cfcase value="survey">
8            <cfset BodyTemplate = "survey/survey1.cfm">
9        </cfcase>
10       <cfcase value="cat">
11           <cfset BodyTemplate = "catalog/catalog.cfm">
12       </cfcase>
13       <cfcase value="log">
14           <cfset BodyTemplate = "login.cfm">
15       </cfcase>
16       </cfswitch>
17
18    </cfif>
19
20    <cfinclude template="#BodyTemplate#">
```

Before you include the BodyTemplate in the switchboard template, specify the style you want.

Setting this value in the switchboard means that the style is applied to all included pages. If you want to change the style, you change it in just one place.

Use the HTML <link> tag to include the style sheet with the Web page.

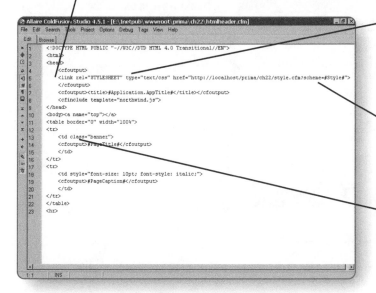

Specify the type of the linked file as text/css. This is required in addition to the <cfcontent> tag in the ColdFusion template.

In the href attribute, add the url variable scheme and set it to the Style value specified in the switchboard template.

Add the class attribute to the banner table cell to tie in the .banner class from the style sheet to this table cell.

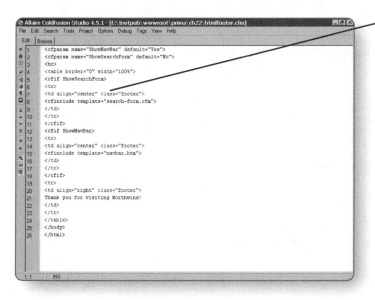

Add the class attribute to the footer table cells to assign the .footer class from the style sheet to this footer table.

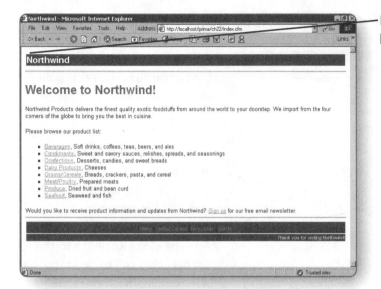

Now the Northwind Web site has a new look.

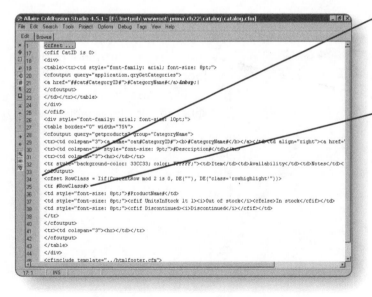

Use the Iif function to assign the .rowhighlight class from the style sheet to alternating rows in the product-listing table.

Note that if the CurrentRow is an odd number, this variable will be empty and no class will be assigned to the table row.

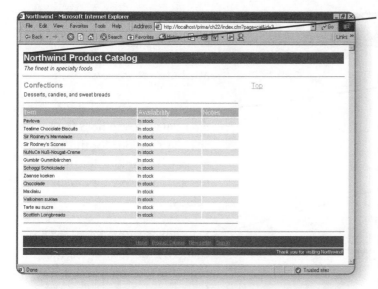

Note that the product catalog Web page has the same new look. Each page included on the switchboard inherits the same scheme.

This is a simple example of changing font sizes and colors using a dynamic style sheet. You can use the same techniques to create dynamic style sheets that adjust layouts based on the browser type or change color schemes based on a visitor's customized settings.

Using JavaScript to Create Dynamic Elements

JavaScript is a scripting language that most modern browsers use for more dynamic control over the document. JavaScript (or JScript on Internet Explorer), in conjunction with cascading style sheets, is what makes HTML dynamic. The scripting language enables you to manipulate windows, form elements, and HTML style elements during runtime.

In this example, you return to the invoice reports of Chapter 7, "Dynamic Query Building." You can use JavaScript to create a dynamic form that selects the region upon which to base the report. You can then enable the users to select a large region that dynamically uses a <select> element to populate the page with more specific regions.

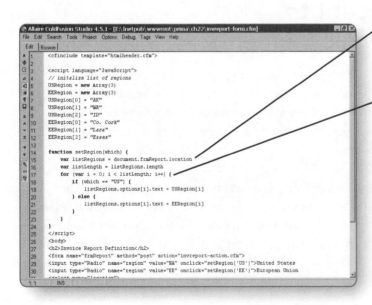

You start a JavaScript snippet by placing it inside the HTML `<script>` tag with the `language` attribute set to `JavaScript`.

Create two arrays of three elements each to hold the list of shipping regions for the two aggregate regions for the form. Next, you hardcode the array values.

You then create a function to be called by the form when the radio buttons are clicked. The form passes the value of the clicked button to the function as the variable `which`.

Now, you set a reference to the `<select>` list and find out how many options it has.

You loop over the length of the list. Set the `text` of the `options` to the values in the arrays, depending on the value of `which`.

The `onclick` attribute of the form elements named `region` invokes the `setRegion` JavaScript function when the users click the button of the form element. The form element invokes the function containing the value of the radio button that was clicked.

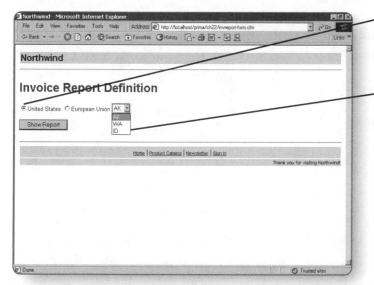

The radio buttons control the list of regions in the drop-down list.

The three states in the drop-down list are the same as the states in the JavaScript array, USRegion.

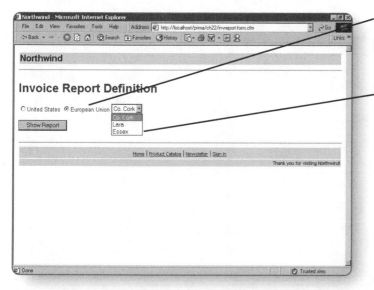

Upon selecting the European Union, the select list dynamically resizes.

The regions from the EERegion JavaScript array now populate the <select> list.

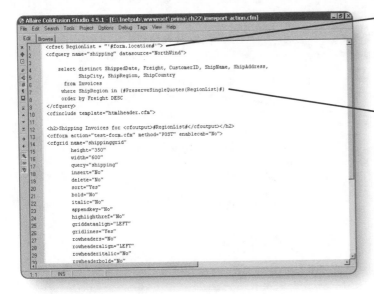

You set the `RegionList` to the value of the `form.location` field. Note the single quotes used with the value.

Include the `RegionList` in the `where` clause of the SQL statement, preserving the single quotes.

Note that the dynamic action of this form was limited to the client's Web browser. There were no additional hits on the Web server, the ColdFusion server, or the database to achieve this dynamic effect.

The selected region is displayed in the header as a descriptive title.

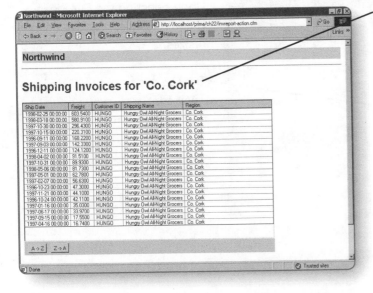

Using ColdFusion and JavaScript to Create Database-Driven Elements

ColdFusion is well suited for working with JavaScript in client browsers. Because a JavaScript snippet is nothing more than code embedded in an HTML page, you can use ColdFusion to generate dynamic JavaScript. In other words, you use ColdFusion code to write JavaScript code that is sent to the browser.

Here, you will convert the JavaScript snippet in the previous example to a dynamically generated script. Query objects replace the hardcoded array values, and standard `<cfoutput>` tags write the new JavaScript arrays. The JavaScript function does not change substantially from the previous example.

This query retrieves a distinct list of country names occurring on the invoices of the set of European countries listed in the `where` clause.

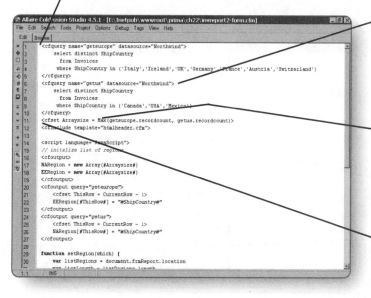

This query retrieves a distinct list of country names occurring on the invoices of the set of North American countries listed in the `where` clause.

The `Max` function returns the larger of the two arguments. In this case, you want to know which query returned more rows.

The `Arraysize` variable determines the size of the `<select>` list on the form.

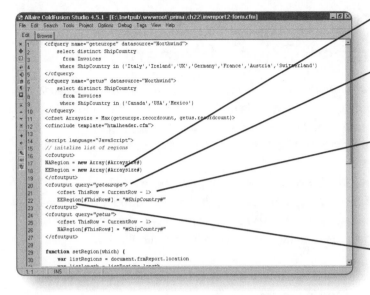

Use `Arraysize` to set the size of the JavaScript arrays.

Loop over the queries to initialize the arrays for each aggregate region.

Because the arrays in JavaScript use zero-based indexes, you need to subtract one from the `CurrentRow` index of the result set.

Using `ThisRow` as the array index, you set the value to the current `ShipCountry` value.

The JavaScript function is almost unchanged from the previous example. The array names and the `which` value are the only alterations.

The `<select>` option list is generated in a loop. The `Arraysize` determines the number of `<option>` tags you need to accommodate.

The `<option>` values are empty or undefined until the users select an aggregate region.

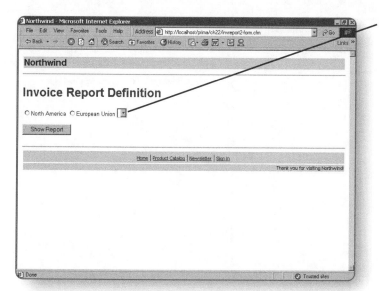

No aggregate region selection has been made, so the `<select>` list is empty.

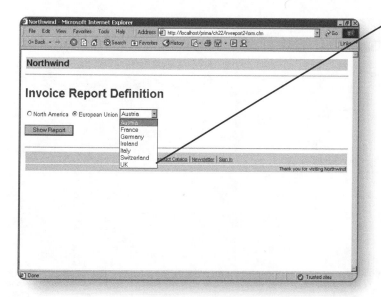

The `<select>` list is populated with European countries when the European Union radio button is selected on the left.

The SQL statement has changed because you are using `ShipCountry` rather than `ShipRegion` for this report.

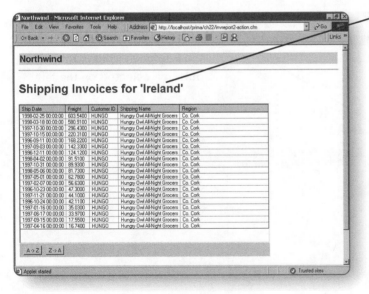

Here is the report of invoices to Ireland. Looks like Northwind is doing business only with the County Cork.

Converting Data Structures with XML and WDDX

XML, the Extensible Markup Language, is emerging as a new standard for information exchange and layout on the Web, and ColdFusion supports XML through the WDDX (Web Distributed Data Exchange) language extension. ColdFusion provides the `<cfwddx>` tag to serialize and deserialize data. The `action` attribute supports four operations: `cfml2wddx`, `wddx2cfml`, `cfml2js`, and `wddx2js`. The `input` attribute is required to supply the data to be converted. The `output` attribute is required only for the `wddx2cfml` operation; if it is not specified in the other three operations, the result of the `<cfwddx>` tag operation is output into the current document.

This example script is taken from the sample code in the ColdFusion online documentation on WDDX. I adapted it to use the Northwind datasource

> **NOTE**
>
> The term *serialization* refers to converting or encoding data from the original platform to the WDDX format. *Deserialization* is decoding the data from WDDX to the original platform format.

This query provides the record set for conversion with the `<cfwddx>` tag.

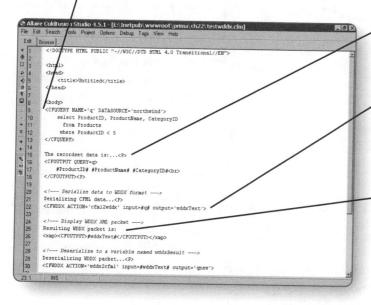

First, you display the results of the query for comparison purposes.

Now, you serialize the query record set, `q`, to WDDX format and store the result in the variable `wddxText`.

The resulting WDDX packet is displayed to illustrate the XML formatting of the data.

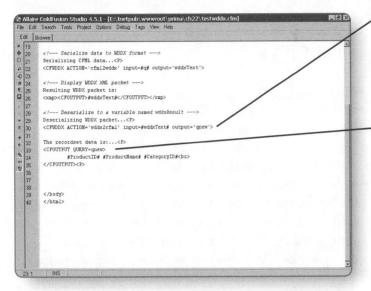

You now use the wddx2cfml operation to deserialize the WDDX packet back to a ColdFusion query object named qnew.

Here is the output of the new query object using the familiar <cfoutput>.

With WDDX and the <cfwddx> tag, you can send data of any type from your ColdFusion applications, via HTTP, to any other application that can deserialize the WDDX packet.

Here is the original query object from the <cfquery>.

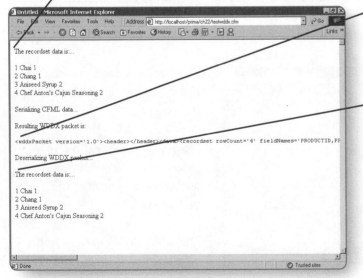

Here is the WDDX formatted data from the query object. You have to scroll to see the whole string.

And here is the new query object deserialized from the WDDX packet. It looks like an exact match of the original.

For applications with complex JavaScript components running on the client browser, you can use WDDX to provide these components with complex data from ColdFusion queries. You can also send complex data structures as JavaScript data to any server that can run JavaScript, such as a Windows Scripting Host like Internet Information Server (IIS). WDDX is also an excellent tool for building cross-server applications.

PART V

Getting the Job Done

23

Building Your Own Tags

You can extend the functionality of ColdFusion by building your own tags. The `<cfmodule>` tag provides a structure that you can use to create customized ColdFusion tags. Custom tags enable you to modularize and encapsulate code that you tend to write repeatedly into tags. You can then reuse these tags in all your Web applications. In this chapter, you learn how to:

- Use the `<cfmodule>` tag to write custom tags
- Pass information out of custom tags
- Pass information into custom tags
- View ready-to-use custom tags

What Are Custom Tags?

Custom tags are separate ColdFusion templates that you can call from other templates as though they were regular ColdFusion tags. Custom tags can have attributes, and they can return values or directly output text into your template. They have their own scope, so you don't have to worry about inadvertently overwriting a variable from the calling template.

You can call custom tags in one of two ways. You can use the <cfmodule> tag with the template or name attribute. The template attribute requires a relative path to the custom tag template and must include the .cfm extension. The name attribute omits the .cfm extension on the template's name, and <cfmodule> searches for the tag in the ColdFusion CustomTags directory in the ColdFusion installation directory or in your application directory structure. However, by placing your tags in the CustomTags directory, you can make them available to all your applications.

The other way you call custom tags requires that the tag be in the current directory or in the root of the CustomTags special directory. You can reference the custom tag by prepending the filename with cf_ and placing the tag in angle brackets.

Custom tags have the attributes scope. This scope holds all the attributes passed to the tag from the calling template. Custom tags also have the caller scope. Using the caller scope, a custom tag can access variables from the calling—or parent—template and can create new variables in the parent template.

This chapter presents some example custom tags that are fully functional and of practical value in a variety of development projects. Please feel free to use and extend them for your own applications.

Custom Tag Example: Log2File.cfm

One of the most common tasks that developers want their applications to do is log information to a file with a timestamp. Logging is an indispensable debugging and auditing tool. It enables you to assess application performance and viability.

The Log2File.cfm tag takes three attributes. The path attribute specifies the physical path of the file to write. The LogString attribute contains the string that's written to the file. The path and LogString attributes are required. The LogFile attribute specifies the filename; it defaults to errors.log.

This tag contains the default value of the LogFile attribute.

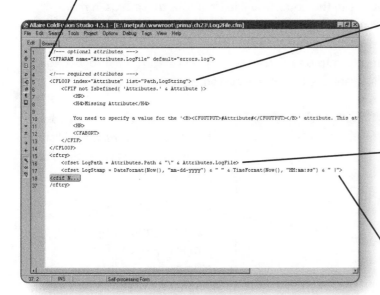

The ColdFusion Studio Custom Tag wizard generates this loop. It loops over the list of required attributes and returns an error if any attributes are missing from the attributes scope.

The LogPath is set by concatenating the attributes.path and the attributes.LogFile variables.

You create a timestamp for the log file by calling DateFormat and TimeFormat with the Now ColdFusion function.

Here, you determine whether the file referenced in LogPath exists. If not, you create it.

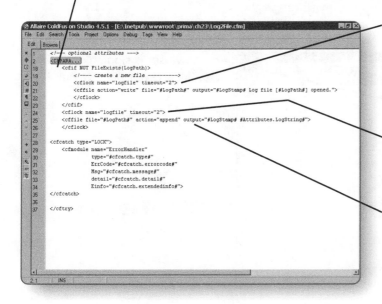

Set a lock on the <cffile> operation to ensure no collisions. Write a special "file opened" string as the first entry in the log file.

Set another lock for the append operation now that the file exists.

Now the output to the log file contains the LogStamp and the value of the LogString passed to the custom tag.

Notice the unusual `<cftry>` and `<cfcatch>` tags in this listing. These are ColdFusion tags that handle exceptions in the code. You'll learn about these tags in more depth in Chapter 24, "Handling Errors."

As an example, you can return to one of the forms from Chapter 4, "Processing and Validating Forms," to illustrate the use of this custom tag.

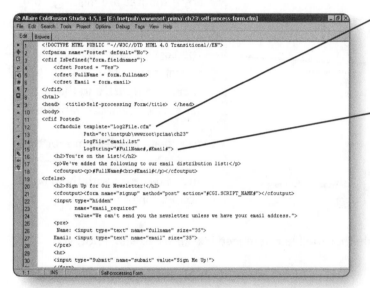

Here is the call to the custom tag that writes the e-mail list. Note the three attributes being passed to the tag.

Because you used the Log2File custom tag to compile the e-mail list, each entry receives a timestamp so that you know when your users signed up.

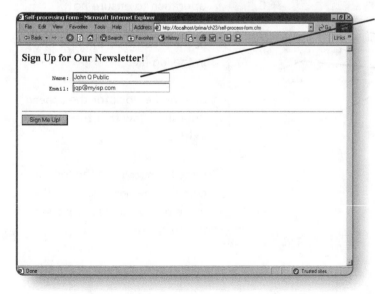

A new user is signing up for the e-mail newsletter.

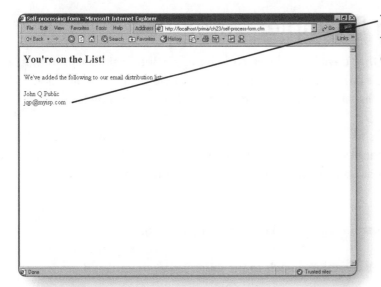

The form has completed its task. A new e-mail address is on the list.

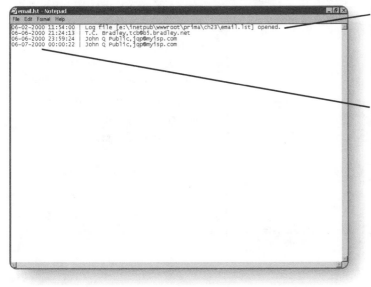

The first line in the text file is the "file opened" message, generated from the file write operation.

Each line has a date and time that mark when the e-mail address was added to the list.

Custom Tag Example: DateSelect.cfm

Another common task that developers write code for again and again is a form that enables users to select a date. You can use a simple text field with date validation, but a set of drop-down lists with the month, day, and year is better way to go.

This custom tag outputs to the parent template three `<select>` form elements for the month, day, and year. It is up to the parent template to provide the `<form>` tag that places these `<select>` elements in context. This custom tag has no required attributes.

You can improve this custom tag by adding leap-year checking.

The Day, Month, and Year variables default to the current day, month, and year, respectively.

This variable determines the range of years shown, both forward and backward, from the current year.

These lists are hardcoded for processing the month. YearBase determines where to start the year `<select>` list.

```
Allaire ColdFusion Studio 4.5.1 - [E:\Inetpub\wwwroot\prima\ch23\DateSelect.cfm]
File  Edit  Search  Tools  Project  Options  Debug  Tags  View  Help
Edit  Browse
1   <!--- optional attributes --->
2   <cfparam name="Attributes.Day" default="#Day(Now())#">
3   <cfparam name="Attributes.Month" default="#Month(Now())#">
4   <cfparam name="Attributes.Year" default="#Year(Now())#">
5
6   <cfset YearRange = "10">
7   <cfset MonthList = "January,February,March,April,May,June,July,August,September,October,November,Decem
8   <cfset MonthDays = "31,28,31,30,31,30,31,31,30,31,30,31">
9   <cfset YearBase = Year(Now()) - YearRange>
10
11  <select name="MonthName">
12  <cfloop list="#MonthList#" index="idx">
13      <cfoutput>
14          <option value="#ListFindNoCase(MonthList, idx)#"
15          #iif(idx is MonthAsString(Attributes.Month), DE("selected"), DE(""))#
16          >#idx#
17      </cfoutput>
18  </cfloop>
19  </select>
20  <select name="MonthDay">
21  <cfloop from="1" to="31" index="idx">
22      <cfoutput>
23          <option value="#idx#"
24          #iif(idx is Attributes.Day, DE("selected"), DE(""))#
25          >#idx#
26      </cfoutput>
27  </cfloop>
28  </select>
29  <select name="Year">
30  <cfloop from="#YearBase#" to="#Evaluate('#YearBase# + (#YearRange# * 2)')#" index="idx">
1:1    INS
```

This `<select>` tag begins the `MonthName` `<select>` element. You loop over the `MonthList` to output the `<option>` elements.

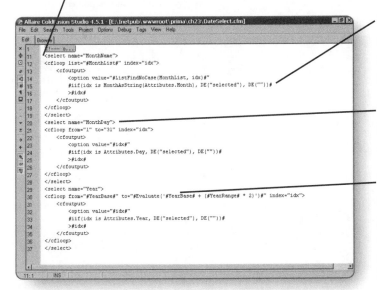

This variable checks the preset value of `attributes.month` for a match. If it matches, you mark this `<option>` as `selected`.

The same structure is repeated in order to output the `MonthDay` `<select>` element.

The last year included is calculated from the starting year plus twice the range of years displayed. In this `<select>` element, a span of 20 years is included.

To test this custom tag, add it to the dynamic query form from Chapter 4.

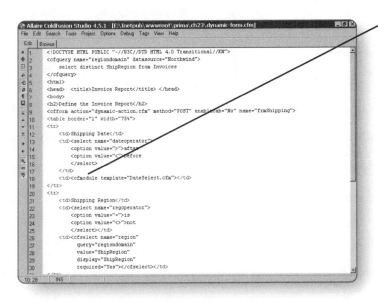

This call to the `DateSelect.cfm` tag makes the code for this form much cleaner and easier to follow.

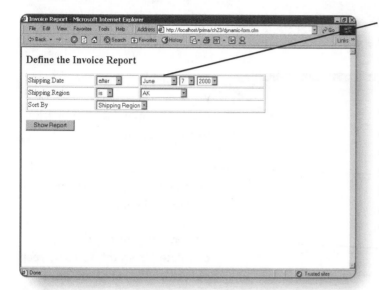

The `<select>` elements default to the current date. This is better than starting with some arbitrary date.

These form elements replace the single date form field with three separate fields. These three fields need to be combined in the form processor in order to create a valid date for the query.

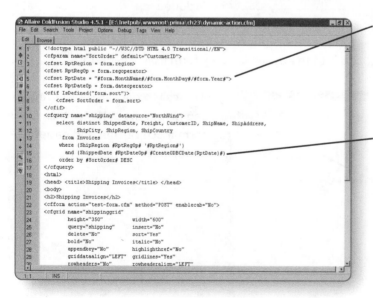

The `RptDate` variable is now set to the combination of the three form fields of the `DateSelect.cfm` tag: `MonthName`, `MonthDay`, and `Year`.

The `CreateODBCDate` function converts the `RptDate` to an ODBC date object.

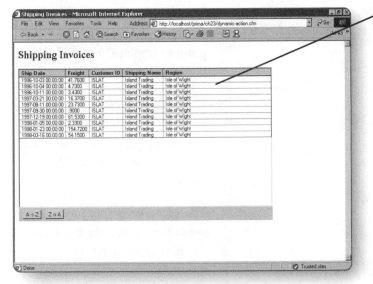

The output of the report is identical to the original. But you saved coding time by creating a custom tag that you can reuse to produce the often repeated code for selecting a date from a form.

Custom Tag Example: LastUpdated.cfm

A good feature to have on any Web page is the date of modification. This information tells the users the age of the data on the page. This feature also helps track changes to ColdFusion templates in your applications. This simple date can place the template in context with other template changes on the site, for instance.

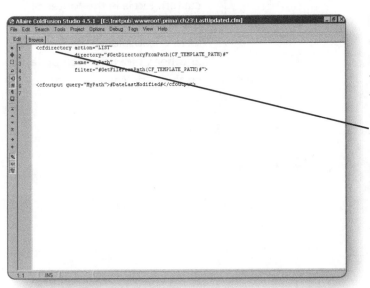

LastUpdated.cfm is a simple custom tag that outputs the last modified date of the parent template file to the parent template.

A call to <cfdirectory> with the appropriate path and filter provides the date the tag requires.

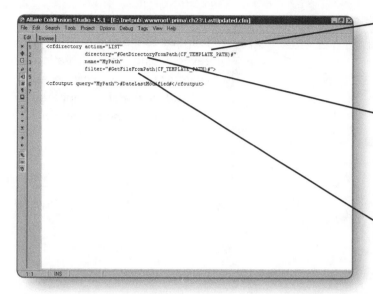

This CGI variable returns the absolute physical path to the parent template, including the filename.

This utility function returns only the path information from the absolute physical path, which is what the directory attribute needs.

This complementary function to GetDirectoryFromPath provides the filter for the list operation.

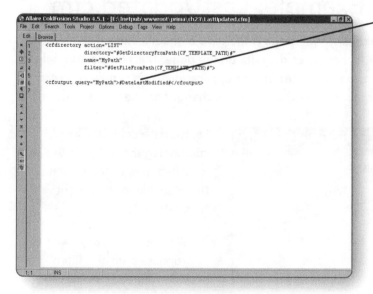

This holds the DateLastModified value from the parent template file's directory listing.

The perfect place for this custom tag is in the footer of the Web site. Of course, you have encapsulated the footer in another ColdFusion template, so this code change is easy.

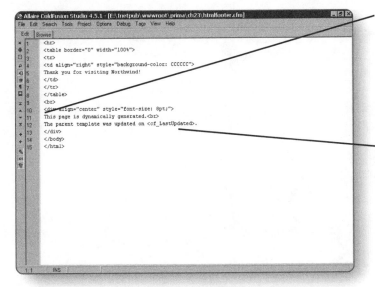

Here is a short disclaimer about the generation of the page. Note that this tag does not determine the date of the last data modification, just the template displaying it.

Here is the alternative syntax for calling a custom tag.

Just to prove you aren't doing anything funny, this example includes the footer of one of the forms from Chapter 4.

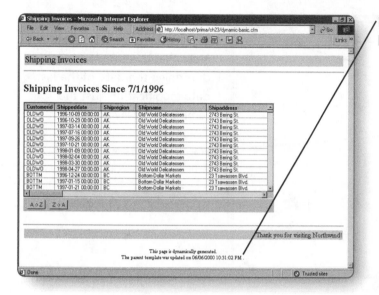

Here is the date the form was last modified.

Custom Tag Example: NavBar.cfm

Navigation bars are ubiquitous on the Web. Your applications will be no different. Because formatting navigation bars is repetitive, they are a wonderful candidate for a ColdFusion custom tag.

```
<cfparam name="Attributes.ButtonArray" default="#ArrayNew(1)#">
<cfparam name="Attributes.LinkArray" default="#ArrayNew(1)#">
<cfparam name="Attributes.LogoutButton" default="No">
<cfparam name="Attributes.LogoutAction" default="">
<cfparam name="Attributes.UseBrackets" default="yes">
<cfif Attributes.UseBrackets>
    <cfset FrameBeginChar = "[">
    <cfset FrameEndChar = "]">
<cfelse>
    <cfset FrameBeginChar = "">
    <cfset FrameEndChar = "">
</cfif>
<cfif Attributes.LogoutButton>
    <cfset foo = ArrayPrepend(Attributes.ButtonArray, "Logout")>
    <cfset foo = ArrayPrepend(Attributes.LinkArray, "#Attributes.LogoutAction#")>
</cfif>
<table width="100%" cellpadding="1" cellspacing="0">
    <tr>
        <cfif ArrayLen(Attributes.ButtonArray) gt 0>
            <cfloop from="1" to="#ArrayLen(Attributes.ButtonArray)#" index="idx">
                <td style="background-color: #FFFFCC;" align="center">
                    <cfoutput>
                    <a class="sidebarlink" href="#Attributes.LinkArray[idx]#">
                    #FrameBeginChar##Attributes.ButtonArray[idx]##FrameEndChar#</a>
                    </cfoutput>
                </td>
            </cfloop>
        </cfif>
    </tr>
</table>
```

The NavBar.cfm custom tag uses two arrays for the buttons and button actions. It offers a logout button and the choice of bracketing the buttons on the display. The output will be a 100% width table to the parent template.

The tag expects two populated, one-dimensional arrays from the parent template, but it defaults to two empty arrays. The `ArrayNew` function calls create these empty arrays when necessary.

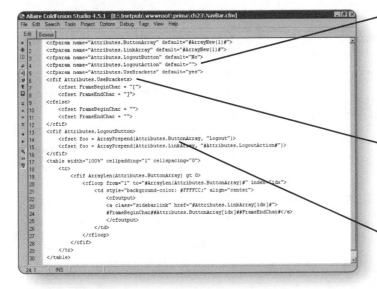

The `Logoutbutton` attribute determines whether a logout button should be displayed. The `LogoutAction` specifies the action to take when the logout button is clicked.

If `attributes.UseBrackets` is true, you set the beginning and ending button characters to square bracket characters.

To create the logout button, use `ArrayPrepend` on `ButtonArray` for the button text and `LinkArray` for the button action. These lines add the logout button to the navigation bar.

Now, you output a table to hold the navigation bar.

You loop over the length of the arrays and determine whether there are any buttons in the arrays to process.

You output a link with the `href` set to the value of the current position in `LinkArray`. The link text is set to the value of the current position in `ButtonArray`.

The framing characters surround the button text value and provide the text button look, if desired.

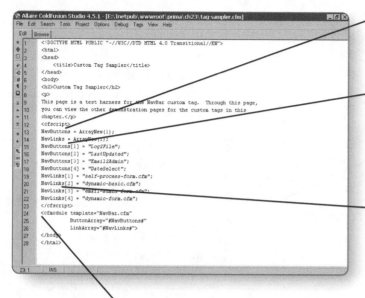

First, you create the two arrays in the parent template to define the navigation bar.

Now, you assign the values of the button text for each navigation button. You address the array elements by number starting with one.

NavLinks holds the buttons' actions (hyperlinks). These match one-to-one with the button text values.

This calls the custom tag. You assign the NavButtons and NavLinks arrays to the appropriate tag attributes.

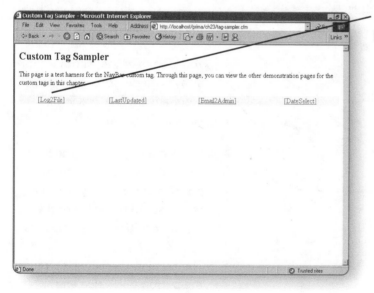

Here, you have the navigation bar.

Custom Tag Example: Email2Admin.cfm

Via e-mail, you can have your server notify you when there is a problem. The Email2Admin.cfm custom tag sends an e-mail to the ColdFusion server's administrator, as configured in the ColdFusion Administrator application. This tag requires a MsgBody attribute and a Subject attribute for the subject line. The tag logs an event when it sends e-mail to a file.

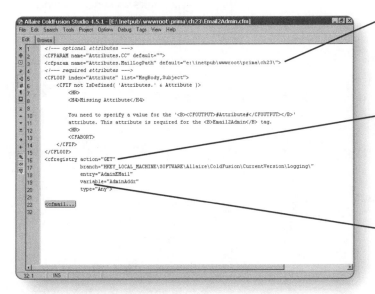

You need to change the path of the mail log file to something appropriate for your environment.

The <cfregistry> tag queries the system Registry for the AdminEmail value. The branch attribute specifies the Registry path to this value.

The value found in the Registry is returned to a local variable named AdminAddr.

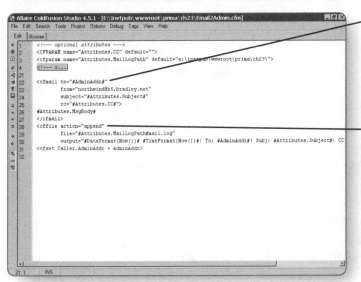

The <cfmail> tag queues the message to be sent to the administrator. Just set the from attribute to something appropriate.

The <cffile> tag writes a line to the mail log containing a time-stamp, the subject, and to whom the message was sent. Use the Log2File custom tag here.

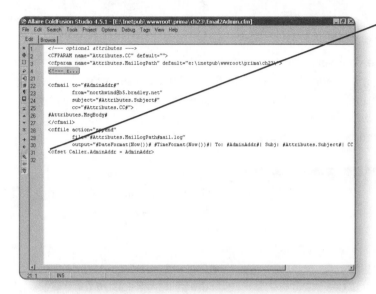

Provide feedback by using the `caller` scope in the custom tag to set a variable called `AdminAddr` in the parent template's scope.

You can also use this tag to enable users to send glowing accolades to the system administrator, but you might want to put a text filter on this form.

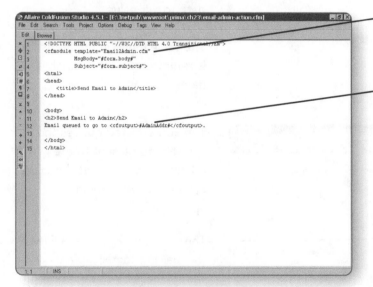

You pass the form variables directly to the custom tag in the form processor.

Here is the administrator's e-mail address that the custom tag retrieved from the Registry.

Don't overlook custom tags as a way to encapsulate unique processing as well as repetitive code. Isolating business logic in separate custom tags can help when that logic needs to change to meet demands.

Custom tags can also decrease your development time. On large projects, spend some time planning the templates with an eye toward building as many custom tags to support your application as possible. Modular code is a great boon when maintaining large applications, especially when you are on a lean budget or your development staff is small.

24

Handling Errors

It isn't glamorous or exciting. You won't get any kudos for it. But a large part of the code you write will be devoted to handling errors. The more complex the application, the more time you will spend writing code to catch errors, or exceptions. Therefore, planning for errors when you write your code is imperative. ColdFusion, as usual, can help. In this chapter, you learn to:

- Understand structured exception handling
- Use the `<cftry>` and `<cfcatch>` tags
- Catch specific types of exceptions
- Throw and catch your own custom errors
- Process transactions using the `<cftransaction>` tag

Understanding ColdFusion's Structured Exception Handling

Errors happen in even thoroughly debugged code. Circumstances that you cannot anticipate will always give rise to exceptions. An *exception* is an error encountered by the ColdFusion engine. Exceptions are encapsulated for processing.

ColdFusion can detect many types of exceptions. All these are recoverable exceptions; that is, the occurrence of one of these errors does not mean necessarily that the ColdFusion engine stops processing the template.

When an exception is encountered, it is said to be *thrown*. To handle a thrown exception of a given type, you must *catch* that type of exception somewhere in your code. To do so, that segment must be enclosed in `<cftry></cftry>` tags, with at least one appropriate `<cfcatch>` tag block.

When an exception occurs in a template inside a `<cftry>` block, ColdFusion checks the current template for a `<cfcatch>` block. If it doesn't find one in the current template, it looks in the template that called the current template. It continues in this manner until it finds a `<cfcatch>` block that can handle the error or until it reaches the top of the template stack, at which time it stops processing all included templates and reports the error. The program then jumps to the exception type's `<cfcatch>` block. Execution of the template continues from that point.

When an exception is thrown, the `cfcatch` scope is created. You use this scope to access information about the error. `cfcatch` has general variables populated upon generation, including `type`, `message`, `detail`, `extendedinfo`, `errorcode`, and `tagcontext`. In addition to these general variables, different exception types have variables related specifically to their purpose. For example, the `lock` exception includes the variables `lockname` and `lockoperation`.

Using `<cftry>` and `<cfcatch>`

You can wrap an entire template or any segment of the template in a `<cftry></cftry>` block, with the appropriate `<cfcatch>` blocks, in order to catch exceptions. For example, you can wrap a `<cfquery>` with a `<cfcatch>` block to catch database errors. A `<cftry>` block must have at least one `<cfcatch>` block to handle exceptions. You can have multiple `<cfcatch>` blocks to catch multiple types of exceptions with the `any` type as the default.

Here is an example template that sends the content of the error to the ColdFusion server system administrator and logs the error to an application-specific log file. To accomplish these tasks, the template uses the custom tags Email2Admin.cfm and Log2File.cfm, which were presented in the last chapter.

This tag has five required attributes: Type, Msg, Detail, ErrCode, and Einfo.

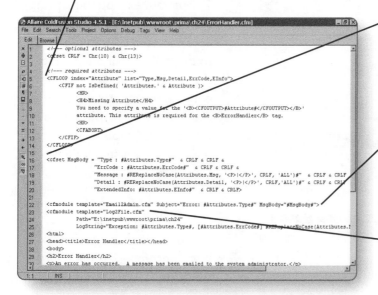

You build the MsgBody by concatenating the attribute values with labels and carriage-return/line-feed combinations. You strip out all the HTML paragraph tags.

First, e-mail a copy of the error parameters to the ColdFusion system administrator using the Email2Admin.cfm custom tag.

Next, log the error to an error log file using the Log2File.cfm custom tag.

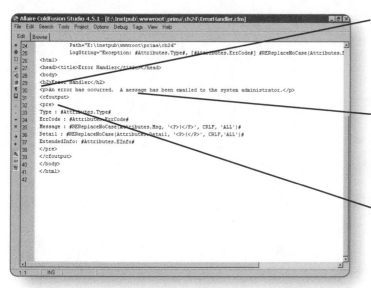

Once the record keeping is done, you need to inform the users that there has been a problem.

Let the users know that the system administrator has already been notified of the problem via e-mail.

Now, output the error information to the browser window.

This information is rarely of practical use to the users, but they often prefer an indecipherable error code to a generic "an error has occurred" message.

To illustrate exception-handling techniques and to exercise the ErrorHandler custom tag, return to the POP e-mail client. Note the <cftry> block around the entire index.cfm template. The catch block is of type Any, so it will catch any type of error that the ColdFusion server finds.

Start the <cftry> block at the top of the template. This block encompasses the entire template.

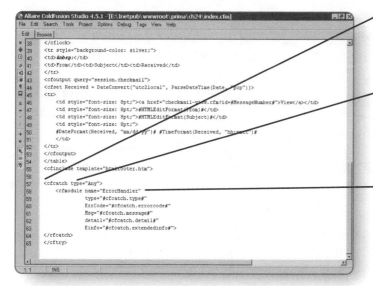

After the last line of the template, add the <cfcatch> tag block.

Because this block is checking for all errors, you set the type attribute of the <cfcatch> tag to Any.

The call to the ErrorHandler custom tag is the only processing you need to do for the exception.

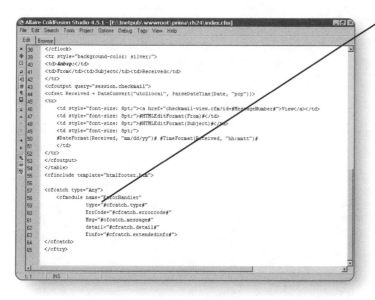

Reference the cfcatch scope variables to pass the information about the exception to the error handler.

Simple enough. Now, it is time to exercise the code. I added errors to the output of the code you see next. Different types of exceptions are caught and reported, based on the types of errors introduced into the code.

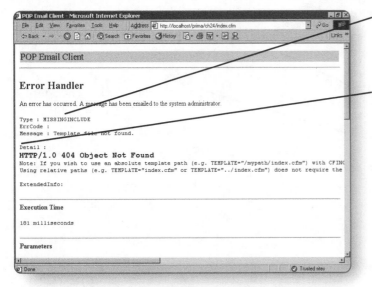

The typo in the task-bar.cfm inclusion generated a MISSINGINCLUDE exception.

The Detail section shows that the ColdFusion server returned an HTTP 404 error, indicating that the file was not found.

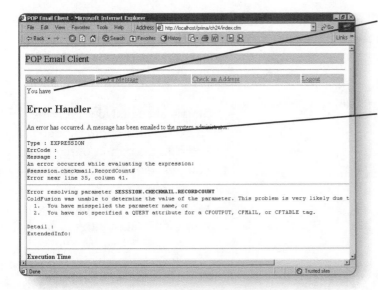

The error handler took over the output to the browser at the point of the error (a typo in a session variable name).

The manufactured typo generated the EXPRESSION exception.

Exception Handling Settings in ColdFusion Administrator

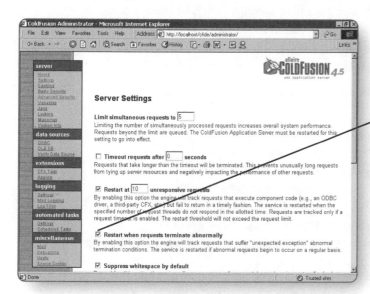

ColdFusion Administrator has some system-wide settings that assist you in handling exceptions in a consistent way.

You can restart the ColdFusion application server if it encounters unexpected exceptions while processing templates.

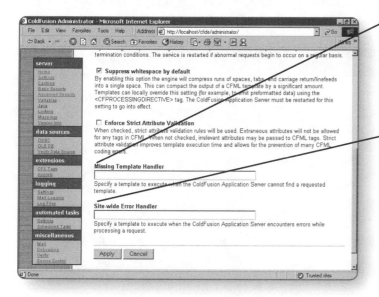

You can specify a system-wide missing template handler, which provides a consistent look to missing template errors across the entire server.

You can also specify a system-wide generic error handler. You basically create a template to call the custom tag ErrorHandler and specify it here.

Catching Specific Errors

Catching specific errors is not much different than catching all errors. You need to know the type of error that you want to catch, which isn't always obvious. For example, you don't need to write a catch block for a database error if you have no `<cfquery>` tags inside the parent `<cftry>` block. Putting these extra `<cfcatch>` blocks in your templates won't hurt, but it won't help either.

TIP

When catching specific exception types, the order of the `<cfcatch>` blocks is important. ColdFusion executes the first block that matches the type of exception. This means that you should always place a catch block of type `Any` at the end, after all other types of catch blocks. This way, ColdFusion matches the specific exception to a matching block type before executing the `Any` block.

The nice thing about catching specific exceptions is that you can usually try to fix the problem and go on with the processing. A good example is catching a `lock` exception. The alterations to the login form template attempt to catch a `lock` exception. Because locks are time-dependent, it is reasonable to assume that the lock on the variable in question is temporary. Therefore, it is reasonable also to try the lock again. The `<cfexit>` tag enables you to loop back to the beginning of a template and have ColdFusion reexecute the template.

The `<cftry>` block encompasses the entire template so that it can catch any type of exception in addition to the `lock` type.

This `<cflock>` tag might generate a `lock` exception.

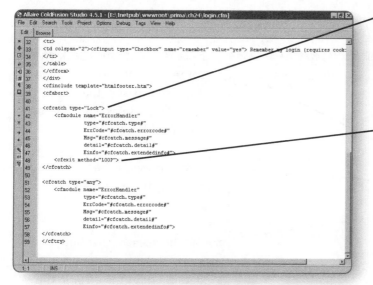

Here is the catch block for the `lock` exception. The first thing it does is use the `ErrorHandler` tag to notify the system administrator and log the error.

The `<cfexit>` tag with the `method` attribute set to loop attempts to reexecute the template. Perhaps the lock on the session variable has now expired.

Throwing and Catching Your Own Errors

Another great feature about ColdFusion structured exception handling is that you can create your own error types to throw around. This is especially useful in larger applications where you need to track the performance of specific segments of code.

You use the `<cfthrow>` tag to generate your own exceptions. The `<cfthrow>` tag takes attributes that match the generally available variables in the `cfcatch` scope of a thrown exception. You can set these attributes to your custom requirements so that this information is passed along when an exception is thrown.

The `<cftry>` block encompasses the entire template.

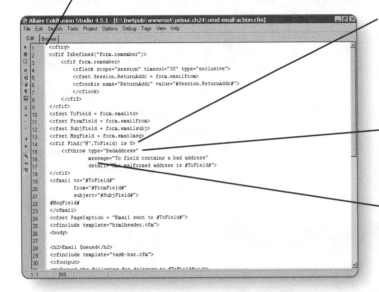

Here is a simplistic check on the `ToField` to look for an @ sign. If it doesn't exist in the string, the `ToField` contains a malformed e-mail address.

If the address is bad, generate an exception of type `BadAddress`.

Set the `message` attribute to a string describing the error. Give details about the error in the `detail` attribute.

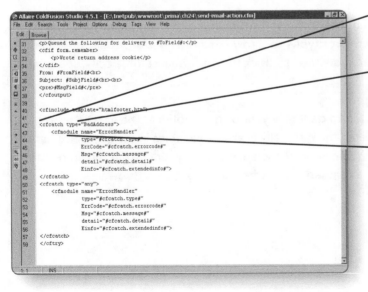

Here is the catch block for the custom exception.

Simply match the `type` attribute to the `type` attribute of the `<cfthrow>` tag.

Report the error to the system administrator and log it.

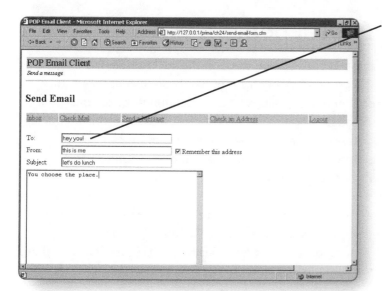

This user does not have a clue about what an e-mail address is.

Here is the custom type of the exception, just as it was set in the `<cfthrow>` tag.

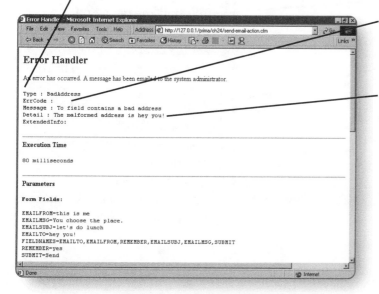

The string from the message attribute of the `<cfthrow>` tag appears here.

Imagine that. "Hey you!" is not a valid e-mail address.

Processing Transactions

ColdFusion provides transaction processing through the `<cftransaction>` tag. Transactions enable you to group together a set of database queries to act in concert with one another. If one query fails, you can discontinue, or roll back, the others. Large relational database engines, such as Microsoft SQL Server or Oracle, provide transaction processing on the database server. Using the `<cftransaction>` tag, you can bring some of this power to databases that do not support transactions, such as Microsoft Access or MySQL.

You can use structured exception handling to organize and control your transactions by leveraging the database type of the `<cfcatch>` tag. With some careful nesting, you can create a string of related queries inside a `<cftransaction>` and use catch blocks to control the commitment or rollback of those transactions.

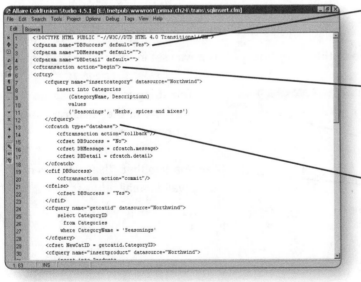

You need to set some variables to hold the error status of the queries.

You start the definition of a transaction by setting the action attribute of the `<cftransaction>` tag to begin.

After the first query, set a `<cfcatch>` block of type database. If you have an exception, discontinue this query by nesting a `<cftransaction>` block with an action of rollback.

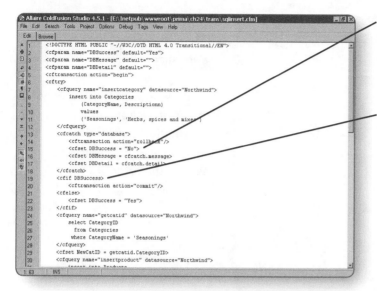

Set the DBSuccess flag to No and update the DBMessage and DBDetail variables to the corresponding cfcatch values.

If the query makes it past the <cfcatch> block, it succeeded. Commit the query with a <cftransaction> of type commit.

The insertproduct query needs the new ID of the category created in the first query.

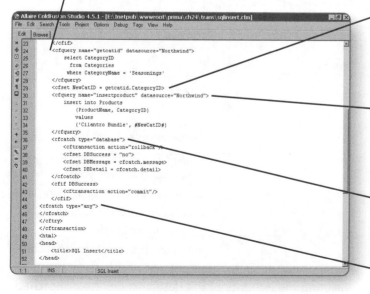

Set the NewCatID variable to the result of the ID query. You can also apply a <cfcatch> block to this query.

Here is the insertproduct query. This should take place only when the category insert query succeeded.

The <cfcatch> block here parallels the <cfcatch> block of the category insert query.

This catch block is required because the last tag inside a <cftry> block must be a <cfcatch></cfcatch> tag block.

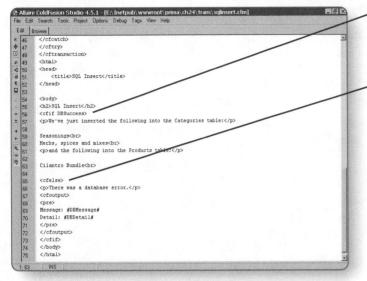

If the transaction succeeded, inform the users that the inserts were successful.

Otherwise, inform the users of the error. Use the exception information captured in DBMessage and DBDetail to explain the error.

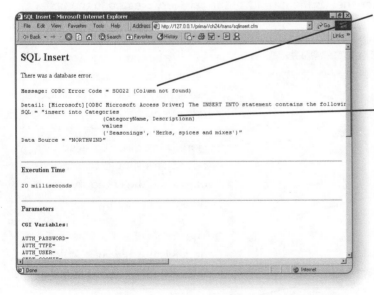

Oops! A typo in the column name of the Categories table caused this exception to be thrown.

Here is the typo. The N key must be stuck.

ColdFusion's structured exception handling gives you great control over your database interactions. Using a carefully nested structure with your queries inside <cftransaction> tags, you can accommodate almost any database error. One of the biggest problems in maintaining a database is ensuring the integrity of the data. Incomplete or botched transactions can cause a database administrator a lot of grief. ColdFusion is here to help you maintain consistent and reliable data.

25

Debugging Your Template

You can't get away from bugs. Bugs plague even the most careful programmer. But make no mistake: programmers write bugs into the code. They do not just appear by themselves. Someone puts them there. Although you can't stop bugs from entering your code altogether, you can use some simple techniques and ColdFusion tools to keep most of them at bay. In this chapter, you learn to:

- Use <cfoutput> to track segments of code
- Debug HTML table formatting
- Use test form handlers
- Configure ColdFusion to display debugging information
- Use the <cfsetting> tag to control information display
- Use ColdFusion Studio and RDS debugging tools

Learning Basic Debugging Techniques

Programmers have a set of tools and techniques they use to debug code. Many such tools are complex and have steep learning curves. These tools are usually effective for finding all manner of bugs and coding errors, but if your debugging needs are modest, these tools are often overkill for the time and money invested in them. Many times, you simply need some tricks to help you figure out small problems.

Using <cfoutput> Creatively

Even the simplest ColdFusion template has a lot of behind-the-scenes processing that you don't ordinarily see. This is true for many programming environments. If you could see what is going on, you could fix the problem. Programmers have been using some variation of the `print` command in various languages for a long time to view those hidden processes while a piece of code is running.

In ColdFusion, the equivalent of the `print` command is <cfoutput>. You can use <cfoutput> to print variables that are not printed to the screen normally or to print intermediate values in a loop. Often, simply viewing the variables' values is enough to understand the bug and fix it.

The idea in this example is simple. You want to check the value of the raw line of data from the log file before you chop it up for display in the HTML table. All you need to do is place a <cfoutput> in the loop to display the data.

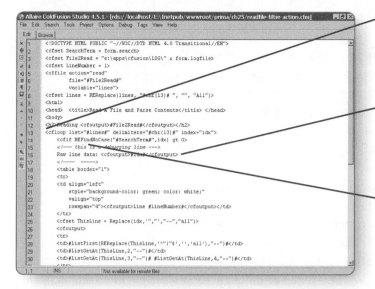

This loop parses each line of text from the log file. The variable idx holds an individual line of raw data for display.

Here is the debug output line. It is a good idea to mark this line with comments so you can identify it later.

Note that the output is inside the search term matching code. If you want to see each line of raw data, move the debug code before this line.

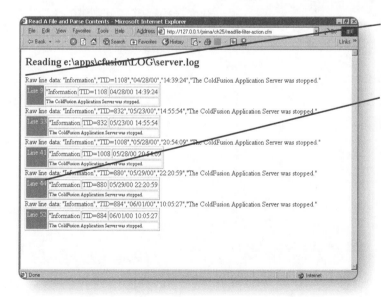

The raw data from the line in the log file appears before each HTML table.

Here's the bug: The first double quote of each line is being displayed. You need to filter out that first quote in the parsing code.

Debugging Table Formatting

HTML tables are a great way to lay out information of all types on a Web page. In fact, with most versions of Netscape Navigator, this is the only way to lay out a complex page. It is easy to become confused with all the table headers, colspans, rowspans, breaks, paragraphs, and so on in the HTML code. And don't forget all the tables within tables. This confusion can result in some pretty strange looking tables, especially when you prefer not to use borders.

A quick way to sort out the table formatting is to include a border attribute for every table on your page, even if you set it to zero width. If the formatting is coming out strangely, return to your HTML code and set all the border attributes to 1 to view the borders. The search and replace function in ColdFusion Studio makes this easy. This method gives you a visual check of the table structures on the page, including embedded tables, cell alignments, empty cells, and so on.

The border attribute of the <table> is set to a width of 1. This frame shows the formatting errors more clearly.

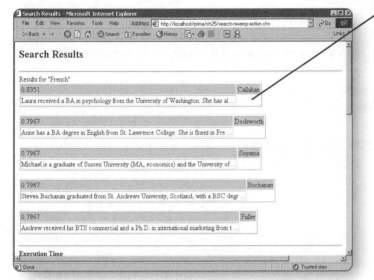

This empty cell should be below the score. It looks like you are missing a `<td>` tag in the second row.

Using Form Handlers

A standard technique for testing segments of code such as functions, procedures, and modules is to create a test harness. A *test harness* is another piece of code whose only mission in life is to provide a framework to test another piece of code. The test harness does not need to be elaborate or even functional, from the overall application point of view. It needs only to enable you to test another piece of code.

As you write ColdFusion applications, especially applications that require a lot of interaction with the users, you will discover that a large part of your development time is devoted to writing Web forms. Forms are the most obvious way to gather data from the users; as such, they often will be front and center in your applications.

Forms are easy to debug; just click buttons and fill in the text fields until something breaks. You can debug your forms this way, but this method is not efficient. An easier and more reliable way of debugging forms is to use a form-processing template as a test harness. You can create a form processor to focus on a specific aspect of the form, or you can use a generic form processor to display the form data and visually check it.

Chapter 3, "Creating ColdFusion and HTML Forms," introduced a test harness of this variety, although it was not labeled as such. You have encountered plenty of ColdFusion code since then, so you might want to review that form processor.

First, you need to determine whether the form scope is present and whether there are form fields to process.

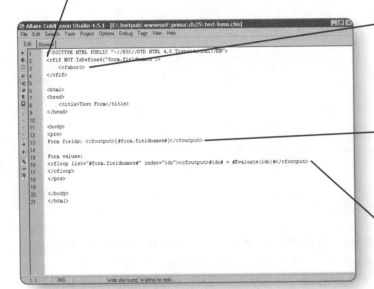

This is a good place to dump some more specific information about the state of the application either to the browser or perhaps to log file.

The list of form fields is another sanity check to make sure that the fields you are expecting have been submitted.

The loop displays all the field/value pairs in the form scope. You might need to adjust this code to account for special form fields or executable data.

ColdFusion Debugging Information

The ColdFusion application server can provide a great deal of useful information about the execution of a template with its built-in debugging information. ColdFusion can display this information at the end of each template output in the browser window. By default, this information is not displayed.

You can configure the type of debugging information in ColdFusion Administrator. Several categories can be turned on and off. You can also tell ColdFusion to send debugging information only to certain IP addresses. By using this service, you can show debugging information on your development machine and hide it from your general users.

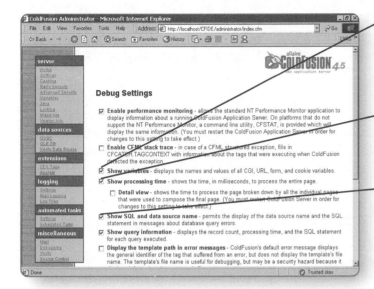

This is the basic level of debugging output. This option can eliminate the need for a generic form processor as a test harness.

The processing time can be useful for tracking down performance issues.

This option, used in conjunction with the query information option, is indispensable for tracking down problems in your database queries.

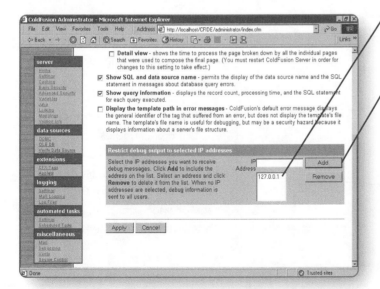

This is the list of IP addresses that receives the debugging information.

To add an IP address to the list, type the address and press the Add button. The page will reload with the address added to the list.

Check out this update form from Chapter 6, "Modifying and Deleting Data," with the debugging information displayed.

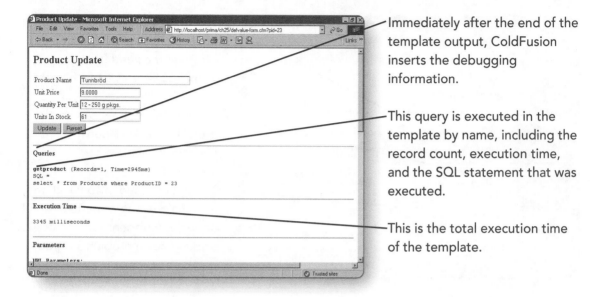

Immediately after the end of the template output, ColdFusion inserts the debugging information.

This query is executed in the template by name, including the record count, execution time, and the SQL statement that was executed.

This is the total execution time of the template.

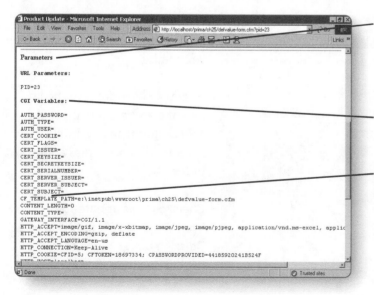

This section displays the cgi, url, and form variables. Note that the PID listing matches the address line.

This area shows the complete set of cgi variables.

This cgi variable is used in the LastUpdated custom tag from the previous chapter. Note the absolute path of the template.

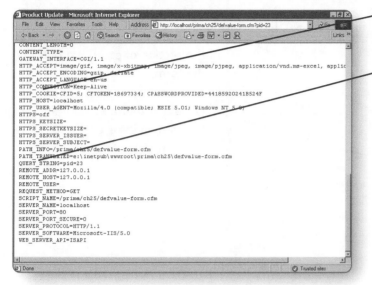

ColdFusion uses this cookie to track a client browser.

The complete query string from the address line is included in this variable.

Using <cfsetting> to Control Information Display

ColdFusion's debugging information is excellent for tracking down code errors. But not everyone needs to see it. True, you can limit its display by restricting the IP address list in ColdFusion Administrator, but in environments where your IP address changes from day to day, this method is ineffective.

ColdFusion offers another solution. You can control the display of this information using the <cfsetting> tag. This tag also enables you to restrict the output of a template to the code inside the <cfoutput></cfoutput> tags.

Using <cfoutput> Only

You can restrict output to code in the <cfoutput></cfoutput> tags by setting the enablecfoutputonly attribute to Yes. Depending on how you placed your <cfoutput> tags, this procedure can greatly reduce the amount of output from your template. Doing so enables you to focus on the output of your ColdFusion code, to the exclusion of plain text or HTML.

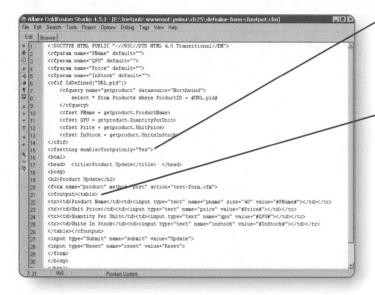

Set the `enablecfoutputonly` attribute to `Yes` before entering the section of code that outputs the form.

Note that the table that holds the form fields is enclosed in the `<cfoutput></cfoutput>` tags.

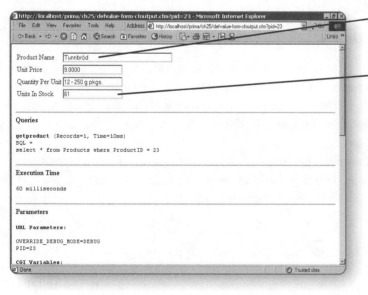

The form is now limited to its table fields and labels.

Some browsers might not react well to you stripping out all the surrounding HTML. Internet Explorer, used here, obviously takes it in stride.

Hiding Debugging Output

For developers who use dynamic IP addressing or who rely on their Internet Service Provider for an IP address, the ability to hide or display debugging information is a great help.

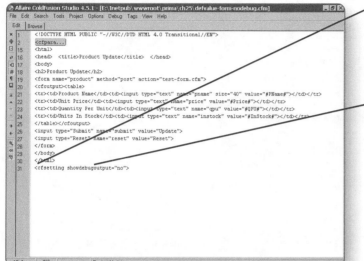

Set the `showdebugoutput` attribute of the `<cfsetting>` tag to `no` to hide the debugging output.

You can place this tag anywhere in the template.

Using ColdFusion Studio and RDS

The integration of Remote Development Services (RDS) with ColdFusion Studio provides you with a full-featured debugging environment. The Studio debugging environment uses RDS to create a debugging session with your ColdFusion application server. This session enables you to set breakpoints in your code, add variable watch windows, evaluate expressions on the fly, step through your code line by line, and view the output of your template in a window.

This section shows you some of ColdFusion Studio's debugging features. Refer to the documentation for a complete description on how to use this tool effectively.

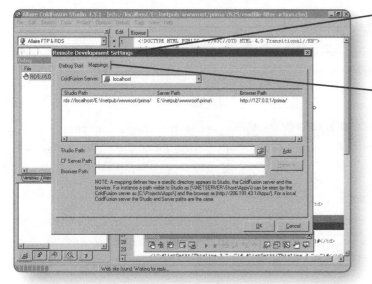

Use the Debug menu to display the Remote Development Settings dialog box.

The Mappings tab enables you to map between the server template path in Studio and the Web server URL.

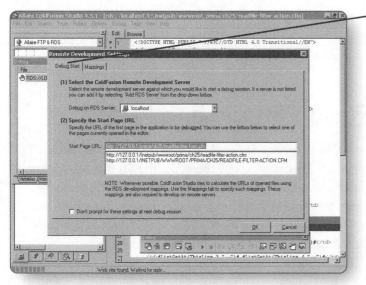

Use the Debug Start tab to configure the starting URL for the debug session. For example, to debug a form processor template, you start with the form template.

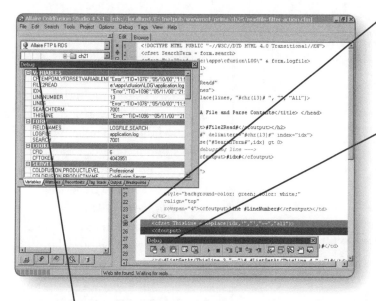

A breakpoint is set on line 25 of the readfile-filter-action.cfm template. ColdFusion has suspended processing of the template at this point.

Reach the Debug toolbar through the Quick Bar or through the Options menu in Customize. You can access all these functions from the Debug menu as well.

Start the Debug window from the View menu. In this view of the window, you can see the complete listing of variable scopes for the current template.

In Watch view, you can specify variables to evaluate on the fly or to monitor as you step through the template.

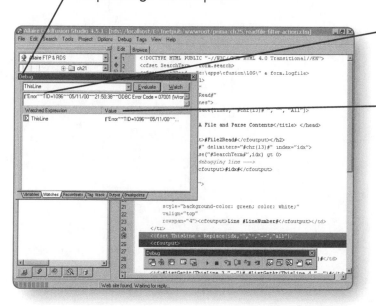

This window displays the current value of the variable when you press the Evaluate button.

The value of the watched expression changes as you step through lines in the template.

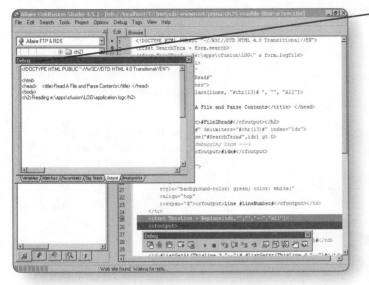

In Output view, you can watch the progress of the template's output.

The ColdFusion Studio debugging tools are powerful. You may find the learning curve a little steep at first, but the extra work will be worth it. You will find these tools to be indispensable for large and small projects alike. You may not use them all every day, but when you need them, you'll be glad you spent the time to learn how to use these debugging tools.

PART VI

Appendixes

A

Installing ColdFusion

Installing ColdFusion is a snap. The installation program is smart enough to determine most of the information it needs in order to install the server. You have to supply locally specific information about your system, such as the desired installation path. In this appendix, you learn how to:

- Install ColdFusion Application Server on Windows
- Configure ColdFusion Application Server

Installing ColdFusion Application Server

Windows NT and Windows 98 are the most common platforms on which to install ColdFusion, so this section covers installation on those platforms. Refer to the ColdFusion documentation for installation instructions for Solaris and Linux.

The system requirements for ColdFusion Application Server 4.5.1 Enterprise Edition for Windows are as follows:

- Windows NT 4.0 with Service Pack 4 or higher or Windows 2000
- Intel Pentium or higher
- 128MB of RAM (512MB recommended)
- 50MB of hard disk space
- A Web server that supports NSAPI, ISAPI, or WSAPI programming interfaces or that supports CGI
- CD-ROM drive (if installing from the CD)

You can get an evaluation copy of ColdFusion Application Server from the Allaire Web site at http://www.allaire.com or from the CD accompanying this book. The installation file is a self-extracting executable (server.exe), so all you need to do is run the file. You can find the file in the directory X:\stuff (where X is the drive letter of your CD-ROM drive). You can launch the file from a command prompt, or you can use the Run menu option from the Start button. After decompressing and setting up some temporary files, the installation program begins.

Remember to close all open applications while you install a new application in order to avoid DLL or system file collisions or failures during the installation. You also need to restart your computer after the installation, so make sure all files are saved and closed at this time. When you are ready to begin, click Next.

The installation program requires that you provide a name and company to continue. The evaluation version places the word "Evaluation" in the Serial number field. If this is the retail distribution, you use the serial number on your ColdFusion box or CD sleeve here. Click Next to proceed. (It isn't grayed out after you fill in all the information.)

The next panel asks you for an installation folder. To change the default installation folder, click the Browse button and navigate to a different folder. Click Next to proceed.

The installation program can detect common Web servers already installed on your system. If there is a different server on your system that you want ColdFusion to use, select the Other Server button on this panel. Click Next to proceed.

The next panel asks you about the document root directory of your Web server. The installation program detects the document root directory of the server you chose in the last dialog box. If this directory is incorrect or you want to specify a different directory, use the Browse button to navigate to another directory. Click Next to proceed.

The next panel asks you about the components to install. You should select ColdFusion Program Files and Documentation as the basic installation components. If you will be using this server to develop ColdFusion extensions with C++ or Java, select the CFX API option. Click Next to proceed.

> ### NOTE
>
> If you are installing the Enterprise version of ColdFusion Application Server, an additional option is in this list: Load Balancing and High Availability.

You need to provide passwords for access to the ColdFusion Administrator application and the ColdFusion Studio Remote Development Services. Enter a password for the administration application in this panel and confirm it in the second field. Click Next to proceed to the Studio RDS password dialog.

On this panel, enter a password that your ColdFusion Studio users will use to access the Remote Development Server services from within ColdFusion Studio and confirm it. Click Next to proceed.

You can change the default Program Folders name on this panel. All ColdFusion Server application icons appear in this folder. Click Next to start the installation.

When the installation is complete, the installation program needs to restart your system. It is highly recommended that you restart now and not delay.

Congratulations! You just installed ColdFusion Application Server. After you reboot your system and log in (if necessary), the installation program brings up a Web browser with the top page of the newly installed documentation for your perusal.

Configuring ColdFusion Application Server

As soon as you install ColdFusion Application Server, you need to configure a few of the basic settings through ColdFusion Administrator. ColdFusion Administrator is a ColdFusion application itself, so loading it is a good way to test the success of your installation.

You can access ColdFusion Administrator at http://127.0.0.1/cfide/administrator/index.htm or http://hostname/cfide/administrator/index.htm, where *hostname* is the DNS name of your system. After it's loaded, Administrator prompts you for the ColdFusion Administrator password you set in the installation procedure.

You need to perform these tasks to configure the ColdFusion Application Server after the installation is complete:

- Add ODBC datasources
- Configure the log settings for ColdFusion
- Configure ColdFusion to use your e-mail server

After these tasks are complete, your ColdFusion Application Server is ready for business.

Adding ODBC Datasources

You can configure ODBC datasources in your Control Panel applet, but you still need to visit ColdFusion Administrator to set up the datasource for use by ColdFusion. However, datasources added with ColdFusion Administrator are also added to your set of system datasources, so you accomplish two tasks at once.

Each datasource requires an ODBC driver for the type of database that the datasource represents. So you need to have an ODBC driver for the database you want to access. Each ODBC driver has different configuration requirements and settings; therefore, configuring a datasource differs for each type of driver.

To use the scripts with the Microsoft Access sample database, Northwind, you need to configure an ODBC datasource in ColdFusion. Follow these steps after installing ColdFusion. From the Start menu, select Program Files, ColdFusion Server 4.5, ColdFusion Administrator. In the browser window that opens, supply the password and select ODBC from the left-hand navigation bar. In the text box under Data Source Name, type **Northwind** and make sure that "Microsoft Access Driver (*.mdb)" appears in the drop-down list. Click Add, then click the first Browse Server button to browse to where your copy of the Northwind.mdb file is located (it should be in the installation directory of your Microsoft Office applications). Click Create. You are now ready to use the scripts from the CD.

You can use these same steps to add other datasources for use by ColdFusion. Simply use a different name and make sure you specify the correct driver for your database.

If you are using one of the major database vendors' products, such as Oracle, DB2, or Informix, you need to contact the vendor for the latest ODBC drivers. You can get the latest ODBC drivers for many databases and data file formats from Microsoft at http://www.microsoft.com/data/.

Configuring ColdFusion Logging

Logging on to the ColdFusion Application Server helps you maintain your server at peak performance. Therefore, make sure you configure the general logging settings immediately after installation. The two most important settings here are the Administrator e-mail address and the log file directory.

After logging in to the ColdFusion Administrator application, select the *Settings* link under *logging* in the navigation side bar. On this page, you can enter the e-mail address that will be displayed on error pages. You can also enter the full path (without a filename) where the log files will be written. This defaults to the LOG subdirectory in the ColdFusion installation directory. Click Apply when you are finished, and the settings will take effect immediately.

Configuring ColdFusion for E-Mail

In order for the `<cfmail>` tag to work without using the `server` attribute with every call, you need to tell ColdFusion which SMTP mail server it should use to send mail.

After logging in to the ColdFusion Administrator application, select the *Mail* link under *miscellaneous* in the navigation side bar. On this page, you can enter the DNS address or the IP address of the SMTP server that ColdFusion should use to send e-mail. You can also specify the port number of the SMTP server. Port 25 is the standard SMTP port; you should not have to change this setting. You can use the Verify button to have the ColdFusion server attempt to connect to the SMTP server. Click Apply when you are done.

That's it. Your ColdFusion server is ready for business.

B

Basic SQL

Structured Query Language (SQL) is a standard set of grammatical rules and keywords used to access data. Although every database vendor has its own unique SQL version, they are all based on the same standard. In this appendix, you learn how to:

- Use the select statement
- Filter a query with conditionals
- Sort a query
- Join tables in a query

Using the select Statement Effectively

The select statement is the most commonly used SQL command; you will use it repeatedly in your applications. All select statements are based on this simple structure: select [column-list] from [table-list] where [condition]. The column-list and the table-list are comma-separated lists, and condition is a simple or compound expression. Using this syntax, you can query your data and retrieve exactly the information you want and in the form you want it.

This statement retrieves the product name and the unit price of each product in the database.

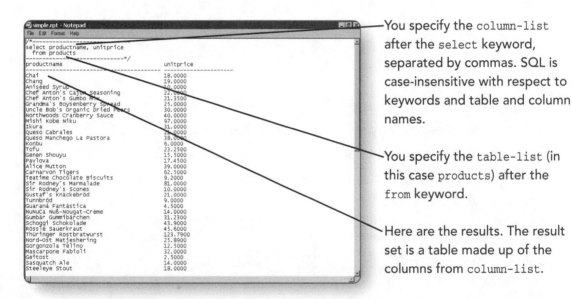

You specify the column-list after the select keyword, separated by commas. SQL is case-insensitive with respect to keywords and table and column names.

You specify the table-list (in this case products) after the from keyword.

Here are the results. The result set is a table made up of the columns from column-list.

You can retrieve all columns from a table without having to know each column name by using the asterisk in place of column-list. The advantage to using the asterisk is that if the table format changes, you do not need to adjust your select statement.

Use the asterisk to return all columns in the result set.

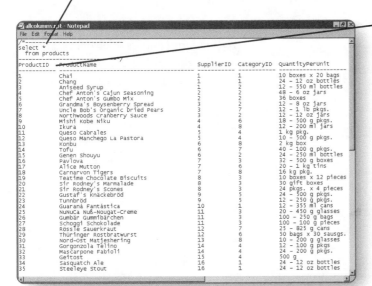

The query returned all the columns from the products table; this view does not show the entire column list.

You can rename a column in the result set by using the as keyword followed by the new column name. Renaming is useful when you use an expression as a column in the column-list or when you need to rename an obscure or long column name to something more appropriate for your output.

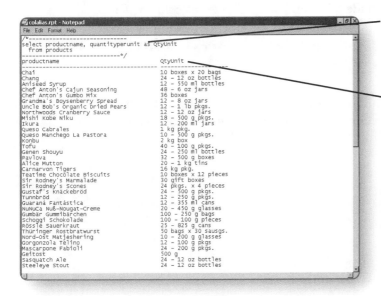

The keyword as renames the quantityperunit column to QtyUnit for readability.

The result set shows the new column name, QtyUnit.

You can use a shorthand alias to reference columns from specific tables in table-list. This alias, often an abbreviation for the table, cuts down on typing table name qualifiers in column-list and condition.

You place the table's alias immediately after the table, separated by a space.

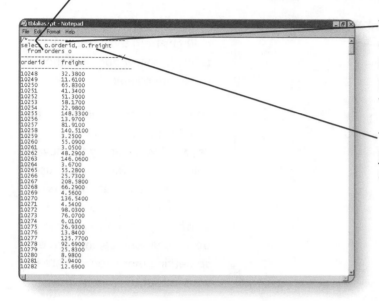

You can now reference the column names in `column-list` by the table alias, which is prepended to the column name with a period.

This syntax is more useful with joins, discussed later in this appendix.

The `column-list` can include SQL expressions as well as column names. *Expressions* are constants, column names, or functions joined by valid operators and parentheses. You can use expressions to create new values in the result set based on column names or the results of functions.

This `select` statement returns the product name, the product's list price, and the list price discounted by 15 percent. The discount price expression in the `column-list` is renamed using the `as` keyword.

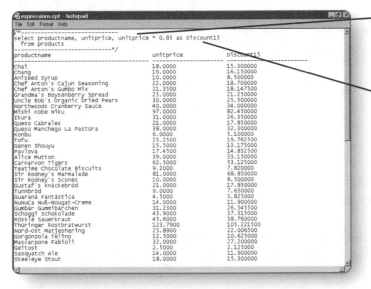

The expression multiplies each value in the `unitprice` column by 0.85.

The new column is called `Discount15` by the as keyword.

You can use functions in `column-list` to return special calculations on the result set, such as counts, sums, averages, minimums, and maximums.

This `select` statement returns a count of all the orders from the `orders` table that had freight costs over $500.

The function `count` takes one argument, most often the asterisk. This function counts the number of matching rows in the result set and returns the single value.

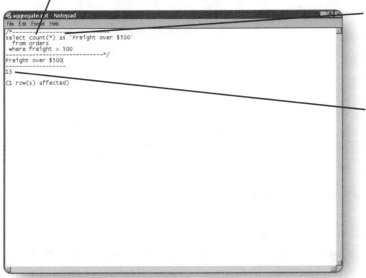

In this example, the new column name contains spaces, so you need to place single quotations around it.

The number of orders with freight costs over $500 dollars is 13.

Using where Clauses to Narrow Your Search

The `select` statement returns all the rows from the tables in the table list by default. However, you might need to return only a subset of the rows in a table. SQL provides the `where` clause to filter the rows in the result set. The `where` clause can be a single or compound expression of column names, operators, and parentheses. The clause is designed to match specific row values in the query result set. You can use operators of equality and comparison, plus the special SQL operators for sets and ranges.

The simple equality `where` clause is the most common conditional clause. This `select` statement retrieves the company name, city, and country of all customers in Spain.

The column-list is a simple list of three of the columns from the `customers` table.

The `where` clause matches rows from the preliminary result set specified by the `select` and `from` clauses.

Because the country is a textual column, you must use single quotations around it (as in 'spain').

The query returns five rows from the `customers` table.

```
where equal.rpt - Notepad
File  Edit  Format  Help

select companyname, city, country
  from customers
 where country = 'spain'
------------------------------------ */
companyname                          city          country
------------------------------------ ------------- -------------
Bólido Comidas preparadas            Madrid        Spain
FISSA Fabrica Inter. Salchichas S.A. Madrid        Spain
Galería del gastrónomo               Barcelona     Spain
Godos Cocina Típica                  Sevilla       Spain
Romero y tomillo                     Madrid        Spain

(5 row(s) affected)
```

You can restrict the result to column values that fall within a certain range. You can also precede the `between` operator with a `not` operator to match values that fall outside the range.

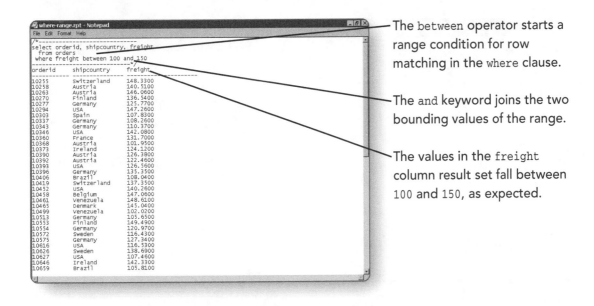

The `between` operator starts a range condition for row matching in the `where` clause.

The `and` keyword joins the two bounding values of the range.

The values in the `freight` column result set fall between 100 and 150, as expected.

You can use sets to match rows. The `in` operator matches values in a set. Specify the set in parentheses following the `in` operator. Use single quotations around each value in the list if the values are textual.

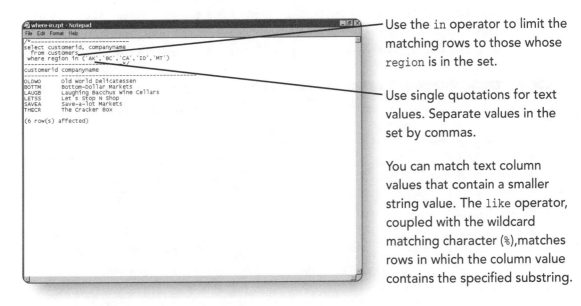

Use the `in` operator to limit the matching rows to those whose `region` is in the set.

Use single quotations for text values. Separate values in the set by commas.

You can match text column values that contain a smaller string value. The `like` operator, coupled with the wildcard matching character (%),matches rows in which the column value contains the specified substring.

In this `select` statement, the query returns the employee ID and last name of any employee with the word `french` anywhere in the text of the `notes` column of the `employees` table.

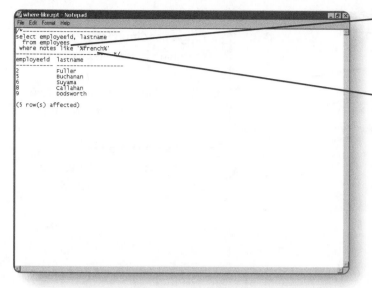

The `like` keyword searches the `notes` column for a string matching the argument.

The percent signs match one or more characters of any type in the value. This syntax, then, matches `french` anywhere in the value.

Sorting the Results

Different databases return query result sets in different orders. The order depends on the database vendor and the configuration of the database server. You can sort the result set with the `order by` clause of the `select` statement. The sort order is affected by the dictionary sort order of your database. The sort order might be a case-sensitive dictionary sort, or it might be case-insensitive. You need to check your database documentation.

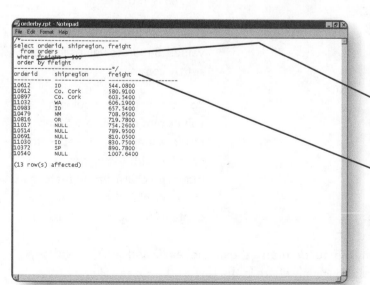

The `order by` clause sorts the result set by the column name or names specified.

The default sort order of the `order by` clause is ascending.

You can change the direction of the sort order adding the desc and asc keywords after the sort list.

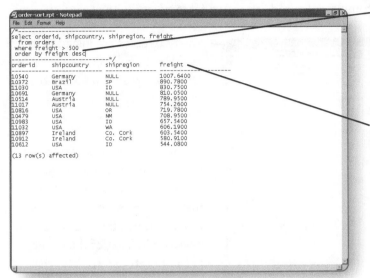

Use the desc (or descending) keyword to specify a reverse sort order. You can use the asc (or ascending) keyword to specify an ascending sort order.

Now the result set flows from the greatest freight cost to the least.

Using Joins

The strength of a relational database is its capability to connect data from one table with another. This process is calling *joining*. A simple join operation matches each row from one table with each row of a second table.

The result of a simple join is the *Cartesian* product of the two tables; in other words, the number of rows returned by a simple join equals the number of rows in the first table multiplied by the number of rows in the second table. Therefore, if you have a three-row table and join it with a five-row table, the join result set will have 15 rows. This simple join can be limited (and usually is) by joining tables with a matching set of columns.

This query selects two columns from the `products` table and one column from the `suppliers` table.

The `from` clause has a comma-delimited list of two table names with aliases.

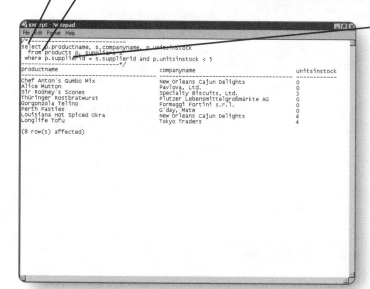

The two tables are joined on the `supplierid` column in each table. Only the rows from each table that meet this condition are returned.

An `outer join` joins two tables on a column and returns all rows from one table and only the matching rows from the other table. You use the `left` or `right` keyword in front of the `outer join` operator to specify which table returns all rows, relative to the `outer join` operator.

This `select` statement performs an outer join of the `employees` and `orders` tables on the `employeeid` column. The result lists all employees and the orders they have sold. It also displays an employee even if he or she hasn't sold an order.

This outer join returns all rows from the first table listed in the `table-list`, as the `left` keyword specifies. The left table in this clause is the `employees` table.

The tables are joined on the `employeeid` column.

The results show that Buchanan has no orders.

Using Web Resources

You can't write applications in a vacuum. You will eventually run into a situation or problem that you just can't seem to figure out or overcome. You need some help. After this book, the ColdFusion documentation is a good place to turn for help. The online help installed on both the ColdFusion application server and ColdFusion Studio offers extensive information about the tags and functions. In most cases, sample code illustrates the use of the language element as well.

ColdFusion also ships with example scripts. However, you should never install the example applications on a production server. Some of the example code can cause a security risk if left open to the public.

Allaire maintains an extensive online knowledge base of problems and guidelines for all their products. If you cannot find what you need from the online documentation or if you feel you've encountered a bug, try the Knowledge Base on the Allaire Web site. You can get to the Knowledge Base at http://www.allaire.com/Support/KnowledgeBase/SearchForm.cfm.

Why reinvent the wheel? Lots of ColdFusion developers are out there, and they have probably seen the same coding problems you are having. Allaire provides a place on the Web site for developers to exchange code and solve certain problems in the form of custom tags. The Developer's Exchange has hundreds of ready-to-use custom tags that solve all sorts of coding problems or enhance your Web applications. The CD with this book has links to sites where you can download custom tags.

If you find yourself thinking of a custom tag that might solve your problem, try the Developer's Exchange first. You might be able to save yourself some coding time. You can find the Developer's Exchange at http://devex.allaire.com/developer/gallery/index.cfm.

Allaire has even more information for developers at the ColdFusion DevCenter. The DevCenter has technical and informational articles devoted to ColdFusion and ColdFusion developers. You will also find links to the Allaire SecurityZone—a clearinghouse of security alerts and information relevant to ColdFusion system administrators—as well as online ColdFusion documentation, user groups, a job bank, and product updates. You can visit the ColdFusion DevCenter at http://www.allaire.com/developer/referenceDesk/index.cfm.

You are well on your way to writing the next great Web application. But be warned! ColdFusion is so easy to use, it's addictive. Enjoy.

D

What's on the CD

The CD that accompanies this book contains ColdFusion Express 4.0, a free noncommercial product from Allaire and 30-day evaluation versions of ColdFusion Server Enterprise 4.5.1 and ColdFusion Studio 4.5.1. The CD also has all the sample code from this book and links to sites where you can download custom ColdFusion tags to extend your ColdFusion applications.

Running the CD with Windows 95/98/2000/NT

To make the CD user-friendlier and take up less of your disk space, no installation is required to view the CD. This means that the only files transferred to your hard disk are the ones you choose to copy or install. You can run the CD on any operating system that can view graphical HTML pages; however, not all the programs can be installed on all operating systems.

To access the CD, follow these steps:

1. Insert the CD into the CD-ROM drive and close the tray.

2. Go to My Computer or Windows Explorer and double-click the CD-ROM drive.

3. Find and open the start_here.html file (this works with most HTML browsers).

NOTE

The first window you see contains the Prima License Agreement. Take a moment to read the agreement, and if you agree, click the I Agree button to accept the license and proceed to the user interface. If you do not agree to the terms of the license, click the I Disagree button. The CD will not load.

The Prima User Interface

The opening screen of the Prima user interface contains a two-panel window. The left panel contains a directory of the items on the CD. The right panel displays a description of the entry selected in the left panel.

Using the Left Panel

If you want to view a sample HTML file, click /Chapters. A drop-down menu appears containing each chapter that has sample files. Next, click the chapter you want to access. To view the programs on the CD, click /Programs and select the program you want.

Using the Right Panel

The right panel describes the entry you choose in the left panel. The information provided tells you about your selection, such as the functionality of an installable program. To download a particular file, position the mouse over the file icon, click and hold the mouse, and drag the file to a folder in an open Windows Explorer window.

Resizing and Closing the User Interface

To resize the window, position the mouse over any edge or corner, click and hold the mouse, drag the edge or corner to a new position, and release the mouse when the size is acceptable.

To close and exit the user interface, select File, Exit.

Setting Up the ODBC Datasource

To use the scripts with the Microsoft Access sample database, Northwind, you need to configure an ODBC datasource in ColdFusion. Follow these steps after installing ColdFusion. From the Start menu, select Program Files, ColdFusion Server 4.5, ColdFusion Administrator. In the browser window that opens, supply the password and then select ODBC from the left-hand navigation bar. In the text box under Data Source Name, type **Northwind** and make sure that "Microsoft Access Driver (*.mdb)" appears in the drop-down list. Click Add, then click the first Browse Server button to browse to where your copy of the Northwind.mdb file is located (this should be in the installation directory of your Microsoft Office applications). Click Create. You are now ready to use the scripts from the CD.

Index

License Agreement/Notice of Limited Warranty

By opening the sealed disc container in this book, you agree to the following terms and conditions. If, upon reading the following license agreement and notice of limited warranty, you cannot agree to the terms and conditions set forth, return the unused book with unopened disc to the place where you purchased it for a refund.

License:

The CD that accompanies this book contains ColdFusion Express 4.0, a free, noncommercial product from Allaire and 30-day evaluation versions of ColdFusion Server Enterprise 4.5.1 and ColdFusion Studio 4.5.1. ColdFusion is included under license from Allaire Corporation. Copyright 1995–2000, Allaire Corporation. All rights reserved. You are licensed to copy the software onto a single computer for use by a single concurrent user and to a backup disk. You may not reproduce, make copies, or distribute copies or rent or lease the software in whole or in part, except with written permission of the copyright holder(s). You may transfer the enclosed disc only together with this license, and only if you destroy all other copies of the software and the transferee agrees to the terms of the license. You may not decompile, reverse assemble, or reverse engineer the software.

Notice of Limited Warranty:

The enclosed disc is warranted by Prima Publishing to be free of physical defects in materials and workmanship for a period of sixty (60) days from end user's purchase of the book/disc combination. During the sixty-day term of the limited warranty, Prima will provide a replacement disc upon the return of a defective disc.

Limited Liability:

THE SOLE REMEDY FOR BREACH OF THIS LIMITED WARRANTY SHALL CONSIST ENTIRELY OF REPLACEMENT OF THE DEFECTIVE DISC. IN NO EVENT SHALL PRIMA OR THE AUTHORS BE LIABLE FOR ANY OTHER DAMAGES, INCLUDING LOSS OR CORRUPTION OF DATA, CHANGES IN THE FUNCTIONAL CHARACTERISTICS OF THE HARDWARE OR OPERATING SYSTEM, DELETERIOUS INTERACTION WITH OTHER SOFTWARE, OR ANY OTHER SPECIAL, INCIDENTAL, OR CONSEQUENTIAL DAMAGES THAT MAY ARISE, EVEN IF PRIMA AND/OR THE AUTHOR HAVE PREVIOUSLY BEEN NOTIFIED THAT THE POSSIBILITY OF SUCH DAMAGES EXISTS.

Disclaimer of Warranties:

PRIMA AND THE AUTHORS SPECIFICALLY DISCLAIM ANY AND ALL OTHER WARRANTIES, EITHER EXPRESS OR IMPLIED, INCLUDING WARRANTIES OF MERCHANTABILITY, SUITABILITY TO A PARTICULAR TASK OR PURPOSE, OR FREEDOM FROM ERRORS. SOME STATES DO NOT ALLOW FOR EXCLUSION OF IMPLIED WARRANTIES OR LIMITATION OF INCIDENTAL OR CONSEQUENTIAL DAMAGES, SO THESE LIMITATIONS MAY NOT APPLY TO YOU.

Other:

This Agreement is governed by the laws of the State of California without regard to choice of law principles. The United Convention of Contracts for the International Sale of Goods is specifically disclaimed. This Agreement constitutes the entire agreement between you and Prima Publishing regarding use of the software.